W.E.B.
Du Bois

W.E.B.
Du Bois

AN ENCYCLOPEDIA

Edited by Gerald Horne
and Mary Young

Foreword by David Levering Lewis

GREENWOOD PRESS
Westport, Connecticut • London

Library of Congress Cataloging-in-Publication Data

W.E.B. Du Bois : an encyclopedia / edited by Gerald Horne and Mary Young ; foreword by David Levering Lewis.

   p. cm.

  Includes bibliographical references and index.

  ISBN 0–313–29665–0 (alk. paper)

  1. Du Bois, W.E.B. (William Edward Burghardt), 1868–1963–Encyclopedias. 2. Afro-Americans–Biography–Encyclopedia. 3. Civil rights workers–United States–Biography–Encyclopedias. 4. National Association for the Advancement of Colored People–Biography–Encyclopedias. I. Horne, Gerald. II. Young, Mary, 1940–

E185.97.D73 W164 2001

305.896'073'0092–dc21   00–035325

[B]

British Library Cataloguing in Publication Data is available.

Library of Congress Catalog Card Number: 00–035325

ISBN: 0–313–29665–0

First published in 2001

Greenwood Press, 88 Post Road West, Westport, CT 06881
An imprint of Greenwood Publishing Group, Inc.
www.greenwood.com

Printed in the United States of America

∞

The paper used in this book complies with the
Permanent Paper Standard issued by the National
Information Standards Organization (Z39.48–1984).

10 9 8 7 6 5 4 3 2

Every reasonable effort has been made to trace the owners of copyright materials in this book, but in some instances this has proven impossible. The editors and publisher will be glad to receive information leading to more complete acknowledgments in subsequent printings of the book and in the meantime extend their apologies for any omissions.

One ever feels his twoness—an American, a Negro; two souls, two thoughts, two unreconciled strivings; two warring ideals in one dark body, whose dogged strength alone keeps it from being torn asunder.

The Souls of Black Folk

Contents

Foreword: The Dissenting Temperament of W.E.B. Du Bois

Born in Great Barrington, Massachusetts, in the year of Andrew Johnson's impeachment and dying ninety-five years later in the year of Lyndon Johnson's installation (1868–1963), William Edward Burghardt Du Bois cut an amazing swath through four continents (he was a Lenin Peace Prize laureate, and his birthday was once a national holiday in China), writing fourteen pioneering books of sociology, history, and politics and, in his eighties, a second autobiography and three large historical novels, complementing the two large works of fiction he wrote in the first two decades of this century. The premier architect of the civil rights movement in the United States, Du Bois was among the first American intellectuals to grasp the international implications of the struggle for racial justice, memorably proclaiming the problem of the twentieth century would be the problem of the color line. What he said precisely one summer day in July 1900 (shortened and made more prosaic three years later) was this: "The problem of the twentieth century is the problem of the color line, the question as to how far differences of race, which show themselves chiefly in the color of the skin and texture of the hair, are going to be made, hereafter, the basis of denying to over half the world the right of sharing to their utmost ability the opportunities and privileges of modern civilization."

Thus, *The Souls of Black Folk*, his 1903 collection of fourteen essays, would transform race relations in the United States with what now seems instantaneous speed and, by redefining the terms of a 300-year-old interaction between blacks and whites, reshaped the cultural and political psychology of peoples of African descent not only throughout the Western Hemisphere but on the African continent as well. Always controversial, Du Bois was to espouse racial and political beliefs of such variety and seeming contradiction as often to bewilder and alienate as many of his countrymen and women, black and white, as he inspired and converted. Beneath the contradictions, however, there is the procrustean bed of race and racism that gives his century-long life collective meaning for us here now at the beginning of a new century. It was therefore as a tribune of civil rights militancy that he became a household name.

By 1910, the problem of the color line in the United States had become so acute that Du Bois gave up his Atlanta University professorship for the editor's desk at the National Association for the Advancement of Colored People (NAACP) in New York. Du Bois' magazine was entirely the editor's creature, its policies virtually independent of the NAACP's board of directors and its extraordinary monthly circulation figures of more than 40,000 by 1915, and more than 100,000 by 1920, due almost entirely to Du Bois' pen. For fourteen epic years, he spoke through *The Crisis* magazine to demand full civil rights and complete racial integration as the NAACP grew from a small operation to a corporate body increasingly staffed by lawyers and lobbyists and run by accountants. But he grew increasingly impatient with the legalistic tack of the NAACP after the onset of the Great Depression.

At a controversial conference held in Amenia, New York, where more than thirty of the nation's leading African American professionals gathered at his invitation in the summer of 1933, Du Bois tried in vain to have the NAACP adopt what he called a concept of "a planned program for using the racial segregation, which was inevitable, in order that the laboring masses might be able to have built beneath them a strong foundation for self-respect and social uplift." The following year, Du Bois tried what can only be called shock therapy to force the NAACP to revise its social and economic agendas by writing two editorials bearing the titles "Segregation" and "Separation and Self-Respect." Since American blacks had to live with segregation, Du Bois called on them to turn it to their advantage. The debate over self-segregation was so fierce, in fact, that rather than renounce his brand of segregation Du Bois chose resignation from the NAACP over removal in 1934, devoting himself thenceforth to teaching and research in the South.

Having failed to reform the NAACP, the years after 1934 saw Du Bois devoted to reading Marx and supervising graduate students. Du Bois' period of Talented Tenth Marxism—from 1935 to 1948—was distinguished by deepening economic radicalism but also by a renewal of his social science meliorism. There was his great 1935 book that was ultimately to transform the historiography of a period, *Black Reconstruction in America*, which appalled most professional historians by positing a general strike by the slaves during the Civil War and a proletarian bid for power in the South after the war. Flaws it certainly had, but Du Bois' sprawling monograph would return the African American to the reconstruction drama as a significant agent. Both Howard K. Beale and the young C. Vann Woodward wrote the author of their admiration for the work and of its influence upon them.

Even as *Black Reconstruction* appeared, Du Bois was intent upon harnessing the great philanthropies in an effort to study race relations of its quagmire, hoping as he now did that the great foundations were far more disposed to support social science research conducted by African American scholars than in his early days. His project was a vast, multivolume *Encyclopedia of the Negro*, for which the Phelps-Stokes Fund provided seed money. The subject outline, worked up with the assistance of historian Rayford Logan and sociologists Robert E. Park and Guy Johnson, was rapidly evolving into a comprehensive masterpiece. Even courtly Jackson Davis, the associate director of the powerful Rockefeller-financed General Education Board (GEB), became an *Encyclopedia* convert, introducing Du Bois to the right New York notables, stroking his own trustees, and lobbying Frederick Keppel, the Carnegie Corporation president, for favorable action on its portion of the $250,000 Du Bois grant application. But the GEB's seven-member executive committee—Raymond B. Fosdick presiding and John D. Rockefeller III participating—rejected the *Encyclopedia* at the beginning of May 1937. A GEB memorandum reveals that Jackson Davis rather inconsistently urged favorable consideration of the *Encyclopedia* by the Carnegie Corporation. "Dr. Du Bois is the most influential Negro in the United States," Davis reminded Keppel. "This project would keep him busy for the rest of his life." Predictably, the Carnegie declined. Then, virtually overnight, the study of the American black was alive again, under different auspices, and directed by a scholar then unknown in the field of race relations, one whose conceptualization of the dominant American race problem was to be distinctly more psychological and less economic than Du Bois'. When Anson Phelps Stokes of the Phelps-Stokes Fund wrote Du Bois, in 1944, that "there has been no one who has been quite so often quoted by [Gunnar] Myrdal than yourself," Du Bois must have savored the bitter irony. Then, that same year, just as he had achieved the near-impossible feat of corralling the bickering presidents of seventeen black land grant colleges into funding a new generation of Atlanta University Studies, the trustees voted his retirement.

Pressured by several members of the NAACP Board, Walter White invited the septuagenarian back as an ornament. "They assumed that my days of work were over," Du Bois chortled. As consulting delegate with Walter White and Mary McLeod Bethune to the founding of the United Nations, in May 1945, Du Bois began what would become ever sharper public attacks upon the policies of an international body whose charter was ambiguous about the rights of colonial peoples. His 1947 UN petition, "An Appeal to the World: A Statement on the Denial of Human Rights to Minorities in the Case of Citizens of Negro Descent in the United States of America," was a bold initiative for the NAACP. Although the NAACP Board had unanimously endorsed the document the previous August, by June 1948, new board member and UN delegate Eleanor Roosevelt made it plain that international circulation of the petition and repeated attempts at General Assembly presentation "embarrassed" her and the nation. By then, Du Bois had virtually endorsed Henry Wallace's Progressive Party candidate, denounced the Marshall Plan and NATO (North Atlantic Treaty Organization) as building blocks in the aggressive U.S. containment of the Soviet Union, and roiled the NAACP directorate by distributing a detailed memorandum for restructuring the national headquarters.

Already shaken in 1947 by historian Arthur Schlesinger, Jr.'s charges in *Life* magazine of Communist infiltration, the NAACP chose Mrs. Roosevelt and fired Du Bois in September 1948.

Now begins what might be called Du Bois' Red Radical period, from 1948 to 1961. Thanks to Henry Wallace, Du Bois was kept afloat financially by a generous subsidy from Anita Blaine McCormick, the Chicago angel of progressive causes. It was an article of faith for him that domestic anticommunism and the foreign policy of containment of the Soviet Union were camouflage for the military industrial complex, of which racism was a central, necessary component. From then on, it was politics in earnest. With Harlowe Shapley, Linus Pauling, and Lillian Hellman, he plunged into the March 1949 Cultural and Scientific Conference for World Peace, chairing the writers' subcommittee with Norman Mailer and A. A. Fadayev at the Waldorf Astoria and delivering an electric closing speech at Madison Square Garden. In April, he gripped the huge crowd attending the Paris World Peace Conference, flaying the Atlantic Pact, Truman, and imperialism.

In 1950, at eighty-two, he ran for the U.S. Senate from New York, on the American Labor Party ticket. Out of 5 million voters, 205,000 liked his campaign speeches enough to vote for him. Parallel with his Senate run, Du Bois also ran, with four others, the new Peace Information Center (PIC), which raised funds and provided speakers to garner 2.5 million signatures for the Stockholm Peace Petition for nuclear disarmament. On July 13, Secretary of State Dean Acheson attacked the PIC in the *New York Times*. On February 9, 1951, he and the officers of the PIC were indicted under the Foreign Agents Registration Act of 1936. Despite an expenditure of several hundred thousand taxpayer dollars searching for evidence in Europe, the Justice Department's case was so farcical that the judge threw it out in midtrial in Washington. But the experience was traumatizing for Du Bois. What wounded him deeply was that, with few notable exceptions, the Talented Tenth ran for cover. However, large numbers of working-class black and white folk attended Du Bois fundraisers across the country. In his 1952 book *In Battle for Peace*, Du Bois predicted what he saw as the co-optation of the rising social and economic tier of African Americans. "In the Negro group, we are going to develop, and indeed have developed, economic classes whose interests clash," he warned. This rising group of what Princeton Professor Nell Painter has called "representative Negroes" found it politically expedient to exclude Du Bois from its inner councils, to shun him socially, and to deplore publicly his patriotic apostasy.

Ably comforted and assisted by his new wife, the author and musicologist Shirley Graham, and new friends on the Left—Esther and James Jackson, Anna Louise Strong, Abbot Simon, Doxey Wilkerson, Herbert Aptheker, Howard Fast, Louis Burnham—Du Bois continued speaking, writing, scolding, and infuriating from his book-lined study at 30 Grace Court in Brooklyn and from his third-floor Manhattan office on 23rd Street. On October 1, 1961, Du Bois applied for membership in the Communist Party of the USA—at ninety-three, five years after Khrushchev's revelation of Stalin Era crimes and three years after the court-ordered return of his own passport. What was the meaning of an act that imposed irrevocable self-exile to West Africa just as lunch-counter sit-ins and freedom bus rides foreshadowed the beginning of the end of the racial segregation in the United States Du Bois had spent his life fighting? The immediate stimulus was the Supreme Court's June 1961 decision upholding the constitutionality of the Subversive Control Board instituted by the infamous McCarran Act of 1950. Partly, he was impelled to an act of Homeric nose-thumbing. Nearing the end, he mischievously conceded, "I would have been hailed with approval if I had died at fifty. At seventy-five my death was practically requested."

Du Bois' broad-gauge explanation of his act was that "today, I have reached a firm conclusion. Capitalism cannot reform itself; it is doomed to self-destruction." The flexible truth he embraced was that just as Africans in the United States "under the corporate rule of monopolized wealth . . . will be confined to the lowest wage group," so the peoples of the developing world faced subordination in the global scheme of things capitalist. Du Bois concluded that for the sake of underdeveloped peoples everywhere all tactics that contained American capitalism were fair. With Russia now a supplicant before the International Monetary Fund (IMF), Du Bois' pronouncement rings oddly enough, perhaps, to make some doubt his stature as one of the twentieth century's prophetic heavyweights. It is unlikely, in an era of crumbling world socialist experiments, that many of us would commend the ideological and geographical choices of Du Bois' last days. It is, I suggest, the significance of his protest and gradual alienation, rather than the solutions he proposed, that are instructive. No doubt he was precipitous in totally writing off the market economy. Yet he might well insist that leaving the market exclusively to solve systemic social problems is an agenda guaranteeing obscene economic inequality in the short run and irresoluble political calamity in the long run. A belief system in which government is the root of all evil and liberal agents of decadence must surely lead to a state of nature best described by Hobbes.

In one of his most prescient essays, "Negroes and the Crisis of Capitalism in the United States," written ten years before his death, Du Bois left a diagnostic of our present turbo-capitalism, admonishing us that "the organized effort of American industry to usurp government surpasses anything in modern history."

From the use of psychology to spread truth has come the use of organized gathering of news to guide public opinion then deliberately to mislead it by scientific advertising and propaganda. . . . Mass capitalistic control of books and periodicals, news gathering and distribution, radio, cinema, and television has made the throttling of democracy possible and the distortion of education and failure of justice widespread. (Du Bois 480)

By the time he wrote *Color and Democracy*, Du Bois' color line had evolved beyond race to become a catholic conception referring to the world's disempowered and dispossessed. The problem of the twentieth century he now said was labor. "The problem of allocating work and income is the tremendous and increasingly intricate world-embracing industrial machine which we have built." From the first things he wrote until the end, Du Bois believed that principled conduct enabled men and women to solve even the most complex, intractable problems. With the intellectual's clarity and the moralist's certitude, he had sternly lectured the readers of his 1896 monograph, *The Suppression of the African Slave Trade to the United States*, that "it behooves nations as well as men to do things at the very moment when they ought to be done."

In the course of his long, turbulent career, W.E.B. Du Bois attempted virtually every possible solution to the problem of twentieth-century racism—scholarship, propaganda, integration, cultural and economic separatism, politics, international communism, expatriation, Third World solidarity. First had come culture and education for the elites; then the ballot for the masses; then economic democracy; and finally all these solutions in the service of global racial parity and economic justice. Du Bois came to see with absolute prescience the perennial utility of wedge politics in the United States, that permanent possibility for using color to legitimize evasion of major economic and social reforms, which would in turn increase, compound, and rigidify poverty, social deformation, and disempowerment until the cost of remediation became stupendous.

In the end, he would offer the best explanation of the dynamic of interior and external forces that had shaped and brought him to his final Pan-African resolution, writing in *The Autobiography*:

Had it not been for the race problem early thrust upon me and enveloping me, I should have probably been an unquestionable worshipper at the shrine of established social order into which I was born. But just that part of this order which seemed to most of my fellows nearest perfection seemed to me most inequitable and wrong: and starting from that critique, I gradually, as the years went by, found other things to question in my environment. (*Autobiography* 155)

David Levering Lewis
Rutgers University

FURTHER READING

Du Bois, W.E.B. *The Autobiography of W.E.B. Du Bois: A Soliloquy on Viewing My Life from the Last Decade of Its First Century.* New York: International Publishers, 1968.

——. *Black Reconstruction in America, 1860–1880: An Essay toward a History of the Part which Black Folk Played in the Attempt to Reconstruct Democracy in America.* New York: H. Holt and Co., 1939.

——. *Color and Democracy: Colonies and Peace.* New York: Harcourt, Brace and Co., 1945.

——. *In Battle for Peace: The Story of my 83rd Birthday, with Comment by Shirley Graham.* New York: Masses and Mainstream, 1952.

——. "Negroes and the Crisis of Capitalism." *Monthly Review* 12, no. 4 (1953): 478–485.

——. *The Suppression of the Slave Trade to the United States of America, 1638–1870.* New York: Longmans, Green and Co., 1896.

——. *The Souls of Black Folk.* Chicago: A. C. McClurg & Co., 1903.

Preface

This book seeks to provide new insight into the protean life of W.E.B. Du Bois by examining individuals, occurrences, themes, places, organizations, and the like. Given that he lived a full ninety-five years, resided on three continents, traveled relentlessly, continually evolved politically and philosophically, and encountered a countless number of individuals, drawing up a list that would do full justice to the man was no small task. Inevitably there are categories that have been excluded that may give rise to quibbles. However, the intent of this project was to include—to the extent possible—entries that point to the leading influences on his rich and instructive life. Cross-references are included that should aid in helping to guide the reader through the thicket of his complex life. The photographs that are included provide a visual guide through various stages of his life. Bibliographic references are included that point the reader toward other sources that shed further light on the life of Du Bois. In that regard, the biography, *W.E.B. Du Bois: Biography of a Race*, by David Levering Lewis and the bibliography, *Annotated Bibliography of the Published Writings of W.E.B. Du Bois*, compiled by Herbert Aptheker are useful starting points.

Introduction

W.E.B. Du Bois (1868–1963) was a historian, sociologist, novelist, journalist, editor, and political activist. During his long and fertile career, he embraced variously Pan-Africanism, socialism, and communism. In those various guises, he served as a founder and a principal operative of the National Association for the Advancement of Colored People (NAACP). He also was a leader of the Council on African Affairs founded in 1937, which over the next two decades spearheaded the struggle in the United States in favor of decolonization of Africa. In 1961, on the verge of departing the United States for self-imposed exile in Ghana, West Africa, he joined the Communist Party, USA.

Though his life and career involved many permutations, there were also certain fixed verities as well: Among these were an abiding interest in all things African and a fierce opposition of white supremacy. These fundamentals are reflected in his many writings over the years. His book on the African slave trade, a publication of research conducted primarily while he was a graduate student at Harvard, continues to be cited as a major source of evidence on this bestial commerce, which propelled the United States into the front rank of nations. In *The Souls of Black Folk* he set the tone for the epoch by noting that the problem of this century was the "color line." He did not limit these words to this nation, nor did he circumscribe this thought by referring solely to "black-white" relations; specifically and pointedly his concept of the "color line" encompassed Asia and Latin America as well.

The Crisis, the journal he edited during his tenure with the NAACP, was wildly successful, attracting tens of thousands of subscribers as it detailed the triumphs and travails of those struggling against the pestilence that was white supremacy. In opening its pages to poets and other creative writers, Du Bois inadvertently served as a principal founder of what came to be known as the "Harlem Renaissance."

Phylon, a journal he founded at Atlanta University, continues to be a leading social science authority on African Americans. It continued the tradition Du Bois himself had initiated with the publication of *The Philadelphia Negro*.

This book was a product of a particular mind-set of Du Bois at the turn of the century, where he believed that if only decent people were apprised of the facts, minds could be purged of the disease of racism. Thus, virtually alone, he formulated questionnaires and spent almost three months and hundreds of hours interviewing 5,000 people. His exhaustive research covered topics such as family histories, community institutions, education, crime, politics, interracial sex and marriage, employment, class distinctions—and much, much more.

Even today this work stands as a monument of sociology. Likewise, perhaps his most significant book—*Black Reconstruction*—still resonates as a milestone in history and historiography. Theretofore, this period following the Civil War had been viewed by many as a roaring failure, an orgy of misrule by untalented and newly enfranchised Africans in the South. Painstakingly and patiently Du Bois' research revealed this canard for the distortion that it was. He demonstrated that those blacks who were able to ascend to high office were pushed by their constituents to enact far-reaching legislation in the realm of public education and other social goods. He detailed how this promising experiment in democracy that the South had never known was aborted as a direct result of extralegal violence by the Democratic Party and its armed wing: the Ku Klux Klan.

One of his least heralded books, *Color and Democracy* is also worthy of consideration decades after publication. Herein he sketched the global dimensions of the "color line," and he lamented the hypocrisy of the United States, which had just fought a war against fascism that posited that Germany had no right to dominate Europe but shrank cravenly away from the Allied notion that Britain and France and Holland and Portugal and Belgium had no right to dominate Africa and Asia.

Du Bois did not write just for the sake of writing; he had a purpose in mind. This simple fact is no better illustrated than in the publication of *In Battle for Peace*. Coming in the wake of his second marriage to Shirley Graham and his trial for being the agent of an unnamed foreign power—presumed to be the Soviet Union—this book revealed, as well, another aspect of Du Bois' life: his political activism. Though well into his eighties, he had taken on the task of being an activist on behalf of the Stockholm Peace Appeal, which sought to outlaw nuclear weapons and was probably signed by more individuals worldwide than any other petition before or since. This notion of "banning the bomb" was also the centerpiece of his race for the U.S. Senate—on a third-party ticket—in 1950. Although he did not receive the most votes in this race, he was a victor of sorts in that the ideas he put forward—seeking to link human rights to peace—have yet to lose their shelf life.

Still, what makes Du Bois unique as an intellectual is his facility as both a nonfiction and fiction writer. He penned novels, short stories, and poems. *The Quest of the Silver Fleece* and *Dark Princess* were among his better-known works in this realm. Here, too, he sought to exert political influence in that a repetitive theme in his fiction was the necessity for peoples of color globally to unite against white supremacy and its close cousins imperialism and colonialism.

Although Du Bois was a unique individual, it is important to recognize that he was not singular in his beliefs. During his lifetime—and even during the last years of his life when he was subjected to vociferous political persecution as a result of the Cold War—he was embraced by a number of comrades in arms. There was Paul Robeson, a graduate of Rutgers and Columbia Law School, who went on to star on stage and screen before becoming embroiled in politics. He was the locomotive that drove the Council on African Affairs from its founding in 1937, and it was Robeson who provided a platform for many of his writings—at a time when he was being shunned by other publications—in his newspaper, *Freedom*.

There was Ben Davis, Jr.—the son of a leading Republican from Atlanta; the younger Davis graduated from Amherst College and Harvard Law School and seemed on a path toward middle-class respectability before being attracted to the defense of Angelo Herndon of the Young Communist League, on trial for his militant protests against the ravages of the Great Depression. In the midst of this trial, Davis, too, joined the party and went on from there to election to the City Council of New York in 1943 and 1945 before being placed on trial and being convicted in 1949 for advocacy and teaching Marxism-Leninism.

And, of course, there was Shirley Graham, a graduate of Oberlin, who was a popular composer, playwright, novelist, and biographer. Born in 1896, she had known Du Bois since she was a young girl. After the unfortunate death of his first wife, Nina Gomer, Du Bois and Shirley Graham were married in 1951 as he faced the imminent prospect of imprisonment because of his peace activism. Her caring and intellectual companionship no doubt added years to his life.

They were among his closest comrades, but there were others who crossed Du Bois' path over the years who are worthy of note: James Weldon Johnson—the NAACP official, writer, and diplomat; Kwame Nkrumah, first leader of independent Ghana, who collaborated with Du Bois at the trailblazing 1945 Pan-African Conference in Manchester; Horace Mann Bond, educator and father of NAACP leader Julian Bond; Herbert Aptheker, historian of slave rebellions, Communist, and editor of many of Du Bois' works.

Of course, all of the personalities who crossed Du Bois' path were not close friends or comrades. Booker T. Washington did not fit into this category of boon companion of Du Bois, for example. Though initially Du Bois had sought assistance from the Alabama Wizard, rather quickly their relationship deteriorated. Du Bois felt sincerely that Washington's overt opposition to voting rights and nonindustrial education for African Americans was dooming this U.S. minority to an uncertain fate.

Marcus Garvey, the Jamaican immigrant who made his mark in Harlem, had been inspired by the praxis of Washington. This helps to explain, perhaps, why he and Du Bois had clashed, particularly after Garvey made overtures to ultra-Right racists.

There are many legacies of Du Bois, but, conceivably, the most fecund is his internationalism. As a graduate student in Berlin in the 1890s he witnessed firsthand anti-Semitism. As a lifelong student of Africa, he pioneered in helping to correct the false image this battered continent had suffered at the hands of unsympathetic writers. In his seminal article "The African Roots of the War," he outlined precisely how the grasping of colonial powers for booty in Africa set the stage for the massive bloodletting that was World War I. Like many African American intellectuals of his era, Du Bois recognized the importance of Haiti to Africans in the diaspora and on the continent. When the Haitians overthrew French colonialism and slavery as the nineteenth century dawned, it was a signal to the United States and other slaveholding powers that this inhumane system could bite back. The events in Haiti convinced France to abandon many of its holdings in the Western Hemisphere, thus leading directly to the Louisiana Purchase. The victorious Haitians lent support to South American nations longing to escape the grip of Spain. Most of all, as Du Bois acknowledged, Haiti demonstrated that brutalizing peoples of African descent did not come without a price.

Du Bois was also a close student of events in Asia. He freely admitted that the independence of India in 1947 was one of the signal events of the twentieth century. Like Washington, Garvey and a generation of African American leaders in the period leading up to the bombing of Pearl Harbor in 1941, he did not dispute Japan's idea that it was a "champion of the colored races." The very existence of Japan, he thought, invalidated the essence of the philosophy of white supremacy. During a time in the 1950s when "Red China" was anathema in this nation, he visited China and was greeted warmly.

And though the Soviet Union was the "bête noire" in the United States from its very inception in 1917, it was not held in such disrepute by Du Bois, particularly during the height of the Cold War. He recognized that the existence of the USSR—and Washington's desire to paint it as a mass violator of human rights—caused the United States to get its own human rights house in order. It was not an accident that desegregation occurred as the Cold War was unfolding.

Du Bois was a founder of the NAACP and editor of its journal. He also was a member of the Communist Party, joining in 1961 when this organization was under dogged assault by the authorities. He was known as the "Father of Pan-Africanism" in no small part because of his devotion to the cause of African freedom. It is this *activism* that separates Du Bois—the intellectual—from many of his counterparts, before or since. He was a man of thought and a man of action. Indeed, his thoughts often were developed and burnished in the crucible of activism; this too sets him apart.

He was a man of encyclopedic interests and actions, and for this reason alone, there are few figures more worthy of encyclopedic treatment than W.E.B. Du Bois.

Chronology

1868	Born Great Barrington, Massachusetts, to Alfred and Mary Du Bois.
1880–1884	Attends Great Barrington High School; graduates as class valedictorian. As the valedictorian speaker, the subject of his speech is "Wendell Phillips."
1885–1888	Attends Fisk University, Nashville, Tennessee; teaches in rural school districts during the summer; receives B.A. in 1888.
1888–1890	Enters Harvard as a junior; receives B.A., graduating cum laude. He is one of the commencement speakers. His subject: "Jefferson Davis: Representative of Civilization."
1890–1892	Begins graduate work at Harvard.
1892–1894	Awarded a fellowship from the Slater Fund after considerable difficulty. Studies at the University of Berlin.
1894–1896	Teaches Latin and Greek at Wilberforce University in Ohio. Marries Nina Gomer.
1894	Receives Ph.D. from Harvard.
1895	His dissertation is published by Harvard University Press—*The Suppression of the African Slave Trade.*
1896–1897	"Assistant instructor" at the University of Pennsylvania.
1897–1910	Teaches history and economics at Atlanta University. Begins the Atlanta University Studies.
1897–1911	Organizes the Atlanta University conference for the study of the Negro Problems; editor of the institution's publications.

1899	Publishes *The Philadelphia Negro*. Death of son, Burghardt.
1900	Secretary of the Pan-African Conference in England organized by Sylvester Williams.
1903	Publishes *The Souls of Black Folk*.
1905–1909	Founder and general secretary of the Niagara Movement.
1906	Founder and editor of *The Moon*, published in Tennessee.
1909	Publishes *John Brown*. Among original founders of the National Association for the Advancement of Colored People (NAACP).
1910–1934	Director of Publicity and Research, member Board of Directors, NAACP. Founder and editor of *The Crisis*, monthly magazine of the NAACP.
1911	Participates in First Universal Races Congress in England. Publishes *The Quest of the Silver Fleece*.
1913	Joins Editorial Board of *The New Review*.
1916	Amenia Conference.
1918	One of the founders of the Harlem Renaissance.
1919	Investigates, for NAACP, treatment of black troops in Europe. The unmasking of the overt racism causes a sensation. Calls Pan-African Congress in Paris.
1920	Receives the NAACP's Spingarn Medal. Exposes U.S. role in Haiti. Publishes *Darkwater: Voices from Within the Veil*.
1920–1921	Founder and editor of *The Brownies' Book*.
1921	Second Pan-African Congress.
1923	Special ambassador representing the United States at the inauguration of President King of Liberia. Third Pan-African Congress.
1924	Publishes *The Gift of Black Folk*
1926	First visit to the Soviet Union.
1927	Fourth Pan-African Congress.
1928	Publishes *Dark Princess: A Romance*.
1934	Resigns from the NAACP.
1934–1944	Returns to Atlanta University as the chair of the Department of Sociology.

1935	Publishes *Black Reconstruction.*
1939	Publishes *Black Folk Then and Now.*
1940	Publishes *Dusk of Dawn.* Founder and editor of *Phylon* magazine in Atlanta.
1944	Returns to NAACP as director of Special Research.
1945	Special envoy to the Founding Convention of the United Nations in San Francisco as a representative of the NAACP. Fifth Pan-African Congress.
1947	Edits for the NAACP and presents to the United Nations "An Appeal to the World," protesting Jim Crow in the United States.
1948	Co-chair of the Council on African Affairs.
1949	Attends Cultural and Scientific Conference for World Peace, Paris. Attends Cultural and Scientific Conference for World Peace, Moscow.
1950	Chair, Peace Information Center in New York. Candidate in New York for U.S. Senate, the American Labor Party. Wife, Nina Gomer Du Bois, dies and is buried in Great Barrington, Massachusetts.
1950–1951	Indictment, trial, and acquittal on charges brought against him by the Justice Department of being an unregistered foreign agent in connection with leadership of Peace Information Center.
1951	Marries Shirley Graham.
1951–1958	Speaking, writing, traveling.
1952	Awarded International Peace Prize.
1954	Publishes *In Battle for Peace: The Story of My 83rd Birthday.*
1957	Publishes *Ordeal of Mansart.*
1958	Awarded Lenin Peace Prize.
1959	Publishes *Mansart Builds a House.*
1961	Joins Communist Party, USA Publishes *Worlds of Color.* Invited to Ghana by President Kwame Nkrumah to edit the *Encyclopedia Africana.*
1963	Becomes citizen of Ghana. Dies August 27 and is buried with a state funeral in Accra, Ghana.

A

ACCOMMODATION VERSUS STRUGGLE

W.E.B. Du Bois was well known for his advocacy of struggle against race prejudice in dramatic contrast with Booker T. Washington's policy of accommodation to the structures of segregation. The two great leaders have become icons of radical versus conservative approaches to social change in twentieth-century African American culture. In his own time, Du Bois was at first cautious in raising his disagreements, because he recognized Washington's leadership skills at Tuskegee Institute and his remarkable ability to communicate publicly with black and white alike. While Washington's achievements were impressive, especially in light of rigid and worsening racism, the younger Du Bois could not long maintain his quiet deference.

After earning his Ph.D. from Harvard in 1895, Du Bois honed his sociological understanding of African American culture and his philosophical outrage with white racism during an early career of writing and teaching at the University of Pennsylvania and Atlanta University. By 1903, with publication of *The Souls of Black Folk*, his clarion call to African American pride and activism, Du Bois blasted Washington for acquiescing to white racism. Du Bois astutely sensed that whatever progress the accommodationist program could produce would be stymied by the rise of avowedly white supremacist politics in the years around 1900.

Much of their different stances on the race question grew from their differing backgrounds. The Southerner Washington was born a slave and had learned to get along with the dominant race as a survival technique. Du Bois was born in Massachusetts, a descendant of a long line of free blacks, and he greeted his first recognition of prejudice as a rude shock to his assumptions of human equality and his lofty ambitions as a bright young man in a mostly white community. Washington was willing to accept separate and inferior treatment and looked to racial progress through vocational education and economic advancement. In contrast, Du Bois indicted racial prejudice itself as a barrier to progress, which he envisioned would only come about through the inspiring leadership of a liberally educated elite. According to Du Bois, Washington's earnest calls for diligent work and political patience would perpetually run into the dark and smoldering ceiling of prejudice. As a result, Du Bois turned his life's work over to political and legal reform and public advocacy. He helped to found the Niagara Movement in 1905 and the National Association for the Advancement of Colored People (NAACP) in 1909, which were devoted to offering public alternatives to Washington's leadership, and he became the unofficial spokesperson for blacks and the widely recognized conscience of the nation on racial matters through his vigorous essays in *The Crisis*, which he edited from 1910 to 1934.

The conflict between accommodation and struggle describes not only the public debate of Washington and Du Bois; these contrasting outlooks were also at war within Du Bois' own mind and heart. For all his fierce antagonism to the systems and assumptions of prejudice, Du Bois was also very much a product of his culture. Much of his conviction grew from his eagerness to become an "insider" in U.S. culture. He was eager to escape the stereotypes of his race and the provincialism of his small-town upbringing. He eventually became a cosmopolitan intellectual with a graceful prose style, fluency in German, and a Harvard degree. Moreover, he conducted his personal life as a model of Victorian sobriety, diligence, and purpose—even if his own driving purpose was the socially radical struggle for black rights.

Du Bois' own approach to the struggle further reflected his cultural stance, since initially he foresaw progress for African Americans emerging with the cultivation of an upper class (the "Talented Tenth") who would serve as a social ideal for the black masses, uplifting them from their ignorance and corruption. And so his elitism often tempered his militancy. His most vehement objections to segregation were directed at the limits it placed on the talented and industrious. Du Bois earnestly expected that, once in place, the better classes of blacks would devote themselves to helping the less fortunate members of their race. In addition, for all the sharpness of his objections to racism, he counseled finesse and courtesy in communicating with its white perpetrators.

Du Bois' ambivalence over accommodation versus struggle emerged most strikingly in his views of integration. He was profoundly committed to the ideal of an integrated society, where blacks would be treated as equal partners with full American citizenship, and his career was a constant struggle to bring that vision to social reality. Since he never witnessed its realization, in the meantime he heartily endorsed African American cultural separatism. Even as he relished the fruits of particularist black culture, he always viewed separatism as a short-run solution, while he longed for eventual integration. Despite his abundant self-confidence, he admitted to feelings of inferiority that led to tortured mixed feelings because he wanted to associate as an equal with whites but dreaded "showing a desire for the company of those who had no desire for me." Du Bois himself accommodated to black separatism even as he struggled for integration.

Late in his long life, as he became more attracted to socialist ideology with its deep critique of American values, Du Bois emigrated to Ghana to escape the intransigence of U.S. racial attitudes. The cosmopolitanism that he so valued in his youth took on even broader political and cultural dimensions. He indicted the greed of capitalism and linked the political economy of European peoples to the oppression of the darker races throughout the world. Becoming a founder of Pan-Africanism, he looked with hope to the solidarity of African peoples throughout the world. When Du Bois died in 1963, just before the major successes of the civil rights movements and the rise of the New Left ideology, he was increasingly recognized as a hero and a prophet. His justification of the capitalization of the word "Negro" because he believed that "eight million Americans are entitled to a capital letter" captures his intellectual drive, taste for irony, and fiery combativeness that appealed to young people eager to fight the Establishment.

Although his commitment to struggle seemed, especially by the 1960s, the antithesis of Booker T. Washington's accommodationism, these two sides of the African American struggle sometimes formed a cooperative synergy. For example, when Washington founded the National Negro Business League in 1901, he pursued an idea suggested by Du Bois' sociological research. In the early twentieth century, when there was so much room for improvement of racial relations, accommodation and struggle each had strong appeal within W.E.B. Du Bois himself and in the African American community as a whole. *See also: The Philadelphia Negro; The Souls of Black Folk*; Washington, Booker T.

FURTHER READING

Du Bois, W.E.B. *The Autobiography of W.E.B. Du Bois: A Soliloquy on Viewing My Life from the Last Decade of Its First Century.* New York: International Publishers, 1968.

——. *Dusk of Dawn: An Essay toward an Autobiography of a Race Concept.* New York: Harcourt Brace, 1940.

——. *The Philadelphia Negro: a Social Study.* 1899. New York: Benjamin Bloom, 1967.

——. *The Souls of Black Folk.* 1903. New York: Penguin Books, 1969.

Lewis, David Levering. *W.E.B. Du Bois: Biography of a Race, 1868–1919.* New York: Henry Holt, 1993.

Paul Jerome Croce

AFRICA

To untangle the proverbial web of racism woven in the United States and to obtain some understanding of the plight of the African American, W.E.B. Du Bois began researching African American history. Through his research he discovered that there was very little written about people of color, and the

W.E.B. Du Bois on lecture tour. Courtesy of Special Collections and Archives, W.E.B.
Du Bois Library, University of Massachusetts Amherst.

information that could be found was negative or inaccurate. This discovery
led Du Bois to believe that there was a culture and history in Africa worth
exploring.

There was a time when African Americans had closer ties to Africa and its
cultures, but this connection and the image of Africa deteriorated because of
distortions and ignorance. The image of Africa in the United States was a
savage land inhabited by equally savage and primitive people. For the most
part, African Americans accepted these images and stereotypes, often dissoci-
ating themselves from Africa.

Unlike some African Americans, Du Bois was not so quick to disavow a
part of his heritage. Despite his light complexion, Du Bois always knew that
he was "Black" and tended to focus on this aspect of his heritage more than
the European aspect.

As Du Bois pursued an education, he found that much of his learning took place outside the classroom. After leaving his hometown of Great Barrington, Massachusetts, and attending Fisk University, he was exposed to blatant racism. As he continued his education, his growing awareness of the connection between race and conflict led him to question why race was such a preoccupation and powerful force within the United States. His experience before attending Harvard University, combined with his experience while attending Harvard, spurred him to study the slave trade and slavery within the United States. He used the information gathered for the study as the basis for his dissertation and his book, *The Suppression of the African Slave Trade to the United States of America, 1638–1870* (1896). Although this book did not focus exclusively on Africa, it did demonstrate that Du Bois saw a bridge between the past in Africa and the present situation in the United States.

As Du Bois extended his research, Africa, the "dark continent," did not appear as dark as had been presented by the mass media. Africa, on the contrary, was rich in raw materials such as rubber, copper, diamonds, and gold, and the technology that its people possessed has sustained civilizations for centuries. With this new information about Africa, Du Bois began to see that the continent, wealthy in land, people, and materials, played a larger role in the context of world power than most people, particularly African Americans, perceived.

The economies of many countries depended on, and continued to depend on, commerce. As a wealthy and unexploited continent, Africa became a primary target for many nations who sought to expand their wealth and power by plundering African riches. So the struggle to possess the continent's wealth erupted into world war. In "The African Roots of the War," published in the May 1915 issue of *Atlantic Monthly*, Du Bois expresses these ideas. He implies that the destructive forces of imperialism and capitalism drove the world economy and were at the root of the problem. He goes on to discuss a firmly rooted product of these forces and the greed that drives it—color prejudice.

Many empires and republics were built because of the labor of the poor and people of color. According to Du Bois, those in power, for example, the wealthy, used the presumption of inferiority as a way to subordinate people of color and maintain power over the poor. So the poor and people of color were pitted against one another as they competed for employment. This competition caused hatred and created a division among the people that allowed those in power to benefit from cheap labor and maintain order and control. Africa was one of many continents exploited by nations to accumulate wealth and establish themselves as world powers. In "The African Roots of the War," Du Bois explains how imperialism and capitalism could be overcome and how everyone could benefit without exploitation. The result of this reconciliation would be a "new peace and new democracy."

Du Bois continued to explore Africa's role in the context of world power, publishing articles and essays in various publications such as *The Crisis*, always keeping abreast of the happenings in Africa. He felt it was "psychologically healthy (for African Americans) to be culturally and spiritually linked to Africa" not only because it was a part of their heritage but also because they could draw strength from the history and perhaps evoke change in the United States. But the United States was not the only place where Du Bois sought change. Through Africa, he sought to change the world. According to Du Bois,

[T]o help bear the burden of Africa does not mean a lessening of effort in our own home. Rather it means an increased interest. For any ebullition of action and feeling that results in an amelioration of the lot of Africa tends to ameliorate the condition of colored people throughout the world. And no man liveth to himself. ("What Is Africa to Me?" 240)

W.E.B. Du Bois was not a man who lived only for himself. He dedicated much of his life to the plight of exploited people, particularly people of African descent. In his essay "What Is Africa to Me?"—in *Dusk of Dawn: An Essay toward an Autobiography of a Race Concept* (1940)—he writes that "it is unity that draws me to Africa," and it is unity that became his goal.

Toward the end of his life, he returned to Africa to work on the *Encyclopedia Africana* under the urging of Kwame Nkrumah. According to Nkrumah, the book would "open the eyes of Africans," showing them all that their continent possesses, uncovering its history and relating it to their present status. Du Bois died before completing this work, but before his death, he was hindered in renewing his passport due to his joining the Communist Party; thus he became a Ghanaian citizen and resided in Ghana until his death at the age of ninety-five. *See also*: Azikiwe, Nnamdi; Belgium and the Belgian Congo; Council on African Affairs; Ethiopia.

FURTHER READING

Du Bois, W.E.B. "The African Roots of the War." *Atlantic Monthly* (May 1915): 707–714.
——. "Not Separatism." *The Crisis* (February 1919): 166.
——. "Reconstruction and Africa." *The Crisis* (February 1919): 165–166.
——. "What Is Africa to Me?" In *Dusk of Dawn: An Essay toward an Autobiography of a Race Concept*. New York: Harcourt Brace, 1940.

Ebony Green

AFRICAN METHODIST CHURCH

In *The Negro Church*, No. 8 of the Atlanta University Studies, published in 1903 and edited by Du Bois, the terminology *African Methodist Church* is employed to mean those congregations that would later evolve into the African Methodist Episcopal (AME) and African Methodist Episcopal Zion (AMEZ) denominations. It is observed herein that "persecution by the whites was the moving cause. They, black parishioners, were compelled to protect themselves against the yoke sought to be imposed on them, by worshipping among themselves." The author continues charting the history of this evolution, discussing the parallel movements that operated in New York and Philadelphia and spread forthwith to the other free states.

In the southern states, he writes that "the establishment of colored Methodist Churches . . . as in Maryland, under the direction of the whites, illustrated one of the instances of special missionary effort." This statement is followed by capsule biographies of Richard Allen and Absalom Jones and a brief note of the general conference of the African Methodist Churches held in Philadelphia on April 11, 1816, at which Allen was elected first bishop of the AME denomination.

In some of Du Bois' earliest writings, for example, his columns that appeared in the *New York Globe*, Du Bois regularly detailed the doings of the AMEZ Church—in his hometown of Great Barrington, Massachusetts—that had been founded by free men and women from the South and that was the center of religious and social life for its small black community. He and his mother sometimes attended this church. In several issues of *The Crisis* he details happenings within the AME Church in particular. For example, there is editorial comment on three of the church's senior bishops in the July 1915 issue and a report in the May 1916 issue that his "Pageant" (*The Star of Ethiopia*, written in 1911 as a fund-raiser for the National Association for the Advancement of Colored people [NAACP] and first performed in New York in 1913) will be performed in Philadelphia to celebrate the Centennial Conference of the AME. This is noteworthy alone in that Du Bois wrote in 1915 about the traditional attitude of the church toward drama, believing it too frivolous an activity for religious purposes. There was also a lengthy editorial in the August 1920 issue "explaining the complications arising from [church] control of [Wilberforce University] and . . . state support of the [Normal and Industrial Department]" within the university in that both shared the same campus but had different objectives. In the October 1928 issue Du Bois writes of rumors of corruption in the AME Church, saying they must be overcome "and that can be done by truth and honesty." In a "Postscript" in the July 1932 edition, he observes that the "recent general conference of the AME church was memorable insofar as it cleansed the church of man fakers and frauds and frauds at its top." *See also*: Jesus Christ; Religion.

FURTHER READING

The Crisis (March 1918).
"Opinion." (August 1920).

William M. King

AMENIA CONFERENCE

Following Booker T. Washington's death in 1915, Du Bois organized the Amenia Conference to reconcile the difference among the various African

American leadership factions. The first Amenia Conference was held August 8–26, 1916, at the New York estate of Joel Spingarn. Coming at the end of the Washingtonian era, the conference's goal was to find new ways of improving the life of blacks.

The conferences brought together perhaps the most distinguished African Americans—Kelly Miller, John Hope, Charles Chestnutt, Mary Church Terrell, a young Ralph Bunche—assembled in years. There were no proclamations, and its declarations held no resentment or acrimony. But all those present agreed to work quietly and sincerely for the enfranchisement of African Americans, the abolition of lynching, and the enforcement of laws protecting civil liberties.

With a composed but firm consensus among the black leaders, African Americans could more unswervingly and intelligently chart a course in concert with their allies. *See also*: Bunche, Ralph; Johnson, James Weldon.

FURTHER READING

The Amenia Conference: An Historical Negro Gathering. Amenia, NY: Privately Printed at the Troutbeck Press, 1925.

Aptheker, Herbert, ed. *Pamphlets and Leaflets by W.E.B. Du Bois*. White Plains, NY: Kraus-Thomson, 1986, 210–16.

Du Bois, W.E.B. "Youth & Age at Amenia." *The Crisis* (October 1933).

Mary Young

ANTI-SEMITISM

No black intellectual had spoken more pointedly on the subject of blacks' relationship with Jews than W.E.B. Du Bois. Du Bois' service to the National Association for the Advancement of Colored People (NAACP) placed him in a unique position; he was juxtaposed between the black community and white liberals—many of them Jewish—who supported the organization in its early years. Indeed, many of his closest friends were Jewish, including Joel Elias Spingarn, who was considered the most powerful and influential white in the history of the NAACP and a pivotal figure in the early black civil rights movement. In 1940, one year after Spingarn's death, Du Bois dedicated his autobiography, *Dusk of Dawn*, "To keep the memory of Joel Elias Spingarn—A Scholar and a Knight." Following Spingarn's lead, Jews would continue to actively participate in the civil rights movement, facilitated by the endorsement of Du Bois and his perception of their common interest in the civil rights struggle and the abolition of racism and anti-Semitism.

Not only did Du Bois respect Jews on a personal level, but he also recognized the ability many of them possessed to identify with and aid the black cause. In a 1923 interview with the *Jewish Daily Forward*, Du Bois stated, "The Negro race looks to the Jews for sympathy and understanding." Clearly, this "sympathy and understanding" arose from the American Jews' constant battle with anti-Semitism, a sentiment that Du Bois at first hesitated to equate with racism but nonetheless despised. Initially Du Bois viewed Jews as fellow pariahs, a people subjected to undue discrimination but insulated from racism per se by their skin color. He later wrote that "race problems at the time were to me purely problems of color, and principally of slavery in the United States and near-slavery in Africa" (Sundquist 470).

His opinion, however, was greatly altered by a firsthand experience with anti-Semitism in 1893. A student at the University of Berlin, Du Bois journeyed throughout eastern Europe; as he traveled, his awareness of the Jewish problem gradually heightened. His consciousness crested when, while dining with a German student in a small German town, he noticed a distinct uneasiness in the room. His friend reassured him, " 'They think I may be a Jew. It's not you they object to, it's me.' I was astonished. It had never occurred to me until then that any exhibition of race prejudice could be anything but color prejudice" (Sundquist 470). The experience was truly life altering; never again would Du Bois see color as the only factor inherent in racist behavior and attitudes. Indeed, after this and similar incidents, he began to understand the interconnectedness of race, class, and gender in the maintenance of racism, anti-Semitism, and capitalist exploitation.

After returning from Europe, Du Bois repeatedly denounced the "poison" of anti-Semitism and confessed its presence among some blacks as well. He now classified Jews as "one of many groups . . . who form the great majority of the inhabitants of the earth and are also excluded from fellowship with the world aristocracy" (Review of Essays 199–200). Because he believed that a parallel history of suffering predisposed Jews to understand the problems of blacks, Du Bois welcomed the aid of the many Jews with whom he worked at the NAACP. Yiddish newspapers of the day expressed an empathy for the black plight and recorded the appreciation blacks felt for the Jewish contribution to their own fight. In turn, Du Bois helped the Jews—whom he referred to as "our best friends"—in their own struggle. Always ready to step out in front of controversial issues, Du Bois, as editor of *The Crisis*, quickly endorsed the appointment of Louis Brandeis to the Supreme Court, presuming it would realign the Court's policy on race because "as a Jew [he] knows what it is to be 'despised and rejected of men' " (Diner 150). The black leader also condemned the rising anti-Semitism in the country and called for "a great alliance . . . between the darker people the world over, between disadvantaged groups like the Irish and the Jew and between the working classes everywhere" to shatter the privileged world of the "oppressive" white elite. In seeking to facilitate this alliance, Jewish groups frequently requested NAACP officials to speak on black issues. Naturally, Du Bois, one of the most gifted intellectuals in American history and an excellent orator, was a highly popular and regularly requested lecturer. After he spent a day among Jewish groups in Oakland, California, one rabbi lamented, "It is a pity that so able a man, with so genuine a message, spends but one day in our community. May he return to us" (Diner 139).

Having been so enlightened by his first trip to Europe, Du Bois returned to Germany and Poland twice more in his lifetime. While in Germany in 1936, he witnessed with astonishment the shameless policy toward Jews under Hitler's Third Reich and the support it had among the people. Unable to write of the atrocities while still within the country, he had to wait until he was outside the border to castigate Germany's treatment of the Jews and warn of its terrible possibilities. Three years before the attack on Poland and many years before the world would learn of the horrific death camps, Du Bois wrote: "There is a campaign of race prejudice carried on, openly, continuously and determinedly against all non-Nordic races, but specifically against the Jews, which surpasses in vindictive cruelty and public insult anything I have ever seen; and I have seen much" (Lewis 735). The severity of the situation for the Jew was in fact so great in 1936 that it compelled Du Bois to aver, "There is no tragedy in modern times equal in its awful effects to the fight on the Jew in Germany. It is an attack on civilization, comparable only to such horrors as the Spanish Inquisition and the African slave trade" (Lewis 81).

Such an assertion reveals the dramatic change that took place in Du Bois' mind from an initially color-oriented classification of racism to a much broader generalization of race prejudice. This evolution was due in no small part to Du Bois' several trips to eastern Europe. In "The Negro and the Warsaw Ghetto," an address delivered at the *Jewish Life* "Tribute to the Warsaw Fighters," the black leader related the profound impact his travels had on his own life and ideology: "The result of these three visits . . . was a real and more complete understanding of the Negro problem" (Foner 253). Hence, Du Bois' encounter with anti-Semitism inspired not only a greater compassion for persecuted Jews but also a realization of one oppressed race's relation to another. In the commonality between anti-Semitism and color-based bigotry, he discovered two problems of race, each as intolerant and narrow-minded as the other. He came to understand the true nature of racism, concluding that "race prejudice . . . is an ugly dirty thing. It feeds on envy and hate" (*Jewish Life*, May 1957).

Du Bois called on blacks and Jews—indeed, all peoples "despised and rejected of men"—to draw upon their mutual experiences to fight for democracy "not only for white folk but for yellow, brown, and black" (Lewis 741). Unfortunately, the groundwork Du Bois laid in black-Jewish relations is today often ignored or misunderstood by some blacks, who are resentful of Jews' rapid socioeconomic rise, and romanticized by some upper-class Jews anxiously clinging to their historic self-image as progressives with a compassion for the oppressed (West 73). *See also*: Racism.

FURTHER READING

Diner, Hasia R. *In the Almost Promised Land: American Jews and Blacks, 1915–1935.* Westport, CT: Greenwood, 1977.

Du Bois, W.E.B. *Dusk of Dawn: An Essay toward an Autobiography of a Race Concept.* New York: Harcourt Brace, 1940.

——. *Essays on Anti-Semitism,* ed. K. S. Pinson. *The Crisis* (September 1942): 200.

Farley, Christopher John. "Enforcing Correctness." *Time* 7 (February 1994): 37.

Foner, Philip S., ed. *W.E.B. Du Bois Speaks: Speeches and Addresses.* New York: Pathfinder, 1970.

Lewis, David Levering, ed. *W.E.B. Du Bois: A Reader.* New York: Henry Holt, 1995.

Review of Essays in Annals of the American Academy of Politics and Social Sciences, 1942.

Sundquist, Eric J., ed. *The Oxford W.E.B. Du Bois Reader.* New York: Oxford University Press, 1996.

West, Cornel. "On Black-Jewish Relations." In *Race Matters.* Boston: Beacon, 1993.

Alphine Jefferson

APTHEKER, HERBERT (1915–   )

Born in Brooklyn, New York, on July 31, 1915, Aptheker became Du Bois' "literary executor" after they had established a deep comradeship while working in the same office. After receiving his Ph.D. from Columbia (New York) in 1943, Aptheker began a scholar–activist sojourn that would not only help shape and change how the field of African American history is understood but also help the United States make the "revolutionary" social change after World War II that led to the desegregation of public institutions. Aptheker's career achievements are the editing and writing of over eighty books (of which over forty volumes are of Du Bois' personal letters and scholarly works). His wife Fay, whom he married in 1942, ably assisted him in these scholarly efforts.

Even though he was born of affluent Russian immigrants, Aptheker noted that a black woman and nursemaid, Angelina Corbin, helped elevate his racial horizons as a child. Aptheker reflected that "Annie raised me as much as mother. I loved her and mother loved her." His intellectual curiosity was challenged by a biography of Ulysses S. Grant that asserted American slaves were stereotyped as "sambo." Reflecting on the strength of character of Annie, Aptheker said of this historical interpretation, "It can't be true. It was impossible that her people were like that." Searching for historical truth, Aptheker's master's thesis analyzed Nat Turner's rebellion, and his dissertation was a comprehensive interpretation of "American Negro Slave Revolts." When his dissertation was published in 1943, it became a watershed in the historiography of slavery. His social consciousness had been pricked after traveling in the depression South and seeing how the "barbarism" of peonage and Jim Crow exploited the black populace. Returning, he wrote a regular column, "The Dark Side of the South," in his high school paper exposing this racial injustice.

Aptheker joined the Communist Party in 1939 and edited and wrote for Masses and Mainstream. It was one of his reviews of Du Bois' publications that led Du Bois to realize Aptheker's scholarly talents. Du Bois told Aptheker that his review of *Dusk of Dawn* was the best he had seen of this work. Aptheker remained in the Communist Party until his resignation in 1992.

His commitment to the oppressed masses led him to join a black effort at eliminating peonage in Oglethorpe County, Georgia. He served on an anti-peonage committee that included the black activist William Patterson, folk singer Woody Guthrie, and blues singer Huddie Ledbetter, popularly known as Leadbelly. Aptheker's dedication led him to Oglethorpe County in the late 1930s disguised as an insurance salesman with the name "H. Biel." H. Biel's mission was to distribute bus tickets to black peons seeking "flight" from the oppressive system of debt peonage.

During World War II, Aptheker, on his request, commanded an all-black artillery battery. This international struggle against fascism in Europe only strengthened Aptheker's struggle against similar ideas in the United States. Understanding that the war was being fought on two fronts, fascism in Europe and racism at home, prompted Aptheker to lead an unusual march. Aptheker led his artillery unit on a midnight march through Pollock, Louisiana, where a sign was posted saying, "No Niggers Allowed." At the appropriate moment, the entire unit began singing "John Brown's Body."

After the war, a Guggenheim Fellowship permitted him to begin his research on a documentary history of African American people. Today, this research is indispensable for those trying to understand the American reality of race. It was during this period of the late 1940s that Du Bois asked Aptheker to share his National Association for the Advancement of Colored People (NAACP) office with him. A close comradeship developed between these office mates, and Du Bois in 1946 asked Aptheker to be his "literary executor." Aptheker recalls that he developed a love and respect for Du Bois no less than what he felt for his own father. When Du Bois, under the auspices of President Kwame Nkrumah, left for Ghana in 1961 to work on the *Encyclopedia Africana*, he entrusted the overwhelming majority of his letters and papers to Aptheker and his wife Fay.

As one of the intellectual and theoretical doyens of the civil rights movement, Aptheker was kept under constant surveillance by the Federal Bureau of Investigation (FBI). Commenting on Kenneth O'Reilly's book *Racial Matters: The Secret File on Black America, 1969–1970* (1989), Aptheker suggested that these files revealed that the agency contemplated underwriting a book-length reactionary critique of his writings. To understand this effort to discredit Aptheker, one must keep in mind that as late as 1976 Aptheker ran for the U.S. Senate seat against Daniel Patrick Moynihan, and over 25,000 voters supported his candidacy.

Years of threats, intimidation, and physical abuse by his political enemies have not daunted Aptheker's will to struggle against racism and oppression. In 1993 his book *Anti-Racism in U.S. History* demonstrated that his vision is still clearly focused.

FURTHER READING

Fisher, Jack. "One Man Who Changed History." *San Jose Mercury News*, February 20, 1994: IA.

Horne, Gerald C. *Black and Red: W.E.B. Du Bois and the Afro-American Response to the Cold War, 1944–1963.* Albany: State University of New York Press, 1986.
Interview by Malik Simba conducted at Herbert Aptheker's home, October 27, 1995.
Lewis, David Levering. *W.E.B. Du Bois: Biography of a Race, 1868–1919.* New York: Henry Holt, 1993.

Malik Simba

ART AND ARTISTS

In much of his writing, Du Bois kept his reading audiences apprised of black artistic achievements to which he applied the same standards as he did to literature. Du Bois delineated his philosophy of creativity in "Criteria of Negro Art" (*The Crisis*, 1926). His view that "all art is propaganda," according to Sundquist, "refers first of all to Du Bois' deeply held belief in the ethical and politically responsibility of art and literature" (304). For Du Bois art must be truthful, an accurate representation of the race: "Negro art is today plowing a difficult row, chiefly because we shrink at the portrayal of the truth about ourselves. We are so used to seeing the truth distorted to our people that whenever we are portrayed on canvas, in story, or on the stage, as simply humans with human frailties, we rebel" (310). Blacks resist images because so many have been negative.

Du Bois' greatest consideration was that "a black artist is first of all a *black* artist" (*Chicago Defender*, January 26, 1946). On the death of Countee Cullen, Du Bois charged that African Americans ignored art created by blacks. "Thus, we starved Richard Brown . . . we lost Henry O. Tanner. Somehow, we as a people, need a 'sort of united determined effort' to really preserve, honor, and nurture our creative genius" (*Chicago Defender*, January 26, 1946).

Du Bois defined "art" very broadly, not limiting his definition to literature but including visual and performing arts, music, theater, and dance. He defined his standards in "Negro Art and Literature" (*The Gift of Black Folk*). He confirmed his skill for appraising and appreciating many areas of black creativity.

Blacks developed and incorporated the music they brought from Africa into U.S. culture and produced great but neglected composers: Jay Hemmenway, A. J. Connor, Justin Howell, and the Anglo-African Samuel Coleridge-Taylor (1875–1912). Coleridge-Taylor, who collaborated with poet Paul Laurence Dunbar on several musical works, was a good friend of Du Bois'. Du Bois also supported William Grant Still (1895–1978), who was the first African American to have a symphony performed by an American orchestra (1931), the East Rochester Philharmonic. In 1940 Du Bois complimented Still for the success of his ballad "And They Lynched Him on a Tree." Du Bois also reviewed musical performers, pointing out Roland Hayes, "the tenor whose fine voice has charmed London, Paris, and Vienna and who is now one of the leading soloists of the Boston Symphony Orchestra."

Du Bois frequently called attention to black contributions to American cul-

ture, observing that African Americans were the "greatest originators of danc-
ing in the United States and the world" (Sundquist, 313). Blacks originated,
for example, the "cake walk," a dance in which the couples performed the
most intricate steps to receive cakes as prizes. The great debt owed to blacks
was seldom acknowledged; however, some white performers conceded their
indebtedness to blacks. Vernon (British dancer, 1887–1918) and Irene Castle
"always told their audience that their dances were of Negro origin" (*Crisis*,
1924).

Du Bois positioned Scipio Moorhead as the ancestor of African American
art just as he situated Phillis Wheatley as the foundation of an African American literary tradition. Moorhead engraved Wheatley's portrait in the frontis-
piece in her 1773 volume of poetry *Poems on Various Subjects, Religious and Moral.*
Du Bois also commended the accomplishments of E. M. Banister (1828–1901)
of Rhode Island, who did not travel to Paris like other black artists of his
generation, claiming he wanted to "paint like an American."

Steadfastly promoting black creativity, Du Bois also championed Henry Os-
sawa Tanner (1859–1937), who was known for his paintings rooted in traditional black culture. Du Bois did not omit women from his discussions of art.
In his columns he recognized sculptors Edmonia Lewis and Meta Warrick
Fuller, a pupil of Rodin. Nevertheless, Du Bois chastised blacks for not supporting black artists, suggesting that every black church adorn its interior with
a Tanner painting.

Commenting on black creativity on the stage, Du Bois explained that "on
the stage the Negro has naturally had a most difficult chance to be recognized."
This lack of recognition was perhaps due to European American negative
portrayals of blacks, especially the minstrel shows. Du Bois observed that the
customary role of blacks as buffoons or fools must give way, for the "most
dramatic group of people in the history of the United States is the Negro."
Continuing, he adds, "[I]t would be very easy for a great artist so to interpret
the history of our country as to make the plot turn entirely upon the black
man" ("The Negro and the American Stage," *The Crisis*, June 1924).

The white negative characterization of blacks did not deter some black actors
because eventually "there appeared Cole and Johnson, . . . Williams and Walker." Bert Williams was the first African American to achieve celebrity on
Broadway, performing in eight productions of the Ziegfeld Follies. Despite his
fame, the blatant racism of the time forced Williams to perform in black face.
Nevertheless, "Their [William's and Walker's] development of a new light
comedy marked an epoch and Bert Williams was . . . without doubt the leading
comedian on the American stage" ("The Negro and the American Stage," *The
Crisis*, June 1924).

On the legitimate stage, Du Bois applauded Ira Aldridge (1805–1867), who
spent his entire career in Europe because of the racial climate in the United
States. Considered one of the greatest interpreters of Shakespeare, Aldridge
went to Europe, possibly with the aid of Edmund Kean (1787–1833), a British

actor who, too, was famous for his interpretations of Shakespeare. Aldridge died at Lodz, Poland, while on tour. Aldridge "had practically no success until Charles Gilpin triumphed in *The Emperor Jones* in New York (1920–21)" (Sundquist, 321). Du Bois paid Roland Hayes the highest compliment, noting that Robeson's performance was the "first time since Ira Aldridge that the character of Othello was played by a Negro, which despite critics was undoubtedly the type that Shakespeare had in mind" (*Phylon* Vol. III, No. 4, 1942). *See also*: Gilpin, Charles Sidney; Hayes, Roland.

FURTHER READING

Sundquist, Eric J., ed. *The Oxford W.E.B. Du Bois Reader.* New York: Oxford University Press, 1996.

Malaika Horne

ART AND LITERATURE

Better known for his work in sociology and history, Du Bois also saw himself as a creative writer. During his lifetime, he published five novels and several poems and short stories. In "Credo" (*The Independent*, 1904) Du Bois articulated his desire for a "Life lit by some large vision of beauty and goodness and truth." Applying his beliefs, Du Bois, in an introductory note to *The Quest of the Silver Fleece* (1911), echoed his *Independent* article: "He who would tell a tale must look toward three ideals: to tell it well, to tell it beautifully and to tell the truth." *The Quest of the Silver Fleece* fulfilled part of his promise to himself to "practice art, as well as science." The novel is a tale of love and economic analysis that emphasizes, among other themes, the intelligence and abilities of black women. Du Bois' conclusion that the race problem "at bottom is simply a matter of ownership of women; white men want the right to own and use all women . . . and they resist any intrusion of colored men into this domain" expresses an acute awareness of the relationship between economics and racism and sexism.

An ardent supporter and critic of black art, Du Bois, in an October 1926 *Crisis* article ("Criteria for Negro Art"), again used "beauty," "goodness," and "truth" among his criteria for black art. Added to his trilogy of ideals was propaganda:

[A]ll art is propaganda and ever must be. . . . I stand in utter shame and say that whatever art I have for writing has been used always for propaganda for gaining the right of [black folk] to love and enjoy. I do not care a damn for any art that is not used for propaganda. But I do care when propaganda is confined to one side while the other is stripped and silent. (Sundquist, 328)

White propaganda as art demonized blacks. Thus, it seems that Du Bois' doctrine demanded that black artists manipulate their creative impulses to present positive images of blacks and to articulate implicitly certain political and economic ideologies.

Reproaching black writers, Du Bois concluded that the artists were following the demands of the marketplace by writing for an implied white audience. Though Du Bois was aware that writing for an implied white audience was not only tempting but corrupting, the chief reason for creating should be the "revelation in his [the artist] own soul, and the picturing of his own problems and his own people" (*The Crisis*, July 1929). Du Bois recognized the need for black artists to have freedom to create, but he also understood the pressures to focus that creativity in a racist society.

Du Bois reiterated this view of artists and society in a 1929 Norfolk (Virginia) *Journal and Guide* article, writing that "it is more and more necessary for Black artists and writers to create not for white but rather for Black people." Art is part of the freedom that blacks are seeking, but they should create their own art, not an imitation of white America. This true black art would allow African Americans to define themselves, instead of accepting white definitions of blackness. Du Bois took this position because he believed that blacks have different values that reflect their unique experiences and perspectives and perhaps a different view of beauty. These differences could only be adequately expressed in literature written by blacks for blacks.

Earlier (1921) Du Bois had condemned the conservative tendencies of some blacks who demanded that writers glorify blackness, presenting African Americans in a positive milieu. Arguing that such exaltation is not art, Du Bois concluded that "we need not be afraid of the truth that our art will flourish" (*The Crisis*, June 1921). Nevertheless, he continued, these positive depictions did not always represent the truth. Yet in his reviews of some Harlem Renaissance writers, Du Bois seemed to prefer those novelists who wrote of middle- and upper-middle-class blacks instead of the working class. He praised Jessie R. Fauset's *Plum Bun* (1929) for her depiction of the ordinariness of black life instead of the exotic, as in Carl Van Vechten (*Nigger Heaven*, 1926) and Claude McKay (*Home to Harlem*, 1928; *Banjo*, 1929). Though admiring McKay's poetry, Du Bois was particularly disparaging of McKay's prose fiction. In 1931 with the installation of the Du Bois Literary Prize, Du Bois hoped "the award will turn our writers away from the Van Vechten and the later McKay school" toward a "more human and truthful portrait of the American Negro in the 20th century" (*The Crisis*, 1931).

As Du Bois praised Fauset's work, he also reviewed Nella Larsen's *Quicksand* (1928) positively: "a fine, thoughtful and courageous piece of work." In the same column ("The Browsing Reader," 1928), Du Bois continued his attacks on Claude McKay. Reviewing *Home to Harlem*, Du Bois wrote that the book "nauseates me."

For Du Bois, art should be beauty, goodness, truth, and propaganda. This literary or artistic endeavor would promulgate a specific political, economic, and social philosophy and redefine the image of blacks while educating and entertaining. *See also*: Art and Artists; *Dark Princess*; Fauset, Jessie Redmon; McKay, Claude; Poetry; *The Quest of the Silver Fleece*.

FURTHER READING

Aptheker, Herbert. *The Literary Legacy of W.E.B. Du Bois*. White Plains, NY: Kraus International, 1989.

"The Browsing Reader." *The Crisis* (June 1928).

Byerman, Keith E. *Seizing the Word: History, Art, and Self in the Work of W.E.B. Du Bois.* Athens: University of Georgia Press, 1994.

Rampersad, Arnold. *The Art and Imagination of W.E.B. Du Bois*. New York: Schocken Books, 1990.

Courtney Young

ASIA

As the most populous continent, Asia is home to some of the world's oldest cultures. During much of its history, foreigners, principally Europeans, have exploited and controlled it and its people.

Largely inhabited by people of color, Asia intrigued Du Bois. His interest and concern for Asia—especially India and China—were long-standing and intense. Du Bois' interest probably sprang from the fact that both countries—unlike Japan—were under European domination, and Du Bois understood the interconnectedness between the "colored" people of Asia and black America.

Admitting that he had learned little of India, or Asia, while a student, Du Bois wrote that "the one tenuous link which bound me to India was skin color." More than just the country, the leader of its independence movement, Gandhi, appealed to Du Bois. In 1929 Du Bois asked Gandhi to send a message to American blacks. Gandhi responded by writing in "Gandhi and the American Negroes" (*The Crisis*, May 1929): "Let not 12 million Negroes be ashamed of the fact that they are the grandchildren of slaves.... There is dishonor in being slave-owners. But let us not think of honor or dishonor in connection with the past. Let us realize that the future is with those who would be pure, truthful and loving." As Gandhi came to personify India for him, Du Bois was sometimes critical of other Asian Indians.

The relationship between the Indians of Asia and the Black people of the United States has not been very good. A reason is the tendency of Indian visitors and students here to keep away from our problems; an illustration is the recent conduct of Madame Pandit, now the Indian Ambassador in Washington, where she has adopted that city's Jim Crow pattern. ("As the Crow Flies," August 12, 1950)

Though critical of the behavior and attitudes of Madame Pandit and other Asian Indians in the United States, Du Bois never lost sight of the parallels between African Americans and Indians.

Despite his earlier assessment of Madame Pandit, in 1947 Du Bois wrote that African Americans should express their appreciation to her for her successful fight in the United Nations General Assembly for a resolution condemning the racism practiced by South Africa against Indians (*The Chicago Defender*, January 18, 1947).

More important than individual personalities was the independence movement that involved India's attempt to throw off its colonial bonds. In 1929,
the year of Gandhi's essay, Du Bois emphasized his attitudes toward colonialism and predicted its collapse.

In the 19th century it was assumed that the world belonged to and always would belong
to the superior peoples of white Europe and America; no longer is this true and the
changes came with the World War, the Bolshevik Revolution, the struggle of independence in India, and the great changes in Japan and China. The fight for independence
intensifies—North, East and West. In the van of this fight are the Afro-American millions. (*The Crisis*, October 1929)

Even so, in writing of India's struggle he consistently stressed India's ties to
the "colored" world.

Supportive of wars of independence, Du Bois welcomed the Chinese Revolution (1949) just as he had supported Gandhi in India. Du Bois first visited
China in 1936 and was impressed by its long history and civilization. "Where
Europe counts its years in hundreds, Asia counts its in thousands" (*Autobiography*, 44).

For Du Bois the Chinese Revolution carried a message for Europeans, especially the British. He noted the embryonic uprising in China and the prophetic message it carried for those "who cannot conceive a world where black,
brown and white are free and equal" (*The Crisis*, February 1911).

Du Bois revisited China in 1959, stressing his theme that China is a land
of "colored" people, and he observed that the Chinese

know, as no other people know, to what depths human meanness can go. I used to
weep for American Negroes, as I saw what indignities and repressions and cruelties
they had passed; but as I read Chinese history in these last months and had it explained
to me stripped of Anglo-Saxon lies, I know that no depths of Negro slavery in America
have plumbed such abysses as the Chinese have seen for 2,000 years and more. They
have seen starvation and murder, rape and prostitution; sale and slavery of children;
and religion cloaked in opium and gin. (*Freedom*, June 8, 1959)

Again, as in the case of India, Du Bois stressed the similarities between the
Chinese and African Americans.

As he had supported China and India, Du Bois did not endorse Japan's
hostilities against China. He wrote that Japan should "cease their warfare and
unite" (*The Crisis*, January 1933). The two countries and India would then "be
able to drive the white exploiters from all Asia." On the other hand, he later
wrote, "Japan is convinced that European influence in China will make her
very existence insecure unless she herself dominates China" ("A Chronicle of
Race Relations," 1939). In the same article he warned, "Japan is fighting Europe in the war it wages in China; however, Japanese militarism is a menace
and should it conquer China this would be a calamity for civilization."

However, with the bombing of Hiroshima and Nagasaki, Du Bois queried:

Just what does the Colored and Colonial world say to the atomic bomb? Will it assure domination by Europe and the United States? Probably not, because in the first place, the white nations do not trust each other, and in the second place, why is it assumed that nations such as China, India, and Japan will not be able to produce the bomb? (*The Chicago Defender*, January 5, 1946)

In 1947 Du Bois' focus on Asia turned to Vietnam, warning that France was seeking to form a French Union similar to the British Commonwealth to replace her colonial empire. By 1950 he was no longer referring to the French colony as Indo-China but as Vietnam, identifying its real leader as Ho Chi Minh, the person who rendered the French army powerless. And he predicted the eventual victory of the Vietnamese freedom fighters, although the United States, at the suggestion of Vice President Richard Nixon, was increasingly helping France in its war. Understanding the importance of a non-European-dominated Asia to the world and to African Americans, Du Bois' interest did not diminish. *See also*: China; Japan; Mao Zedong.

FURTHER READING

"A Chronicle of Race Relations." *Phylon* (Vol. 1, No. 1, 1939), pp. 90–97.
"As the Crow Flies." *The Chicago Globe* (May 20, 1950).
"As the Crow Flies." *The Chicago Globe* (August 12, 1950).
The Autobiography of W.E.B. Du Bois. New York: International Publishers, 1968.

Mary Young

ATLANTA, GEORGIA

W.E.B. Du Bois first came to Atlanta, Georgia, in 1897 to teach at Atlanta University and remained there until 1910. These years were some of the most productive of his long life and were some of the most horrifying years as well. Living on the campus at Atlanta University, Du Bois had limited contact with the rest of the city and the people of Atlanta. The political climate of Atlanta deterred him from even voting. During these years blacks were not allowed to vote in Georgia's "white primary," which, in a state controlled by the Democratic Party, decided the outcome of most elections.

Several events commanded Du Bois' attention during this period in Atlanta. In 1899, a white mob in the city lynched and dismembered a black farmer, Sam Hose. A month later Du Bois' two-year-old son died. The year of 1906 brought the infamous Atlanta Pogrom, which occurred while Du Bois was working in Alabama. Upon hearing of the riot, he returned home and in transit wrote a memorable poem entitled "Litany of Atlanta." Du Bois comments in his *Autobiography* that although many people he knew owned pistols, he had never purchased or carried one. However, after the 1906 riot he kept a double-barreled shotgun in his home. He writes: "If a white mob had stepped on the campus where I lived I would without hesitation have sprayed their guts over the grass."

Du Bois jumped at the opportunity to leave Atlanta in 1910 to assume a position with the National Association for the Advancement of Colored People (NAACP). When he was pushed out as editor of *The Crisis*, Du Bois was afforded the chance to return to Atlanta University in 1934. He remained there until his controversial dismissal in 1944. *See also*: Atlanta University; *The Crisis*, Georgia; National Association for the Advancement of Colored People (NAACP); Poetry.

FURTHER READING

Broderick, Francis L. *W.E.B. Du Bois: Negro Leader in a Time of Crisis.* Stanford, CA: Stanford University Press, 1959.

Du Bois, W.E.B. *The Autobiography of W.E.B. Du Bois: A Soliloquy on Viewing My Life from the Last Decade of Its First Century.* New York: International Publishers, 1968.

Lewis, David Levering. *W.E.B. Du Bois: Biography of a Race, 1868–1919.* New York: Henry Holt, 1993.

Marable, Manning, *W.E.B. Du Bois: Black Radical Democrat.* Boston: Twayne Publishers, 1986.

Moore, Jack B. *W.E.B. Du Bois.* Boston: Twayne Publishers, 1981.

Mary Ellen Wilson

ATLANTA UNIVERSITY

W.E.B. Du Bois twice made Atlanta University his professional home. In 1897 Du Bois departed the University of Pennsylvania for Atlanta, where he taught social science and supervised the Atlanta University Conference for the Study of the Negro Problems. Atlanta's racial climate posed a stern challenge for Du Bois' beliefs in the power of social science. While he produced celebrated studies of black life and culture, white Atlantans participated in a free-for-all of racial violence that culminated in the 1905 Atlanta Race Riot. This climate helped turn Du Bois' career toward reform activity. During his Atlanta tenure, Du Bois emerged as an articulate opponent of Booker T. Washington's program of racial accommodation. Speaking for an emerging black middle class, Du Bois demanded social and political equality, in contrast with Washington's emphasis on economic gain. In 1905 he played a crucial role in founding the Niagara Movement, an organization dedicated to this agenda. Du Bois cofounded the National Association for the Advancement of Colored People in 1910 and resigned his Atlanta University position to become its secretary. Twenty-four years later at the age of sixty-six, Du Bois returned to Atlanta for a second tenure at the university. Before his resignation in 1944, Du Bois produced another round of influential and lasting scholarship, including his *Black Reconstruction in America* (1935). Du Bois' return to the South during the most violent and repressive period of white southerners' successful program of resegregation and racial intimidation decisively turned an idealistic young social scientist toward the political task at hand and made the scholar an activist. *See also*: Atlanta, Georgia.

W.E.B. Du Bois at Atlanta University circa 1909. Courtesy of Special Collections and Archives, W.E.B. Du Bois Library, University of Massachusetts Amherst.

FURTHER READING

Du Bois, W.E.B. *Black Reconstruction in America.* New York: Russell and Russell, 1935.

Drew VandeCreek

AZIKIWE, NNAMDI (1904–1996)

Azikiwe was a Nigerian politician, an advocate of Pan-Africanism, and the first president of Nigeria (1963–1966). Like most African intellectuals of his day, Azikiwe was active in the Pan-Africanist movement and was also an African nationalist. Educated at Howard University and Lincoln University (Pennsylvania) during the late 1920s and 1930s, Azikiwe became intimately acquainted with the philosophies of Pan-Africanists such as Marcus Garvey and W.E.B. Du Bois. In 1937, Azikiwe returned to Nigeria and founded a chain of newspapers that advocated self-rule for Nigeria, then a British colony.

The end of World War II heralded significant changes for colonialism in Africa. The rise of an educated African elite during the interwar years bolstered Pan-Africanism. The Fifth Pan-African Congress held on October 15–21, 1945, in the Chorlton Town Hall at Manchester, England, was convened to honor Du Bois as the "Father of Pan-Africanism." Every major African nationalist was in attendance, including Azikiwe. After the Manchester conference, Du Bois continued to chronicle Azikiwe's career. He noted the seminal role that Azikiwe played in placing Nigerian demands for independence before the British during the 1940s and 1950s.

After a visit to Nigeria in 1960, to attend the inaugural of Azikiwe as the first governor general of Nigeria, Du Bois wrote an extensive report in the *People's Voice* on the history of Nigeria, focusing on the struggle against colonialism. Like his assessments of other postindependence African leaders, Du Bois believed that Azikiwe greatly contributed to the liberation of his country from British rule. *See also*: Africa.

FURTHER READING

Jones-Quartey, K.A.B. *A Life of Azikiwe.* Baltimore, MD: Penguin, 1965.
"Pan-Africa." *The People's Voice* (November 8, 1947).

Stephen G. Hall

B

BANDUNG CONFERENCE

In April 1955 delegations from twenty-nine Asian and African nations met at Bandung, Indonesia to discuss issues common to the recently decolonized nations, including economic development, resistance to racism, and the prospects for remaining nonaligned in the context of the Cold War. Although this conference was pivotal in the formation of the Non-Aligned Movement, nonalignment was not required for participation, and several countries with strong ties to superpowers, including Turkey (a U.S. ally) and China (which had not yet split with the Soviet Union), were present. Independent delegations, including several black Americans, were also invited to address the assembly. Bandung was the first meeting in the era of the modern world system that attempted to unite "Third World" nations outside the hegemony of the West, and as such it was celebrated as a historic moment by both Du Bois and many other African American intellectuals. For example, Richard Wright wrote *The Color Curtain* about the conference.

Du Bois was invited to address the conference, but (with Paul Robeson) he was unable to attend because the U.S. Department of State denied him a passport due to his political stance. It is not going too far to say that Du Bois had spent the last forty years working toward Bandung. Ever since he began to organize Pan-African Conferences in 1919, his global politics identified the colored peoples of the world as the group capable of uniting against racial colonialism and the global expansion of capitalism for the purpose of creating a more just world system. His attentiveness to Gandhi and issues of Indian decolonization, leading to the analysis of Asian-African relations in his journalism and in *The World and Africa* (1947), began early in the 1920s. During his participation in the peace movement in the 1940s and 1950s, he proposed that the maintenance of the colonies was the primary issue preventing world peace and that the neutrality of people of color in the Cold War was therefore central to avoiding another world war. In this context, Du Bois declared of Bandung that "in another half century the colored world is going to date the beginning of its integrity, unification, and self-conscious progress on the great Pan-Colored meeting of 1955" (*Spotlight on Africa*, January 1955).

Denied the opportunity to attend the conference, Du Bois sent a short, general statement to be read aloud, which consisted of a "Greeting" from "the twenty-five million colored peoples of America" and a "Declaration of Independence" of the peoples of Africa, asserting that "Africa is for Africans. . . . Hereafter it will no longer be ruled by might nor by power . . . but by the spirit of all its gods and the wisdom of its prophets" (*Spotlight on Africa*, January 1955). The conference statement is noteworthy for at least two things it does not address. First, in a piece published in *Spotlight on Africa* in January 1955, Du Bois emphasized that strong ties between Africa and Asia can and should be made at this date because of the history and continuing presence of racism in the world system:

Since the Renaissance, skin color has been made a reason for oppression, discrimination and war, and therefore it is of great significance that the peoples of Asia and Africa have recently arranged to have a joint meeting in Indonesia to drive a wedge between socialists (and Communists) and the Western nations so as to hide the real problem of exploitation of Asian and African colonies by the west.

He continued, stating that the United States is trying to "bribe American Negroes to join Big Business by some relaxation of the color line." Thus, Du Bois' chief concern about the conference addresses the intervention of the great powers (particularly the United States) through their proxies—African American attendees among them. *See also*: Asia; Cultural and Scientific Conference for World Peace; Peace Movement.

FURTHER READING

Du Bois, W.E.B. "The Bandung Conference." In *Writings in Periodicals Edited by Others* 4: 237–247. Millwood, NY: Kraus-Thomson Organization, 1982.
——. "Pan-Colored." In *Writings in Periodicals Edited by Others* 4: 225–236. Millwood, NY: Kraus-Thomson Organization, 1982.
Wright, Richard. *The Color Curtain*. Jackson: University of Mississippi Press, 1995.

Kenneth Mostern

BELGIUM AND THE BELGIAN CONGO

Located in northwest Europe, Belgium, approximately the size of the state of Maryland, gained its independence in 1839. In 1865, with the ascension of Leopold II (1835–1909) to the throne, Belgium became interested in founding an overseas empire. The scramble for Africa began five years later.

In 1876, Leopold II employed Sir Henry Stanley, who was famous in Europe for his search for Dr. David Livingstone, to acquire as much land in the Congo basin as he possibly could. The land was not intended to become a Belgian colony but a private state, owned exclusively by Leopold. Stanley negotiated treaties with the Congolese that gave Leopold exclusive ownership of the land.

Europeans and Americans set up a conference in Berlin to discuss dividing Africa evenly. With the treaties that Stanley had obtained, Leopold legitimately claimed the Congo. He did anything to gain the area's wealth—rubber, ivory, gold, copper, and diamonds—through the use of forced labor. By the mid-1890s, the Congo Free State (its name under Leopold) had become the scene of the worst scandals in modern colonial history, and tales of forced labor and massacres emanating from the country shocked the world. The inhabitants "were saddled with taxes in food or rubber deliveries or in porterage" (Ascherson 252). Others reported seeing "men shot . . . fishing instead of rubber gathering . . . and watched a boy sawing off the hand of a victim who was not yet dead" (Ascherson 252). An Antwerp newspaper reported a raid against an idle village: "We fell upon them all and killed them without mercy . . . he [the commander] ordered us to cut off the heads of the men and hang them on village pallisades, and also their sexual members, and to hang the women and children on the pallisades in the form of a cross" (qtd. in *King Leopold's Rule in Africa* 129). Like Du Bois, much of Europe frowned upon these reported atrocities, which led to the end of Leopold's rule. His financial backing eroded to the point that Leopold required loans from the Belgium government. Additionally, investigation of the brutal treatment and exploitation of the Congolese led to the annexation of the territory and the establishment of the Belgian Congo, which became independent in 1960.

In 1907, before Leopold formally ceded the area to the Belgian government, Du Bois was reporting (*The Horizon,* January 1907) Belgium's "shameful" exploitation of the area. He also noted the infusion of U.S. capital—especially Rockefeller's—and direly warned: "The day of reckoning is coming."

Nonetheless, after the Belgian government assumed control of the Congo, the savagery did not end. Du Bois reported that he had received correspondence verifying the flogging of women by employees of American firms. Apparently the United States "is doing Africa as badly as ever Belgium did" (*The Crisis,* January 1924).

In a review of F. Seymore's book *E. D. Morel, the Man and His Work*, Du Bois declared, "Morel's best claim to fame was his exposure of the atrocities committed by King Leopold's company in the Belgian Congo. . . . [S]lavery in its most virulent form exists in the Belgian Congo" (*The Nation,* May 25, 1921). E. D. Morel, in his reports on the atrocities in the Congo, almost single-handedly exposed Leopold. In 1904 Morel visited the United States to ask President Roosevelt to intervene in the Congo. Instead, a branch of the Congo Reform Association (CRA) was formed under the leadership of Booker T. Washington.

As late as 1947, Du Bois was reporting the brutality in the Congo. "An unnamed official, returning from the Belgian Congo, reports conditions have not improved from what they were before the war [World War II]" (*The People's Voice*, September 6, 1947). *See also*: Africa.

FURTHER READING

Ascherson, Neal. *The King Incorporated. Leopold II in the Age of Trusts*. Garden City, NY: Doubleday and Co., 1964.

Emerson, Barbara. *Leopold II of the Belgians. King of Colonialism*. New York: St. Martin's Press, 1979.

Morel, E. D. *Great Britain and the Congo: The Pillage of the Congo Basin*. 1909. New York: H. Fertig, 1969.

——. *King Leopold's Rule in Africa*. Greenwood Press Reprint. London: 1904.

Mary Young

BELLEGARDE, DANTES (1877–1966)

Born in Port-au-Prince, Haiti, educated and trained for the law, Dantes Bellegarde was a leading educator in his country before entering government service. As a representative of Haiti, he, eventually, became not only Haitian minister to France but also a member of the Permanent Court of Arbitration of the Hague and minister and member of the Commission of Experts on Slavery and Forced Labor.

In 1914, under the Monroe Doctrine, the U.S. Marines intervened in Haiti. In 1924, Bellegarde, the Haitian delegate to the League of Nations, sought League sanction against the United States. Although the League refused to place the matter on its agenda, it was a victory for Haiti that Bellegarde was allowed to place the issue before the League at all.

In the February 1923 issue of *The Crisis*, Du Bois published a letter from Bellegarde about his League presentation. Later, in April of 1926, he devoted his *Crisis* column to Bellegarde, reporting on his achievements. He ended the column with words of praise for Bellegarde. "More power to Dantes Bellegarde! More shame to America in Haiti!" *See also*: Haiti.

FURTHER READING

Bellegarde-Smith, Patrick. *In the Shadow of Powers: Dantes Bellegarde in Haitian Social Thought*. Atlantic Highlands, NJ: Humanities Press, 1985.

Mary Young

BIRTH CONTROL

Although African Americans have been using birth control for centuries, the debate over contraception became increasingly public during the 1920s and 1930s with the rise of the larger birth control movement and the use of science as a legitimate discourse. Within this context, Du Bois became one of the first African Americans to express approval of birth control as a mechanism for racial progress.

Cognizant of the harsh social and economic conditions African Americans faced, and the circumstances of black women in particular, Du Bois asserted the woman of the future must have access to birth control technology in addition to the right to choose motherhood at her own discretion. But his support of birth control went beyond personal access and human rights. Observing that other populations in the modern world were breeding and training for intelligence and efficiency, Du Bois imagined birth control would offer a better chance of survival for African Americans as a race. Arguing that African Americans needed birth control more than any other group, Du Bois maintained "ignorant Negroes" were breeding carelessly, believing in the "fallacy of numbers." Comparing human races and groups to vegetables, he suggested African Americans, particularly those of lower socioeconomic status, needed to learn that quality rather than quantity is what counts. The influence of the eugenics movement is apparent in Du Bois' rhetoric, particularly through his promotion of "prudent breeding" to create "quality" African Americans, or the "Talented Tenth." Expressed within the prevailing discourse of science, Du Bois viewed birth control as a tool for breeding desirable physical and mental characteristics for the "race," which were essential for its survival. *See also*: Marriage and Race.

FURTHER READING

Du Bois, W.E.B. "Black Folk and Birth Control." *Birth Control Review* 16 (June 1932).
Hart, Jamie. "Who Should Have the Children? Discussions of Birth Control among African American Intellectuals, 1920–1939." *Journal of Negro History* (Winter 1994).

Jamie Hart

THE BIRTH OF A NATION

This landmark film, directed by D. W. Griffith, glorifies the Ku Klux Klan's role in overthrowing "Black Reconstruction" of the defeated South. Based on Thomas W. Dixon's (1864–1946) novel, *The Clansman, The Birth of a Nation* portrays Reconstruction as a tragic era of governmental malfeasance and suffering for white Southerners. Attempting to enlist the sympathies of a national audience, the film depicts the Old South as a land of gracious planters and contented slaves. After the Civil War, however, a band of vengeful Northern radicals, personified by Congressman Austin Stoneman, a thinly disguised Thaddeus Stevens, unleashes upon the prostrate South the freedmen, painted in coarse stereotypes as lustful beasts who equate emancipation and civil rights with access to European American women. *The Birth of a Nation* embodied views of Reconstruction widely supported by mainstream historiography and painted a picture of African Americans and the Ku Klux Klan that exercised a long and persistent hold on the imagination of white Americans.

Technically brilliant, the film pioneered such techniques as flashback and montage to depict Civil War battles and avenging Klansmen and was embellished by an orchestral score featuring Wagner and Grieg. Starring such box-office heavyweights as Lilian Gish, *The Birth of a Nation* played to full houses throughout the nation and stands as one of the most financially successful motion pictures of its era. Even in an age of expanding Jim Crow, however, many Americans, including Oswald Garrison Villard, Booker T. Washington, and Du Bois found the film's vilification of African Americans foul and dangerous. From the film's release, Du Bois was involved in efforts to ban *The Birth of a Nation*, and he, along with the National Association for the Advancement of Colored People (NAACP) and many local chapters (1915), picketed theaters that showed the film. *See also*: National Association for the Advancement of Colored People (NAACP): Racism; Villard, Oswald Garrison; Washington, Booker T.

FURTHER READING

"The Clansmen." *The Crisis* (May 1915).
The Crisis (April 1915).

Trent Watts

BLACK BUSINESS

Du Bois was generally supportive of black efforts to start and control businesses. His involvement with the study and observation of black business began early in his career. As the editor of the Atlanta proceedings for the study of African Americans, Du Bois wrote much of *The Negro in Business* (1899). The study detailed the scope of the involvement of African Americans in industry and in their own businesses. In *The Crisis*, he infrequently commented on the state of black business as a whole but showed his approval by listing its achievements.

In Du Bois' lifetime, black business grew significantly, mostly in the North, with prominent exceptions in the South. Black insurance companies did well in Harlem and other predominantly black communities. At least one woman, Madame C. J. Walker, headed an extremely successful beauty products company.

Overall, African Americans increased their share of businesses, usually at the expense of agriculture in the South. Southern farming showed a decline when African Americans moved northward during the Great Migration.

More than a million African Americans moved to the urban North from 1916 to the mid-1920s in hopes of securing industrial employment. There was a corresponding rise in black business, especially retailing in the burgeoning black sections of northern cities.

Du Bois himself was part of a rapidly growing black business—newspapers and magazines. Newspapers like *The Chicago Defender* displayed tremendous growth in the early 1900s, and black editors founded many newspapers in cities all over the country. Du Bois took pride in his "own" business—*The Crisis*, the organ of the National Association for the Advancement of Colored People (NAACP). In the early years of the periodical, he was pleased that it showed a profit. On the other hand, he rejected certain advertisers, and certain advertisers rejected him, which led to a decline in circulation. He resigned from the periodical in 1934.

In *The Crisis*, he despaired when black business failed and sometimes attributed the failures to racism. When black entrepreneurs succeeded, Du Bois would either write about their success in detail or list an individual's achievements in the "Men of the Month" section.

Du Bois believed that African Americans should support black businesses but not exclusively as more race-conscious members did. This may have had something to do with his general disapproval of the separatism of Marcus Garvey, whose black-owned steamship line was supposed to benefit African Americans. However, it was more likely his general belief in integration that spurred this notion. After all, the NAACP was a mixed-race organization.

Du Bois did become more wary of black business and businesspersons as he got older, and his politics became more leftist. In the 1930s, he suggested to a conference on "The Economic Status of Negroes" (1933) the abandonment of the idea of profit. In the 1940s, he decried the way successful black businessmen were becoming too much like white businessmen. They were becoming more concerned with profits than people. This focus on profits caused him some anguish. He increasingly believed that the capitalist system itself was flawed, and he hoped it would be reformed, if not overthrown. *See also: The Crisis*; Garvey, Marcus; National Association for the Advancement of Colored People (NAACP).

FURTHER READING

"As the Crow Flies." *The Amsterdam News* (October 10, 1942).
"The Economic Future of the Negro." *Publications of the American Economic Association* (February 1906).

Jonathan Silverman

BLYDEN, EDWARD WILMOT (1832–1912)

Blyden was born in St. Thomas, Danish West Indies, on August 3, 1832, of free, literate parents. He became the foremost black nationalist of the nineteenth century who advocated African regeneration. St. Thomas had a racial hierarchy that placed Blyden and all other "pure Negroes" below the mulattoes and the whites. This experience led Blyden to denigrate mulattoes as a reactionary class. But because he became a Western-educated elite himself, Blyden developed a contradictory consciousness in which he alternately blamed blacks themselves and then whites for black deprivation.

As a young man, Blyden came under the tutelage of the missionary John Knox. In 1850, while in New York City with a Mrs. Knox, Blyden was introduced to the Liberian colonization effort and became convinced that Africa could be redeemed from its "benighted" state through Christian evangelization. After arriving in Liberia, Blyden continued his education and excelled enough to be appointed principal of Alexander High School in 1858 and editor of the *Liberian Herald* newspaper. He also attained the pastorate of the Presbyterian Church of Monrovia.

Blyden vigorously argued for continued colonization in *Voice from Bleeding Africa* (1856). He became a staunch advocate for elevating the mental faculties of Liberian womanhood. Blyden became professor of ancient languages when Liberia College was inaugurated in 1862.

He challenged the domination of mulatto Americo-Liberian coastal elites and retreated into the interior where he embraced Islam. His book *Christianity, Islam and the Negro* (1888) advocated the positive dimensions of Islam in the regeneration of the Negro personality. After a period of exile, due to political friction with the mulatto elites, Blyden returned to Liberia and assumed the presidency of Liberia College in 1881, only to be suspended for moral and financial indiscretions a few years later. He was exiled again in Sierra Leone, Lagos Colony, and the United States between 1885 and 1897. Blyden returned and briefly assumed the acting presidency of Liberia College in 1901. He was soon forced to resign this position, due in part to criticism that he was teaching Islam and advocating polygamy, which he practiced in his personal life. Blyden died on February 10, 1912.

Du Bois knew Blyden by reputation and admired him. Both advocated "Africa for Africans," and Du Bois published Blyden's writings in *The Crisis*. In 1909 Du Bois wrote to Blyden, requesting his assistance in compiling writers for Du Bois' proposed *Encyclopedia Africana. See also*: Liberia.

FURTHER READING

Benjamin, George J., and Edward W. Blyden. *Messiah of the Black Revolution.* New York: Vantage Press, 1979.

Malik Simba

BOND, HORACE MANN (1904–1972)

A younger contemporary of Du Bois, Bond established his reputation in the early 1930s with a series of articles on black education in the southern states published in both academic journals and popular magazines and several major scholarly studies, one of which was *Negro Education in Alabama. A Study in Cotton and Steel* (1969) impressed Du Bois most favorably when he reviewed the book for the April 1940 issue of the *American Historical Review*. He was not uncritical of the work, writing that "the least satisfactory part of Mr. Bond's book is his interpretation of the economic development of Alabama and its relation to the country and the world." What pleased him the most was the support provided in the book for Du Bois' "unproved contention that the so-called enormous Reconstruction debt heaped up by Negro suffrage in Alabama was a false accusation." In the same year (1940), Bond, having become president of Fort Valley Teachers College in Georgia in 1939, became one of the contributing editors of *Phylon*, a journal that Du Bois began editing that year during his second tour at Atlanta University and that he hoped would continue the traditions of the earlier Atlanta University Studies that he had edited from 1897 to his departure in 1910. Finally, in Du Bois' column in *The Chicago Defender* (May 18, 1946), titled "New Day at Lincoln University," there is a recapitulation of Bond's presidency over the past year when he was named the first Negro president of the school that had been founded in Pennsylvania in 1854. *See also*: Atlanta University.

FURTHER READING

"As the Crow Flies," *The Amsterdam News* (October 28, 1939).
Urban, Wayne J. *Black Scholar: Horace Mann Bond, 1904–1972*. Athens: University of Georgia Press, 1992.

William M. King

BOSTON GUARDIAN

The *Boston Guardian* was a crusading African American national weekly newspaper founded and published in Boston by William Monroe Trotter from 1901 until his death in 1934. Du Bois, often an ally and supporter of the irascible publisher, recalled no other paper "that for sheer biting invective and unswerving courage, ever quite equaled the *Boston Guardian* in its earlier days." He remembered that Booker T. Washington and "his followers literally shriveled before it," although it was "often as unfair as it was inspired" (*The Crisis*, June 1927).

Trotter used the *Guardian* to promote the Niagara Movement that he and Du Bois founded in 1905, but the two men broke in 1907 during the third annual conference in Boston. George Forbes, Trotter's partner, also quit the paper in 1904. After that, Trotter operated the newspaper with his wife, Geraldine Louise ("Deenie") Pindell Trotter until her death in 1918. Du Bois recalled she gave up the thought of children and gave him utter devotion while working with him and even lost their home in Roxbury. Later Trotter's sister, Maude Trotter Steward, helped him in operating this militant paper. Despite the efforts of his wife, sister, and friends, Trotter was an erratic businessman and inefficient accountant, so the paper was often in financial jeopardy. By the 1920s its literary style also suffered from Trotter's hectic schedule and chronic overwork. Covert opposition from Booker T. Washington's Tuskegee Machine also frustrated Trotter's efforts to promote militant civil rights and other liberal causes in his newspaper. Nonetheless, as 1 of only 200 African American newspapers at this time in the country, the *Boston Guardian* had an influence far beyond its modest circulation. *See also*: Niagara Movement; Trotter, William Monroe; Washington, Booker T.

FURTHER READING

Fox, Stephen R. *The Guardian of Boston: William Monroe Trotter*. New York: Atheneum, 1970.

Peter C. Holloran

BROWN, JOHN (1800–1859)

John Brown's one-man war on slavery made him the nineteenth century's most controversial citizen, and in 1909, Du Bois appropriated his image in a biography dedicated to attacking the Progressive era's racial mores. Brown was born in 1800 in Torrington, Connecticut, and raised among northeast Ohio's transplanted Yankees. Although he was an indifferent businessman, the cause of abolition he learned from his parents fired Brown's imagination. As he aged, the idea seemed to dominate his thinking, and in 1855, Brown sent five of his sons to Kansas to join in the struggle between Free-Soil and pro-slavery settlers vying for control of that territory after passage of the Kansas-Nebraska Act. Brown soon followed, in a wagon laden with weapons and ammunition. On the night of May 24, 1856, the Browns responded to pro-slavery ruffians' sack of Lawrence, Kansas, by brutally murdering five random slavery supporters at Osawatamie. Brown declared himself an instrument of God.

Brown returned to Massachusetts obsessed with the thought of ending slavery and found wealthy and influential men willing to support his cause. The struggle in Kansas had polarized Northern political opinion, and abolitionists became increasingly willing to countenance violence against the entrenched slave system. In 1859 Brown decided upon Harpers Ferry, West Virginia, as the site for a bold offensive into the South. On October 16 of that year, Brown and twenty-one men took the federal armory there, part of a vague plan to provide Virginia's slaves with arms for an insurrection. However, the expected slaves failed to materialize. Only the Virginia militia and the U.S. Marines, under the command of Robert E. Lee, arrived. The marines took back the armory that night and captured Brown. He was tried for treason and hanged on December 2, 1859. Brown's eloquent attacks on slavery and depiction of himself as an instrument of Divine Providence touched important nerves in U.S. civil religion, however, and he became a potent political symbol. To Northerners he represented an appeal to a higher law defying the South's political machinations in defense of slavery. In the "white" South he embodied the North's abandonment of the constitutional order in favor of a violent attempt to dictate a new way of life to the South.

W.E.B. Du Bois cast John Brown as a symbol of struggle against white supremacy. In 1906 he led a march of Niagara Movement protestors on Harpers Ferry to commemorate Brown's ill-fated attack. His 1909 biography (*John Brown*) of Brown served more as a political interpretation casting Brown as a hero of the black race than as a full-fledged biography. Du Bois largely avoided ethical evaluations of Brown's actions and instead chose to celebrate his bold fight against the institution of slavery. Du Bois received unaccustomed luke-warm reviews for a work one reader termed "hero worship," but the biography stands as an integral part of his turn from the "professional discourse" of social science and decisively toward the use of scholarship in the cause of protest and freedom. The book struck a literary blow against white supremacy, as well as Booker T. Washington's policy of racial accommodation. It also ironically echoed Du Bois' own Yankee upbringing in Great Barrington, Massachusetts, when as a young man he imbibed his white neighbors' religious and political traditions, which doubtlessly included the story of John Brown. *See also*: Great Barrington, Massachusetts; Slavery; Washington, Booker T.

FURTHER READING

Du Bois, W.E.B. *John Brown*. International Pub., 1974.

Drew VandeCreek

THE BROWNIES' BOOK

In January 1920 the first issue of *The Brownies' Book*, a magazine for "children of the sun," was published. Du Bois was the editor and publisher; Augustus Granville Dill, a former Atlanta University professor, was the business manager; and Jessie Redmon Fauset, author and mentor to many African American writers, was the literary editor.

Of its many goals, *The Brownies' Book* wanted to develop black pride, teach black history, and expose 1920s adolescents to black role models. These goals were necessary because there were few children's magazines. Movies and books seldom portrayed blacks, and if they did, the portrayals were minor or stereotypical. *The Brownies' Book* sought to show African American children that the history and achievements of black people were worthy of study and emulation, for example, Frederick Douglass, Sojourner Truth. The magazine also included poetry, stories, plays, and current events.

Twenty-four issues were published between January 1920 and December 1921. Although *The Crisis' Brownies' Book* was short-lived, it was profoundly influential, showcasing some of the best-known young African American writers of the Harlem Renaissance. *See also*: Fauset, Jessie Redmon; Harlem Renaissance.

FURTHER READING

Aptheker, Herbert, ed. *Selections from the Brownies' Book*. Millwood, NY: Kraus-Thomson Organization, 1980.

Johnson-Feelings, Dianne, ed. *The Best of the Brownies' Book*. New York: Oxford University Press, 1996.

Malaika Horne

BROWNSVILLE RAID

The aftermath of the so-called Brownsville Raid led Du Bois to regard Theodore Roosevelt as an arch foe of black Americans. And later when William Howard Taft ran for president, Du Bois vigorously opposed him chiefly because he had been the secretary of war who carried out Roosevelt's orders on this matter.

The Brownsville Raid concerns a shooting incident that took place around midnight on August 13, 1906. Black soldiers of the segregated 25th Infantry Regiment were blamed for attacking a section of Brownsville, Texas, and killing a bartender and wounding one or two others, all white. After determining that there was a conspiracy of silence, Roosevelt in November summarily disbanded the entire army unit. Except for a handful, all were discharged "without honor."

Evidence suggests that paranoid whites reacting to a sensationalized newspaper article triggered the incident. The newspaper, the Brownsville *Daily Herald*, had a headline that read:

INFAMOUS OUTRAGE
Negro Soldier Invaded Private Premises
Last Night And Attempted to Seize
A White Lady

After that edition of the paper hit the street, the commander of the black military unit canceled, as a precautionary measure, all passes and restricted his men to the barracks. Later that night, however, shots were fired outside of Fort Brown, and many of the black soldiers awoke to alarm bells and believed that they were under attack by angry whites.

Exactly what transpired that night remains less than clear, but even at the time there were those who questioned the official report. Roosevelt branded opponents "short sighted white sentimentalists" and "self-seeking demagogues." One of the skeptics was Senator Joseph Benson Foraker, of Ohio, who forced a Senate investigation.

In March 1907, writing in his monthly newspaper *The Horizon*, Du Bois admonished Roosevelt to reconsider his actions in light of the Senate hearings.

But slowly, surely the wrong you have done a hundred black men and their ten million fellows has struggled doubtingly, determinedly to the light and sits today in silent judgment on your soul. I will not say that the 25th Infantry have absolutely proven their entire innocence, but I do say, and the whole country agrees, that they have raised a doubt as to their guilt. . . . You know that their innocence is so near proven that the nation sits dumb before their testimony. The nation is watching you. The black millions are waiting. Theodore Roosevelt, are you an honest man? If you are speak!

Roosevelt refused to rescind his order, although he did concede on January 27, 1909, a month before leaving office, that Companies C and D were innocent, while "the bulk of Company B ... are guilty to a degree." Earlier Roosevelt had characterized the Senate investigation as an "academic discussion." In his autobiography Roosevelt completely omits the Brownsville incident.

In 1972, all 167 soldiers were given honorable discharges, including the last living survivor of the regiment, Private Dorsie Willis, who was then eighty-seven years old.

FURTHER READING

Aptheker, Herbert, ed. *Writings in Periodicals Edited by W.E.B. Du Bois: Selections from* The Horizon. White Plains, NY: Kraus-Thomson Organization Limited, 1985.

Hart, Albert Bushnell, and Herbert Ronald Ferleger, eds. *Theodore Roosevelt Cyclopedia* New York: Roosevelt Memorial Association, 1941.

Lane, Ann J. *The Brownsville Affair: National Crisis and Black Reaction.* Port Washington, NY: Kennikat Press, 1991.

Weaver, John D. *The Brownsville Raid.* College Station: Texas A & M University Press, 1992.

Roger Chapman

BUNCHE, RALPH (1904–1971)

Born in Detroit, Michigan, Bunche was probably the most influential and gifted diplomat of the twentieth century. He graduated summa cum laude from the University of California at Los Angeles in 1927, and he was the first African American to receive a doctorate in political science from Harvard University. Before leaving for graduate school at Harvard, Bunche wrote Du Bois, asking for his assistance in obtaining a summer position that would benefit the race. Bunche did not receive an assignment (Henry 1).

Subsequently, in August 1933, Bunche and other young Turks attended the Amenia Conference, where they assailed the ideology of Du Bois and James Weldon Johnson (Henry 50). Bunche was appointed to a committee established to formulate specific recommendations. The committee's report was heatedly debated but ultimately rejected.

After receiving his Harvard degree, Bunche became a member of the faculty at Howard University (Washington, D.C.), where he organized and chaired its first Department of Political Science. While in this position, he also began writing. In *A World View of Race* (1936), Bunche complimented Du Bois on his continuing militancy and his refusal to compromise his principles.

Throughout his life, Bunche was active in the civil rights movement, eventually becoming an expert on European colonialism in Africa. Working at the State Department from 1944 to 1947, he concentrated on the future of African colonial territories. He was also a member of the U.S. delegation at the Dumbarton Oaks Conferences (1944), which led to proposals for an international organization. Additionally, he was present at key meetings concerning the newly formed United Nations in 1945. Du Bois was present at many of these meetings as consultant to the U.S. delegation.

Bunche resigned from the State Department in 1947 to take a permanent post with the United Nations. Appointed acting UN mediator in Palestine, he successfully brought to conclusion, in 1949, the armistice agreements between Israel and the Arab countries. For brokering the armistice, Bunche was awarded the Nobel Peace Prize in 1950. After becoming a Nobelist, Du Bois wrote: "Perhaps then it was good counsel of perfection to have hoped that Ralph Bunche would have stood fast for justice, freedom and the good faith of nations and his race—perhaps; but God knows I wish he had" (Henry 180).

Bunche long played a primary role in organizing and directing UN peacekeeping operations, and in 1955 he was appointed undersecretary of the UN Secretariat. From 1957 to his retirement in 1971, he was undersecretary for Political Affairs. *See also*: Africa; Amenia Conference; Cold War; Council on African Affairs; Harvard; Johnson, James Weldon; National Association for the Advancement of Colored People (NAACP); United Nations.

FURTHER READING

Bunche, Ralph. *A World View of Race*. Washington, DC: Associates in Negro Folk Education, 1936.
Henry, Charles P. *Ralph Bunche*. New York: New York University Press, 1999.

Courtney Young

C

CHINA

Du Bois became fascinated with China and its culture. Having made two trips to China, first in 1936 and again in 1959, he was also able to contrast pre-Communist and post-Communist China. His first visit was coupled with a trip within the Soviet Union. Having expressed very positive comments about the Soviet Union, Du Bois compared China unfavorably to its northern neighbor. While in Shanghai in 1936, he was struck by the large number of foreigners residing in the city. Although commenting on the beauty found there, he was disturbed by the numbers of foreign soldiers patrolling the streets of Shanghai. He was appalled at the way native Chinese were treated in the city and compared their treatment to the discrimination suffered by blacks in Mississippi.

Returning to China for his second visit in 1959 and in defiance of a U.S. State Department prohibition (China was now ruled by Mao Zedong and his Communist regime), he regarded the People's Republic of China as a miracle. Spending approximately eight weeks in the country, he traveled extensively and visited Beijing, Shanghai, Nanjing, and Canton, among many other places and cities. He observed rural areas, various smaller villages, and communes. As Du Bois writes in his *Autobiography*, he had "never seen a nation which so amazed and touched me as China in 1959." Having read Chinese history in preparation for this trip, Du Bois was appalled at the horrible conditions that the average Chinese had endured for over 2,000 years. He concluded that the slavery African Americans had been subjected to was not as awful as conditions endured by the Chinese. This 1959 journey to China coincided with his ninety-first birthday. Obviously touched by the fact that his birthday was declared a Chinese national holiday, he could not help but point out that the United States ignored the memory of his birthday.

In China 1967 with Mao, Dong, and others viewing anniversary parade from balcony of ancient Royal Palace in Peking. Courtesy of Special Collections and Archives, W.E.B. Du Bois Library, University of Massachusetts Amherst.

In his writings on the People's Republic of China, Du Bois was completely uncritical and, in fact, displayed much naïveté. Asserting that the Chinese Communist proved that human nature could be changed, Du Bois described Communist officials as "incorruptible, their merchants . . . honest." Admitting that China was certainly no utopia, he opined that "envy and class hate are disappearing in China." Du Bois did not publicly embrace communism during his latter trip to China, but a few years after his last journey, he did so.

Late in life Du Bois concluded that there was a kinship between China and Africa. Believing that China had successfully thrown off the shackles placed on it by certain Western nations, Du Bois maintained that Africa could look to China as a role model. He encouraged the development of a relationship whereby Chinese experts would visit Africa, and African students would be sent to China for education. *See also*: Asia; Mao Zedong; Russian Revolution and the Soviet Union; Socialism/Communism.

FURTHER READING

Du Bois, W.E.B. *Writings*. New York: Library of America, 1986.
Lacy, Leslie Alexander. *The Life of W.E.B. Du Bois: Cheer the Lonesome Traveler*. New York: Dial Press, 1970.

Mary Ellen Wilson

COLD WAR

The phrase "cold war" describes the antagonistic rivalry between two blocs of nations led by the United States and the Soviet Union following World War II. At the end of that war, United States, British, and Russian troops occupied important parts of Europe that they had not previously controlled. Both the United States and Great Britain on one side, and the Soviet Union on the other, claimed that this development was necessary for self-defense. However, neither side was willing to go to war to drive the other back to its prewar position but used economic blockades or propaganda to weaken its opponent. The result was a "cold" war, as opposed to a "hot" or shooting war.

The United States based its official policy upon the belief that the inefficiency of socialism in the Soviet Union would lead to collapse from within, and the U.S. monopoly of the atom bomb would prevent an attack on the country. During the early stages of the Cold War, each of the primary antagonists, and its allies, believed that its way of life was threatened by the other and that coexistence was impossible.

At the beginning of the Cold War period of international politics, Du Bois cautioned that "Red baiting" (*Soviet Russia Today*, 1946), if adopted as part of foreign policy, would lead the United States toward "overturning the great landmarks of human liberty which have been raised in the last four centuries." By 1951 Du Bois was attacking the Cold War more aggressively, insisting that the U.S. ruling class was responsible for it and that the potential for war lay in the system of colonialism that World War II had not crushed.

Openly attacking the Truman administration, Du Bois argued that there was a need to reverse the Cold War and abandon the current policy on international politics. In later writings and speeches, Du Bois did not change his position on the Cold War. Paralleling the Cold War with colonialism (*Peace is Dangerous*), Du Bois argued that the Cold War was the result of "the desperate American attempt to revive colonial imperialism with the United States in the saddle instead of Britain." *See also*: Bunche, Ralph.

FURTHER READING

Du Bois, W.E.B. *Peace is Dangerous*. New York: National Guardian, 1951.
"The Sane Liberal." *Soviet Russia Today* (September 1949).

Mary Young

COLONIALISM

Colonialism and *imperialism* are mutually related terms. *Imperialism* refers to the practice of extending political power, especially through the acquisition of conquered territories, colonies. *Colonization* has—coincidentally—distributed knowledge and culture and led to the "discovery" and "development" of lands. It, however, has also caused bloody wars of conquest and the destruction of peoples who stood in the paths of the establishment of empires.

The chief motives for establishing colonies have been to get control of trade already existing between a territory and the rest of the world, to control possession of precious metals, gems, or raw materials, to establish new markets, to provide an outlet in the colony for surplus populations, and to take advantage of and exploit the indigenous people. For Du Bois, the aspect of colonialism that was most disquieting was that capitalism and profit led to this exploitation, mostly of people of color.

Besides exploitation, Du Bois believed that colonialism had been the root cause of World War I. Unless excised, colonialism would encourage wars and risks of wars in the period following World War I. According to Du Bois, the world's many ills are derived from colonialism, particularly from the envy arising from European nations over colonial aggrandizement. Du Bois' solution was that the world's people of color should unite in the face of colonialism. In the United States, African Americans should not rush to follow Garvey and his "back to Africa movement." For Du Bois, Garvey's program could have deeply challenged the system of colonials. Instead, Du Bois felt that Garvey had allied himself with the forces of reaction, even the Klan.

Du Bois continued to blame colonialism for world wars. At the end of World War II, he devoted an article to the efforts after World War I to bring the question of colonialism to the diplomats at Versailles through the 1919 Pan-African Conference. Du Bois speculates that the efforts did not succeed in influencing the organization, and that is one reason for World War II and the present need for the United Nations not to dismiss the question of colonialism. Though no clear-cut stands against colonialism emerged in San Francisco, Du Bois believed that there were many signs that the United Nations would stand against colonialism. Further, at its thirty-eighth annual convention, the National Association for the Advancement of Colored People (NAACP) affirmed that the United Nations is the greatest hope for abolishing colonialism in the world.

During the presidential campaign of 1944, Du Bois asked, "Shall this land be a new realm of private profit, exploitation, or a new land of socialized wealth, medicine, and opportunity?" He continued, stating that "the greatest single question is the ending of colonialism. For unless this is done, the world cannot be democratic. This is the problem to which I propose to devote the remaining years of my life" (*The Amsterdam News*, August 19, 1944). *See also*: Africa; Garvey, Marcus; Ku Klux Klan; National Association for the Advancement of Colored People (NAACP); Pan-Africanism; United Nations.

FURTHER READING

Frankel, Benjamin. *The Cold War, 1945–1991: Leaders and Other Important Figures in the U.S. and Western Europe*. Detroit: Gale Research, 1992.

Mary Young

COLOR AND DEMOCRACY

W.E.B. Du Bois wrote at the beginning of this century, "The problem of the twentieth century is the problem of the color line—the relation of the darker to the lighter races of men in Asia and Africa, in America and the islands of the sea" (*Souls of Black Folk*). He believed that what made the color line "the problem of the 20th Century" was its use by powerful forces in Europe and in North America to discredit and undermine the democratic ideal. Democracy is predicated on the assumption that the collective will of all the people, freely arrived at and freely expressed, will produce the highest good. This was a fundamental belief for which Du Bois worked throughout his lifetime.

Those who engaged in and supported the enslavement of human beings well into the modern era were required to provide a justification for that enslavement. Despite evidence to the contrary, attested to by reports of early European travelers and adventurers to the African continent and surviving, pre-European slavery, precolonial records, and archaeological and architectural remains, the image of the heathen African savage was created and widely propagated. This propaganda was created to counter the inevitable, democratic-spirited, humanist antislavery sentiment of ordinary folk emanating from the early Christian ideals and beliefs that accompanied the Enlightenment.

Some unchanging and unchangeable traits or marks were required to explain what made Africans savage, uncivilized, and uncivilizable—fit only to be slaves. The only mark that truly distinguished the African from the European was color. And thus color was made the raison d'être. In 1920 Du Bois wrote, "Ever have men striven to conceive of their victims as different from the victors, endlessly different, in soul and blood, strength and cunning, race, and lineage. It has been left, however, to Europe and to modern days to discover the eternal, world-wide work of meanness—color" (*The Crisis*, January 1920).

There are at least four areas of great importance in European scholarship on Africa that were either ignored, severely distorted, or deliberately lied about: the African reality *prior to the slave trade and colonial exploitation*; the devastating upheavals on the African continent caused by the European slave trade; the actual conditions of life and work imposed upon the slave by the European and African slave traders and slave holders, particularly in the Deep South of the United States and in the Caribbean; and the extent and nature of resistance to slavery *by the slave*. Each of these areas speaks to the character of the African. Each of these areas was researched and extensively reported on by Du Bois.

Du Bois understood that associating color with ethnicity as an explanation for racial inferiority and racial superiority undermined the democratic ideal. By so doing, not only was slavery and colonialism on the African continent justified, but European hegemony in a world four-fifths colored was not only justified but inevitable. In 1915, W.E.B. Du Bois declared, "Most men in this world are colored. A belief in humanity means a belief in colored men. The future world will, in all reasonable probability be what colored men make it" (*Negro*, 242). Du Bois knew that that future world would only be possible if democracy prevailed globally. *See also*: Africa; Colonialism.

FURTHER READING

Du Bois, W.E.B. *Color and Democracy: Colonies and Peace.* New York: Harcourt, Brace, and Company, 1945.
———. *The Negro.* New York: Henry Holt, 1915

David Du Bois

COOPERATIVES

Du Bois believed that cooperatives, organizations that carry on any of a variety of economic activities for the mutual benefit of their members, were the economic wave of the future for African Americans. With his anticapitalist stance and insisting that production for private profit was antithetical to the interests of blacks, Du Bois felt that cooperatives would be a primary economic solution. Economic depression, unemployment, and tenacious segregation continued to afflict blacks. The effect of monopolization, chain stores, failure of vocational education, and continued racism assured the survival of capitalism.

Admonishing blacks against copying white America, Du Bois recommended that African Americans develop a different type of system—cooperatives: a system that would be created, operated, and used by blacks.

Arguing that cooperatives had been in wide use after the Civil War, he gave several examples: black schools, fraternal organizations, insurance companies, cemeteries. Since Reconstruction, segregation and race prejudice had grown, and the use of cooperatives had diminished.

Since the evils of racial bias had grown, the obvious conclusion was to organize, learn to cooperate, and use machines. Du Bois cited examples of successful black cooperatives, for example, the Dry Dock Company in Baltimore led by Isaac Myers, which lasted twelve years, forcing white shipbuilding unions to accept black members; others were a black railroad in Wilmington, North Carolina, and a street railway company in Jacksonville, Florida.

Early cooperatives eventually declined, perhaps because of the rush of blacks to become Americans or deliberate destruction by European Americans. At any rate, Du Bois reiterated that cooperatives were not palliatives as some of his detractors suggested. They could serve as important educational tools, and they had worked in many places and assisted thousands of people. *See also*: Black Business; Racism.

FURTHER READING

"A Forum of Fact and Opinion." *The Pittsburg Courier* (September 25, 1937).

Mary Young

COUNCIL ON AFRICAN AFFAIRS

The Council on African Affairs was founded in 1937, on the initiative of African American Max Yergan. Yergan was a YMCA field secretary who worked in South Africa for twenty years. Worsening conditions for black South Africans radicalized Yergan, who left the country in 1936.

First called the International Committee on African Affairs, the Council on African Affairs eschewed mass organization, focusing instead as a small group on disseminating information about Africa, lobbying for colonial reform, and providing scholarships for African students. The members came chiefly from academic, philanthropic, and religious circles. They included Yergan; singer–activist Paul Robeson; President Mordecai W. Johnson of Howard University; political scientist Ralph Bunche; and Harvard University political scientist Raymond Leslie Buell, president of the Foreign Policy Association. The Council raised operating funds through donations and subscriptions to its journal, *News of Africa*.

During World War II the Council emphasized African contributions to the war effort and the consequent debt to Africa that Western powers had amassed. The Council pressed for lend-lease assistance to Liberia and unsuccessfully lobbied the State Department to place African issues on the agenda at the 1944 Dumbarton Oaks conference. After the war, the Council sent a food shipment to a South Africa stricken by famine. It supported what it considered allied causes—independence for India and two major petition drives sponsored by the National Negro Congress and the National Association for the Advancement of Colored People (NAACP), respectively, to put the plight of African Americans before the United Nations.

Du Bois joined the Council on African Affairs in 1947. The informational mission of the Council suited his interests and capacity for scholarly advocacy during a time when the NAACP's indifference to disseminating information about Africa and disinclination to activism on African issues displeased him.

The Council on African Affairs had early acquired a reputation for pro-Soviet positions, premised on the USSR's presumed commitment to decolonization. However, founder Max Yergan insisted that it identify itself publicly as nonpartisan. Some members interpreted this stand as a capitulation to opponents of Progressive Party nominee Henry Wallace's candidacy. Du Bois headed a committee charged with resolving the issue. Ironically, the NAACP fired Du Bois the same year because of a dispute between him and secretary Walter White over the nonpartisanship of that organization. Ensuing conflict between Du Bois and Yergan led to the latter's censure for financial irregularities and to Du Bois' resignation from the Council.

Once Du Bois left, Yergan moved to consolidate control, firing W. Alphaeus Hunton, Jr., the Council's only executive staff member. The executive board suspended Yergan for this power play, but resentments and fear of being labeled "red" led to critical resignations of prominent persons. A diminished Council on African Affairs nevertheless survived the 1948 debacle and continued to criticize U.S. foreign policies. The Council finally disbanded in 1955, a casualty of Cold War repression and crippled by a lack of funds. *See also*: Africa; Bunche, Ralph; Cold War; Colonialism; Dumbarton Oaks Conference; Harvard; Howard University; Hunton, Alphaeus; National Association for the Advancement of Colored People (NAACP); Robeson, Paul; South Africa.

FURTHER READING

"American Negroes—Africa." *Freedom* (February 14, 1955).
Du Bois, W.E.B. *In Battle for Peace: The Story of My 83rd Birthday*. New York: Masses and Mainstream, 1952.

Brenda Gayle Plummer

THE CRISIS

The Crisis: A Record of the Darker Races was conceived by W.E.B. Du Bois in 1910 and became the main publication of the National Association for the Advancement of Colored People (NAACP). Under his leadership it became the most popular black periodical in the first half of the twentieth century. At one point its circulation reached 116,000 per month, a noteworthy achievement particularly in an era of rampant illiteracy. Part of the newspaper's success was due to Du Bois' ability to communicate to a cross section of readers on a wide variety of topics including lynching, civil rights, women's suffrage, institutional prejudice, and Pan-Africanism. In reporting on each of these issues, he remained committed to exploring the precarious relationship between race and democracy. Throughout his twenty-four years as editor, Du Bois never compromised his dream of black equality. He publicly denounced those who did not share his point of view as evidenced by his periodic criticisms of the NAACP's leadership, white southern politicians, Booker T. Washington, Woodrow Wilson, and others who disagreed with his assault on racism. He was even willing to criticize groups that he believed were dedicated to fighting for democracy, including suffragists and labor leaders, when their policies were racist.

In the 1920s, *The Crisis* became an important outlet for creative writers who would have had difficulty publishing their work elsewhere. Some scholars have argued that Du Bois' willingness to publish unknown black writers helped usher in the Harlem Renaissance, one of the most important literary and cultural movements in this century. Du Bois, though, should not be given sole credit for the superb journalism of this period. His literary editor, Jessie Fauset, was instrumental in helping to publish poems, essays, and short stories by Langston Hughes, Countee Cullen, Claude McKay, and Jean Toomer. In 1925, *The Crisis* began sponsoring a literary contest that became an important arena to showcase new talent. Even though the *The Crisis* was forced to reduce its size during the depression, it continued to address social, political, and educational matters during this period of political turmoil. It was Du Bois' stand on voluntary segregation that ultimately ended his career as the journal's editor. Concerned that he was becoming too radical, the NAACP's leadership used the article "Segregation" (January 1934) to justify their vote that employees of the NAACP could not criticize the work of the organization in *The Crisis*. Determined not to be under the control of any organization, Du Bois promptly submitted his resignation to the NAACP board and returned to Georgia to become the chair of the Department of Sociology at Atlanta University. Although published periodically, *The Crisis* remains dedicated to reporting issues relevant to the African American community. *See also*: Fauset, Jessie Redmon; Harlem Renaissance; National Association for the Advancement of Colored People (NAACP); Women's Rights.

FURTHER READING

Lewis, David Levering. *W.E.B. Du Bois: Biography of a Race*. New York: Henry Holt and Company, 1993.

Catherine M. Lewis

CULLEN, COUNTEE (1903–1946)

Adopted at the age of fifteen as the son of an influential African Methodist Episcopal (AME) minister in Harlem, Cullen went on to be elected to Phi Beta

Kappa while studying at New York University, then receiving his Master of Arts degree at Harvard in 1926. By 1924 he was already recognized by Du Bois as a significant member of the New Negro Renaissance. Cullen wrote and published in several genres but is best known as a poet. As literary editor of *Opportunity* (1926–1928), he also influenced the rise of other young African American writers.

In a 1926 speech at the National Association for the Advancement of Colored People (NAACP) annual meeting, Du Bois noted that artistic achievements such as Cullen's did not mean the race was now free, and he pointed out that artists feel the weight of oppression, too. This truth is borne out by the theme of many of Cullen's poems—readers need only consult Cullen's seminal work *Color*, published in 1925.

On April 9, 1928, in the social event of the season for Harlem, Cullen married Nina Yolande Du Bois with the blessing of her father. The marriage only lasted two years before Yolande obtained a divorce. Nevertheless, for the rest of his life Cullen enjoyed the friendship and admiration of Du Bois, who gave praise in *The Crisis* book reviews to both *Caroling Dusk* (1927) and *The Black Christ and Other Poems* (1929).

In an obituary following Cullen's death in 1946, Du Bois pointed out how African Americans are positioned best to communicate artistically the plight of their experience. Despite his successes, Cullen never achieved what his genius was capable of creating, and Du Bois held the African American community at least partially responsible, due to its inattention to nurturing the Talented Tenth. *See also*: Art and Literature; *The Crisis*; Du Bois, Yolande; Harlem Renaissance; Talented Tenth.

FURTHER READING

Cullen, Countee. *On These I Stand: An Anthology of the Best Poems of Countee Cullen*. New York: Harper and Brothers, 1947.
Shucard, Alan R. *Countee Cullen*. New York: Twayne, 1984.

Scot Guenter

CULTURAL AND SCIENTIFIC CONFERENCE FOR WORLD PEACE

In the years following the end of World War II, Du Bois devoted himself increasingly to the cause of peace, something that had concerned him from his earliest years as a graduate student at the University of Berlin. Held at the Waldorf-Astoria Hotel in New York City on March 25–27, 1949, and sponsored by the National Council of Arts, Sciences and Professions, an alleged Communist front organization, this conference was noteworthy for the public hysteria whipped up by the New York press and the enmity Du Bois earned for his admitted role in the planning and execution of the meeting. Much of this enmity was due to the temper of the times, in particular the belief that war with the Soviet Union was not only likely but imminent and that anyone who supported its rhetoric about not wanting war in contrast to similar messages emanating from Washington must be "anti-American" and deserving of the condemnation directed at him. Added to this was the fact that there were no identifiable anti-Communist speakers from the Left or the Right on the program. All who spoke, and many of those attending, represented "progressive" positions or came from the intellectual elites that had long been suspected of fostering dissent in U.S. society. At a panel on writing and publishing held in the Starlight Room on March 26, Du Bois gave a short presentation on the nature of intellectual freedom that might be construed as a direct challenge to those working to limit the political vision of the citizenry. And on March 27, at a rally at Madison Square Garden, he spoke to some 20,000 persons on the topic of "Colonial Peoples and the Fight for Peace," a subject he had also addressed at the organizational meetings of the United Nations in San Francisco. *See also*: Peace Movement; Stockholm Peace Appeal; University of Berlin.

FURTHER READING

Review of the Scientific and Cultural Conference for World Peace. Arranged by the National Council of Arts, Sciences, and Professions, held in New York City on March 25–27, 1949.

William M. King

D

DARK PRINCESS

Published in 1928, *Dark Princess* is Du Bois' second novel, and in his later autobiographical accounts, he claimed it his personal favorite. The novel follows Matthew Towns, a talented African American of southern agrarian origins who at the book's opening has just been denied the opportunity to complete his medical degree because of racial discrimination. In anger, he leaves the United States for Europe. There he meets the beautiful dark Princess Kautilya of Bwodpur, a British Colony in the mountains of South Asia, who has received a racial insult from a U.S. expatriate. Towns intervenes and, as a result, is introduced to a conspiracy of the global colored aristocracy against colonialism. The aristocratic and largely Asian makeup of the members of Kautilya's network, however, make the politics of the conspiracy right wing and discriminatory toward people of African descent. The romance of Matthew and Kautilya, the constant deferral of which is the motor of the plot, finally occurs when Kautilya is able on her own initiative to abandon the other aristocrats in favor of global democratic and socialist politics. Kautilya begins working as a box-maker in the United States and ultimately becomes president of the box-makers' union. Thus the explicit consummation of the sexual relationship between Matthew and Kautilya, and then the birth of their child on the last page, is made to represent the potential unity of Third World workers, the most radical wing of which is said to be women industrial workers. The potential unity is, of course, a sign of the limits of Du Bois' faith in working-class politics in 1928. He oscillates throughout the book on the question of whether white workers might become part of this unity, and he requires the spokesperson for this radical politics to have been born a princess.

At a less global level, the book is a psychological study of the ups and downs of Matthew Towns. Du Bois refuses to portray Towns as a model revolutionary. Instead, Towns is as capable of bitter cynicism and political opportunism as he is of radical struggle. For a significant portion of the book he becomes a Chicago machine politician to fund his aesthetic tastes; this 100-page middle section forms a critique of U.S. politics as merely another example of doing capitalist business. Before becoming a politician, Towns for a time conspires with a Marcus Garvey–like figure who has turned violent and plots to blow up a train carrying Klan members. Towns intervenes at the last minute to save Kautilya, who is on the train.

In every sense the novel, as a novel, is excessive, sometimes to the point of being hard to read. In its bizarre juxtaposition of Du Bois' growing commitment to feminism, Third Worldism, and socialism with its idealized sexual romanticism, it is perhaps the most psychologically revealing book he wrote— even more so than his autobiographies. *See also*: Art and Literature; Asia; Garvey, Marcus.

FURTHER READING

Du Bois, W.E.B. *Dark Princess.* Jackson, MS: University Press of Mississippi, 1995.

Kenneth Mostern

DAVIS, BENJAMIN J. (1903–1964)

Davis was born at the turn of the century in Dawson, Georgia, a society existing in the shadow of slavery. His father was noted enough as a Republican politician that Du Bois mentioned him in his writings. Davis attended Morehouse College, attained his B.A. at Amherst College, and earned his law degree from Harvard.

Davis' rubicon occurred when he represented the young black Communist Angelo Herndon, who was indicted by the state of Georgia in 1931 after leading a protest against the effects of the Great Depression. Attending many meetings and rallies for Herndon, Davis witnessed the racial equity of the Communist Party. This experience and his study of Marxism led him to believe that this philosophy should direct blacks in the path of liberation. Davis noted that he "entered the trial as Herndon's lawyer and ended it as his comrade."

In 1943, Davis successfully ran for office, winning a seat on New York's City Council. Davis felt that his election was "another high-water mark in the achievement of the labor-Negro people's progressive coalition." One newspaper headline ran "Black Red elected in New York, White Yankees vote for him." The first bill passed under his sponsorship designated Negro History Week as an official annual event. Davis was allied on the council with the only other elected Communist, Pete Cacchinone.

Davis' political activism and his membership in the Communist Party led to his arrest and eventual conviction under the Smith Act in 1950. Davis, along with his black and white comrades, was imprisoned. Davis spent five years in the federal prison at Terre Haute, Indiana, and was released in 1955. Du Bois was involved in and supported the "free Ben Davis" campaign.

Though he criticized Du Bois early in his career, Davis later became a close confidant, and both issued statements on the dilemma of using "Negro troops in Korea" while the government maintained segregation here at home.

Du Bois headed his reelection committee in 1949. Right before Du Bois left for Ghana, he called for more brave leaders like Davis to further the rights of African Americans. Du Bois also influenced Davis to change his position on how the Communist Party analyzed the "Negro Question/Black Belt Thesis." Benjamin Davis died on August 22, 1964. *See also*: Harvard; Republican Party; Socialism/Communism.

FURTHER READING

Horne, Gerald. *Black Liberational/Red Scare: Ben Davis and the Communist Party*. Newark, DE: University of Delaware Press, 1994.

Malik Simba

DAVIS–DU BOIS, RACHEL

Dr. Rachel Davis–Du Bois (no relation) was a Quaker teacher from New Jersey best known for developing techniques for intercultural and interracial education. Her most important book, *Get Together Americans: Friendly Approaches to Racial and Cultural Conflicts through the Neighborhood-Home Festival* (1943), was described by Louis Adamic as a "practical manual for social interaction among Americans of various racial, national and religious backgrounds" and widely praised by W.E.B. Du Bois. Neighborhood-Home Festivals were spontaneous local gatherings of culturally diverse individuals intended to help alleviate antagonism and suspicion among groups so they could adjust to living together. Such gatherings were intentionally social, frequently involved food, dance, and music, and often took place in churches, homes, schools, Americanization classes, parent-teacher organizations, and community centers. As a proponent of what she terms "cultural democracy" (a free exchange of values among numbers of our various cultural groups), Dr. Davis–Du Bois believed that sharing human resources was an important step to global unity. Dr. Davis–Du Bois was a longtime supporter of Du Bois' program for race uplift, especially his idea of the "Talented Tenth." In her autobiography, she recalls that she was first introduced to Du Bois' ideas through an article titled "Race and War" published in *American Mercury*. Dr. Davis–Du Bois would eventually serve on the National Association for the Advancement of Colored People (NAACP) board and count Du Bois as a close friend and adviser. *See also*: Talented Tenth.

FURTHER READING

Davis-DuBois, Rachel. *Get Together Americans: Friendly Approaches to Racial and Cultural Conflicts through the Neighborhood-Home Festival*. New York: Harper and Brothers, 1943.

Davis-Du Bois, Rachel, and Corann Okarodudu. *All This and Something More: Pioneering in Intercultural Education*. Bryn Mawr, PA: Dorrance, 1984.

Catherine M. Lewis

DEBS, EUGENE (1855–1926)

Eugene Debs was born in Terre Haute, Indiana, in 1855 and rose to become the U.S. labor movement's greatest spokesperson. At the height of his career, he embraced socialism and gathered nearly 1 million votes for the presidency of the United States in 1912.

Debs became involved in labor organizing after working in Terre Haute's railroad shops as a young man. He was an advocate of industrial unionism and an opponent of the limited craft unionism represented by the American Federation of Labor. In 1893 he helped organize the American Railway Union for all railroad workers; the next year he was jailed for his role in leading union workers' national rail shutdown in support of striking Pullman Palace Car Company workers. In prison Debs took up socialism and spent the heart of his career as a socialist orator, journalist, and political candidate.

The U.S. labor movement presented a problem for W.E.B. Du Bois and other black radicals. Although Du Bois' social scientific research convinced him that class exploitation contributed to the general oppression of American blacks, the labor movement itself remained a racist institution. Although Eugene Debs refused to speak before segregated audiences, his American Railway Union voted to ban black membership. In 1911 Du Bois became a member of the Socialist Party, albeit for one year, despite its own uneven record on race. To him the promise of a mass movement for oppressed people overshadowed the particular stumbling blocks presented by even progressive Americans' racism. *See also*: Socialism/Communism.

FURTHER READING

Ginger, Ray. *The Bending Cross: A Biography of Eugene Victor Debs*. New Brunswick, NJ: Rutgers University Press, 1949.

"If Eugene Debs Returned." *American Socialist* (January 1956).

Drew VandeCreek

DOUGLASS, FREDERICK (1817–1895)

By 1900 Du Bois had decided that black Americans should aggressively claim full civil rights, especially "the right of franchise, security of person and property." He wanted the activism of "Garrison, Phillips and Douglass" to be the conscience of the United States at the turn of the century.

Du Bois' scholarly stature was solidified with his publication of *The Souls of Black Folk* in 1903. This stature, along with his admiration for Frederick Douglas, led to a publisher's offer for him to write a biography of the great nineteenth-century abolitionist leader. The firm of George W. Jacobs and Co. offered a contract to Du Bois to write Douglass' biography for their *The American Crisis Biographies* series. The editor of this series, Ellis Paxson Oberholtzer, wrote Du Bois on November 18, 1903, that though several biographies of Douglass had been published, he thought that Du Bois' work would be definitive. Du Bois immediately accepted the offer, but in a letter dated January 25, 1904, Oberholtzer wrote an apologetic letter to Du Bois, explaining that Booker T. Washington had accepted an earlier offer to write the biography of Douglass. Oberholtzer explained that his offer to Du Bois was made in an interim period when he thought that Washington was not interested in doing the project. Oberholtzer noted that "I had written him [Washington] first, but not having heard from him" offered the project to Du Bois because of his "superior historical training." Du Bois graciously accepted this explanation and offered to write a biography of Nat Turner, but this offer was rejected, and a compromise project was agreed upon. This project became Du Bois' biography of John Brown. *See also*: Slavery; Slave Uprising.

FURTHER READING

Du Bois, W.E.B. *John Brown*. Philadelphia: G. W. Jacobs, 1909.
Lewis, David Levering. *W.E.B. Du Bois: Biography of a Race*. New York: Henry Holt and Company, 1993, p. 356.

Malik Simba

DRAMA

Attention given to the works and wide-ranging influence of W.E.B. Du Bois does not usually include his interest in and support of African American drama in the early part of the twentieth century. Du Bois was, however, an integral force in its development. In 1910, appointed editor of *The Crisis*, the monthly magazine of the National Association for the Advancement of Colored People (NAACP), Du Bois almost immediately became mentor to the early black theater. His involvement in African American drama was as playwright, as critic, and, through *The Crisis* magazine play competitions, as mentor to developing black playwrights.

Du Bois perceived the black stage as a means of reaching and educating black Americans about the race. He believed that the stage should serve a purpose, whether in joining people together, in portraying black history, or in raising the morale of the audience. In providing a literal and figurative platform for showing problematic situations and their solutions, drama did not rely on literacy to be understood by or to impact an audience. Further, because drama is a visual art, the figures from black history and life who walked the boards were, in a sense, made real to those who may have had little awareness of black history. To Du Bois, these features made the stage a medium too forceful and invested it with an energy too valuable for a minority population to be spent on entertainment purposes only. In 1926, he summarized this belief, writing that he did "not believe in any art simply for art's sake" and that he did "not care a damn for any art that [was] not propaganda" (Criteria of Negro Art).

Seeing the stage as a powerful tool in the progress of African Americans, Du Bois promoted its use for combating stereotypes seen on the white stage in musicals, song and dance revues, and vaudeville routines. He urged the presentation of accurate, nonstereotyped depictions of African Americans, arguing that African American drama should be "for us, by us, about us, and near us."

Du Bois' work with the pageant form reflected his belief in African Americans controlling their own theaters and, thereby, the depictions of blacks on stage. *The People of Peoples and Their Gifts to Men*, published in *The Crisis* in 1913, is his most important work on the stage. Featuring vignettes and characters from black history, the pageant was written to celebrate the fiftieth anniversary of the Emancipation Proclamation. It was performed, Du Bois wrote, "with a thousand [Negro] actors" and was "given for Negroes and by Negroes." Later entitled *The Star of Ethiopia*, it was produced in New York (1913), Washington (1915), Philadelphia (1923), and Los Angeles (1923). Black educator and writer Alain Locke referred to Du Bois' pageant as a foundation for black drama.

Du Bois held that pageants were "what [black] people want and long for" and that pageants provided "the gown and paraphernalia in which the message of education and reasonable race pride can deck itself." To Du Bois, the pageant form made it possible "to teach the colored people themselves the meaning of their history and their rich emotional life."

In 1919, Du Bois' belief in drama led him to discuss the formation of the Horizon Guild, an organization that would "present pageants of Negro history in the principal centers of Negro population." These plans, however, never materialized.

Du Bois also served as the editor of *The Brownie's Book* (1920–1922), a magazine published by the NAACP. Through this monthly publication, he used drama to give African American youth positive examples of black children and heroes. Langston Hughes' play *The Gold Piece* and four of Willis Richardson's plays were first published in the magazine. Although a few other plays had been written for black children, this magazine was the first time they had been distributed widely.

In a 1924 essay on black drama, Du Bois noted that "any mention of Negro blood or Negro life in America for a century has been occasion for an ugly picture, a dirty allusion, a nasty comment or a pessimistic forecast" (*The Crisis*, June 1924). He looked to the stage as offering a corrective to these perceptions. Du Bois was aware of the resistance white theater owners would have to producing serious plays by African Americans. He, therefore, advocated community-based productions and sought to have African American plays presented in African American churches, libraries, lodges, and community centers.

To carry out such productions, Du Bois urged the establishment of little-theater groups of and for African Americans. Through *The Crisis*, he organized the Krigwa Players. Its name an acronym for *The Crisis* Guild of Writers and Artists, it was active from 1926 through 1935. Krigwa groups were formed in New York, Philadelphia, Baltimore, Washington, and other East Coast cities.

Du Bois wrote nearly thirty sketches and scripts. Among them are two "playlets"—"A Little Play" (1914) and "Christ of the Andes" (1908)—and *Sacco & Vanzetti* (1927), none of which are believed to have been produced. In 1931, he prepared a manuscript of five of his plays along with an introduction; he titled the collection "Playthings of the Night." In 1941, he revised the manuscript, renaming it "The Sorcery of Color." The collection was never accepted for publication and is among his papers at the University of Massachusetts. Despite published claims to the contrary, the play *Haiti*, performed in Harlem by the Negro Theatre section of the Federal Theatre in 1938, was written by a William Du Bois, a white writer.

In 1927, Du Bois wrote to Alain Locke that Carter G. Woodson, the founder of Negro History Week, had approached him about editing a collection of plays on black life. In the end, Du Bois did not work on this collection. Published in 1930, the collection was entitled *Plays and Pageants from the Life of the Negro* and had Willis Richardson as its editor.

Du Bois was the greatest advocate of and contributor to the development of African American drama. Unfortunately, his work in this area has received little acknowledgment. *See also*: Art and Artists; Art and Literature; *The Brownies' Book; The Crisis*; Du Bois, Shirley Graham; Woodson, Carter G.

FURTHER READING

Du Bois, W.E.B. "Can the Negro Serve the Drama?" *Theatre* 38 (July 1923): 12+.
——. "Criteria of Negro Art." *The Crisis* 32 (October 1926): 290–297.
——. "The Drama among Black Folk." *The Crisis* 12 (August 1916): 169+.
——. "Krigwa Players Little Negro Theater." *The Crisis* 32 (July 1926): 134–136.
——. "The National Emancipation Exposition." *The Crisis* 6 (November 1913): 339–341.
——. "The Negro and the American Stage." *The Crisis* 28 (June 1924): 56–57.
——. "Negro Art." *The Crisis* 25 (June 1921): 55–56.
——. "A Pageant." *The Crisis* 10 (September 1915): 230–231.
——. "The People of Peoples and Their Gift to Man." *The Crisis* (November 1913).
——. "Paying for Plays." *The Crisis* 23 (November 1926): 7–8.
——. "The Star of Ethiopia." *The Crisis* 11 (December 1915): 90–93.

Christine Gray

DU BOIS, DAVID GRAHAM (1925–   )

David Graham Du Bois is the stepson of W.E.B. Du Bois. Born in 1925 to Shirley Graham, David assumed the Du Bois surname later in life. He attended Oberlin Conservatory of Music from 1942 to 1943 and later received his B.A.

from Hunter College, now City University of New York. He, later, received his M.A. from New York University. From 1960 to 1972, he served as an editor for the *Arab Observer*. During this period, 1965–1966, he worked in public relations for the Ghanaian government in Cairo. Throughout his career, David Du Bois had varied interests and held a variety of positions. He was the spokesperson for the Black Panther Party, a public relations representative for Ghana, a novelist, an announcer for Radio Cairo, and an editor and a news analyst for the *Egyptian Gazette*. Du Bois also wrote for the *Black Scholar* and served as the editor of the *Black Panther*. In 1975 he wrote *And Bid Him Sing*, published by Ramparts. During his years in China and Africa, David Du Bois deepened his commitment to radical change. *See also*: Du Bois, Shirley Graham.

FURTHER READING

And Bid Him Sing. Palo Alto, CA: Ramparts, 1973.

Laura de Luca

DU BOIS, NINA GOMER (?–1950)

One of three surviving children of Charles Gomer, a Cedar Rapids, Iowa, hotel chef, and his deceased Alsatian wife, Nina Gomer was Du Bois' student at Wilberforce University (Ohio). They married, each for the first time, on May 12, 1896, three months before Du Bois left Wilberforce for the University of Pennsylvania to conduct a sociological study that would culminate in the publication of *The Philadelphia Negro* in 1899. The move to Philadelphia—and the necessity of making their first home near the slums where Du Bois conducted his research—introduced many of the patterns that would shape their fifty-three years together as Du Bois' various academic appointments and his demanding work schedule necessitated numerous moves while severely limiting his participation in family life.

What is known about Gomer Du Bois comes primarily from her husband's autobiographical writings and correspondence held in the Du Bois papers at the University of Massachusetts at Amherst. While Du Bois describes the early years of their marriage as generally happy, letters from the later decades suggest they had grown apart. Although intelligent and educated, Gomer Du Bois did not engage in the kinds of intellectual pursuits her husband performed. Her concerns were for the domestic sphere, and her letters to him deal mostly with family and household matters.

Still, it would be a mistake to understand Nina Gomer Du Bois as disinterested in issues of race and equality. Having spent most of her early years in Iowa, Ohio, and Pennsylvania, she encountered racism in its most virulent forms for the first time when her husband took an appointment at Atlanta University in 1887. Her correspondence indicates she was deeply outraged by the segregation and violence that characterized life for blacks in the South.

Nina Gomer. Courtesy of Special Collections and Archives, W.E.B. Du Bois Library, University of Massachusetts Amherst.

Her anger and anguish became especially acute after the death of the couple's firstborn son, Burghardt, who succumbed to diphtheria in the spring of 1899 at the age of two. Although it is unlikely that the boy would have survived even with the best medical attention available at the time, Atlanta's segregationist policies hindered the couple's efforts to find adequate health care and made his death even more difficult to accept. Gomer Du Bois had always suffered from chronic physical ailments; her son's death cast a pall over her emotional health as well. Her husband would later suggest in her obituary that the child's death pushed his wife into a depression from which she never fully recovered.

The tragedy of Burghardt's death was eased somewhat by the birth of the couple's second child, Yolande, on October 22, 1900. Letters from the period suggest that Gomer Du Bois felt a renewed sense of purpose as she immersed herself in the care of her daughter and adjusted to her husband's frequent work-related absences. Throughout the remainder of the marriage, which ended with her death in 1950, her primary concerns were Yolande's upbringing and her husband's continued success. Nina Gomer Du Bois is buried in Great Barrington, Massachusetts, near the body of their son. *See also*: Atlanta, Georgia; Atlanta University; Du Bois, Yolande; University of Pennsylvania; Wilberforce University.

FURTHER READING

Lewis, David Levering. *W.E.B. Du Bois: Biography of a Race*. New York: Henry Holt and Company, 1993.

Paul Ryan Schneider

DU BOIS, SHIRLEY GRAHAM (1896–1977)

Graham Du Bois was born in Indiana and died in China. Her earliest influence was her father, a pastor, the Reverend David Andrew Graham. During her youth, he was peripatetic, moving his family routinely: Tennessee, Louisiana, Colorado, and the Pacific Northwest were among the stops.

Graham was an excellent student in elementary and high school and was known particularly as a more than capable musician. However, opportunities were not vast for African American women of that era in Oregon and Washington; moreover, her father was rather strict, she was a de facto disciplinarian for her younger brothers, and she yearned to escape. By the mid-1920s she had escaped: She married and gave birth to two sons; however, her marriage was of brief duration, and during this period, she divorced, left her sons with relatives, and moved to Paris to study.

There she developed her musical skills and deepened a friendship with the Harlem Renaissance writer Eric Waldron. At this juncture, her father had moved his brood to Liberia, where he was involved in missionary and educational work. Soon she had returned to the United States, where she lived and worked and studied intermittently in New York and the Washington, D.C. metropolitan area. She also performed piano recitals as a way to supplement her income.

By the early 1930s, she decided to enroll at Oberlin College in Ohio, where she obtained a B.A. and an M.A. Her stated goal was to develop expertise in music to advance the role of Africans worldwide in this field. During this period, she wrote an opera—*Tom-Tom: An Epic of Music and the Negro* (1932) that premiered in Cleveland to favorable reviews.

From Ohio she moved to Tennessee, where she taught college, but found this regimen burdensome; she left for the greener pastures of Chicago, where

Wedding of W.E.B. Du Bois and Shirley Graham Du Bois, February 27, 1951. Courtesy of Special Collections and Archives, W.E.B. Du Bois Library, University of Massachusetts Amherst.

she sought to operate a business with her brother, William Graham. This enterprise was not successful, so she signed on with the Federal Theatre Project (FTP) in Chicago. Funded by the federal government, the troupe that she directed provided stiff competition for independently financed producers. They objected vehemently when her *Swing Mikado* attracted large audiences and sizable revenues. Moreover, the FTP was suspected of being influenced, if not dominated, by the Communist Party. Soon it was no more.

Thus, Graham moved on to Yale Drama School, where she intended to obtain a doctorate. While at FTP and Yale, she acted, played the drums, studied theater and foreign languages, and wrote many plays; along with Langston Hughes, she was considered one of the leading playwrights among African Americans.

However, supporting her two sons while writing plays was not easy. She was compelled to return to Indianapolis, where she directed a center that, among other things, produced plays. But when World War II broke out, she seized the opportunity to move to Arizona, where she toiled for the Young Women's Christian Association, directing the equivalent of a community center for African American soldiers.

There she became embroiled in fighting rampant racial discrimination against these troops and Jim Crow in the West. This brought her into conflict with her supervisors, and she was obliged to leave this post. Consequently, she moved to New York City, where she got a job working for the National Association for the Advancement of Colored People (NAACP).

Her time with the Association—roughly 1942–1944—was the era of this group's most significant growth. Membership expanded almost tenfold to 450,000; along with Ella Baker—who went on to play a role in the direction of both the Southern Christian Leadership Conference (SCLC) and the Student Non-Violent Coordinating Committee (SNCC)—Graham played a pivotal role in bringing on this membership expansion.

However, despite her success in this realm, she still felt the need to write and create and study. Directing a community center in Brooklyn provided her with a more flexible schedule than that provided by the NAACP; thus, she was able to enroll in a doctoral program at New York University and begin work on a series of biographies on such figures as Frederick Douglass, George Washington Carver, and Paul Robeson that won her both fortune—and increased fame.

This prominence brought her into closer contact with Howard Fast, the novelist and then Communist Party member. When her son Robert, died, she was crushed and—as well—felt somewhat guilty in that she had not always been present as he was growing into maturity; in the midst of this anxiety and driven by a desire to transform society so that other mothers might be able to escape the kind of financial travails she endured while raising her sons, she joined the Party.

Her prominence on the Left was evident when in 1948 she played a leading role in the convention of the Progressive Party that led to the third-party nomination for president of the former vice-president under Franklin D. Roosevelt, Henry A. Wallace. Wallace's campaign was supported by Paul Robeson—and W.E.B. Du Bois.

She had known Du Bois since her youth and had reacquainted herself with him intimately in the 1930s. The Wallace campaign and her crusading for him after the NAACP fired him in the fall of 1948 because of differences over the impending Cold War and Red Scare brought them closer together.

At this time she was living in St. Albans, Queens, New York; from time to time her mother, her son David, and the son of a Cuban diplomat resided with her. However, her mother died as Du Bois was being widowed and her son married; they comforted each other and soon decided that marriage would be an ideal way to cement their developing relationship. They married in 1951.

However, that year Du Bois also was put on trial for being an agent of an unnamed foreign power—presumably the Soviet Union—after he spearheaded a massive petition campaign known as the "Stockholm Peace Appeal" that sought to ban nuclear weapons. Her organizing on behalf of her newly wed husband was a signal factor that led to a mass movement that contributed to his acquittal.

Relieved, the couple then moved into a home in Brooklyn Heights, purchased from playwright Arthur Miller. Their home became an important site of resistance against the developing Red Scare and Cold War, as they entertained visiting African students and diplomats from the United Nations, the children of executed "atomic spies" Julius and Ethel Rosenberg, and Communist Party activists.

Graham Du Bois continued her writing of popular biographies, studied Russian at Columbia University, and spoke widely to diverse audiences. However, the political affiliations of herself and her husband meant that obtaining a passport for foreign travel was difficult at best.

Finally, in 1958 they were able to obtain this coveted document. That year and the next and the next found them—but her particularly—abroad almost constantly. She visited England and Holland and France. In the Soviet Union she met with the top leadership and—along with prodding from her spouse— was able to convince the USSR to initiate a major institute for the study of Africa. In China they were wined and dined by the leaders of the Communist Party. In Africa she was embraced by an old friend, Ghana's Kwame Nkrumah, who had led his homeland to independence in 1957.

Returning to the United States, she joined Esther Jackson in founding *Freedomways*, a quarterly that focused on the emerging civil rights movement. The board of this periodical was to include Jack O'Dell, a top aide to Martin Luther King, Jr. King ultimately was pressured to rid himself of O'Dell because of his alleged Communist ties. The board also included John Henrik Clarke, a historian who became a confidant of Malcolm X.

However, the attractions of life in New York City were not sufficiently compelling to keep her from accepting an invitation from Nkrumah to move to Accra, Ghana. There she joined Maya Angelou, Pauli Murray, and scores of other African Americans who repatriated to Africa with high hopes of aiding in a significant transformation.

As they were leaving the United States in 1961, her husband joined her as a member of the Communist Party. Arriving in Accra, she continued her writing and spent considerable time attending to the growing needs of her spouse; W.E.B. Du Bois eventually died in August 1963.

From that year until Nkrumah's overthrow in February 1966, she served as a key adviser of the Ghanaian leader, while working as director of television. In this post, she developed plans to install television watching centers in remote villages and brokered deals with Japanese corporations to provide various electronic appliances. She traveled widely in West Africa, Europe, and Asia, both learning about television production and providing solidarity to allies for the government. She also became a citizen of Ghana.

When Nkrumah was overthrown, she was barely able to escape with her life in that the new government felt she was entirely too close to the ancien regime. She found it difficult to return to the United States. Her son was in Cairo working as a journalist, and after considering residing in East Germany, the Bahamas, Guinea-Conakry (the new home of Nkrumah), and Tanzania, she moved to Egypt.

There she was able to secure a sizable apartment in Cairo's Giza district. She studied Arabic and became a fervent advocate of the policies of the government of G. A. Nasser. Living in Egypt helped to make her an early proponent of "Egypt-centric" viewpoints of Africa that came to be known as "Afrocentrism." This development helped to make her more friendly to Black Nationalism.

Philosophically, she was also moving closer to China in its conflict with the Soviet Union. This was facilitated by her frequent trips to this largest of all nations. At times she made broadcasts for international consumption on Beijing radio.

Such actions complicated her effort to obtain a visa to return to the United States. When the Nixon administration refused her a visa, a campaign that was to include figures as diverse as leading African American intellectuals and future New York City Mayor Ed Koch rose as one in protest. The Nixon administration relented, and she made a triumphant return to the land of her birth.

In the United States she addressed audiences ranging from Harvard students in Cambridge to Black Panthers in Oakland. Her visit was covered widely by the press. The lionized Graham Du Bois decided to stay in the United States for a while and took a teaching position at the University of Massachusetts at Amherst, teaching literature.

However, she continued traveling to China, where she died in April 1977. *See also*: China; Cold War; Douglass, Frederick; Drama; Du Bois, David Graham; National Association for the Advancement of Colored People (NAACP); Nkrumah, Kwame; Robeson, Paul; Rosenbergs; Socialism/Communism; Stockholm Peace Appeal.

FURTHER READING

Horne, Gerald C. *Black and Red: W.E.B. Du Bois and the Afro-American Response to the Cold War, 1944–1963.* Albany: State University of New York Press, 1986.

Gerald Horne

DU BOIS, YOLANDE (NINA YOLANDE DU BOIS) (1900–1960)

Yolande Du Bois is the daughter of W.E.B. Du Bois and his first wife, Nina Gomer Du Bois. As the only daughter of a famous father, Yolande was subjected to much scrutiny. She attended the elite British Preparatory Academy, the Bedales School, and later Fisk University, where she graduated with a degree in fine arts in 1924. While she was in school, her father pressured her to achieve and sent her stern letters about maintaining her discipline academically and socially.

Although she was allegedly infatuated with Jimmy Lunceford, one of the pioneers of swing, on April 9, 1928, she married poet Countee Cullen in Harlem in a huge wedding with sixteen bridesmaids. Countee Cullen's father married the couple in the Salem Methodist Church. Arna Bontemps, Langston Hughes, Edward Perry, and other notable personalities ushered such distinguished guests as the James Weldon Johnsons, the Eugene Kinckle Joneses, Charles Johnson, Mary White Ovington, and various Springarns to their pews. A reception followed at the Walker Studio. After a short honeymoon in Philadelphia, the couple went to Paris because Cullen had received a Guggenheim award. The couple separated that summer due to incompatibility, and Yolande entered the American Hospital for treatment of an undisclosed illness.

Yolande, who worked as a teacher, died in Baltimore, Maryland, while her father was visiting Nigeria. W.E.B. Du Bois buried her beside her mother and her infant brother in Great Barrington, Massachusetts. *See also*: Cullen, Countee; Harlem Renaissance.

FURTHER READING

Du Bois, Shirley Graham. *Du Bois: A Pictorial Biography.* Chicago: Johnson Pub., 1978.

Laura de Luca

DUMBARTON OAKS CONFERENCE

From August 21 to October 7, 1944, representatives of China, the Soviet Union, Great Britain, and the United States gathered at Dumbarton Oaks outside Washington, D.C. to discuss the possibility of creating a world organization to ensure peace that would eventually become the United Nations. The conference's most notable goal was to organize the most powerful nations

Yolanda Du Bois at her Fisk graduation, 1926. Courtesy of Special Collections and Archives, W.E.B. Du Bois Library, University of Massachusetts Amherst.

into a confederacy against aggression. At the close of the proceedings, Secretary of State Edward Stettinius invited representatives of eighty organizations to contribute their perspectives on the peace process. As the National Association for the Advancement of Colored People (NAACP) delegate, Du Bois criticized the Dumbarton Oaks Conference for failing to protect the rights of over 750 million colonized peoples. He argued that peace and security should not hinder any nation's chance to pursue "political rebuilding and social uplift." In the following year, Du Bois would become an active participant in the San Francisco Conference, where the UN charter was drafted. In a letter dated May 16, 1945, he urged the U.S. delegation to include an article for the charter that denounced colonialism, demanded that no nation or group be deprived a voice in their own government, and guaranteed the right to petition the world organization on their own behalf. *See also*: Bunche, Ralph; United Nations.

FURTHER READING

Hilderbrand, Robert C. *Dumbarton Oaks: The Origins of the United Nations and the Search for Postwar Security*. Chapel Hill, NC: University of North Carolina Press, 1990.

Catherine M. Lewis

DUSK OF DAWN

Dusk of Dawn: An Essay toward an Autobiography of a Race Concept (1940) is a remarkable and complicated book of autobiography and dialectical sociology that has not received the attention it deserves. Its autobiographical component is usually viewed as its main narrative. Du Bois is quite insistent, however, that the autobiography is only a minor part of the text as a whole, because interest in his life has its "only deep significance inasmuch as it [is] part of a Problem," that of the color line, which he continues to view as the major problem of the twentieth century. Thus, he presents his personal narrative embedded within an interpretation of world history during the years of his life, beginning not with his birth (as a conventional bourgeois autobiography would) but with the end of the Civil War, positioning himself not as the primary actor but as a subject—history. The description of his own subjectivity is then a means to an end—the explanation of the meaning of race, or the "race concept," in his historical period. Thus he describes how the imperatives of his life, as the life of a "Negro"—that is, one socially interpolated into a minority race and oppressed caste—created the cultural, psychological (he refers to Freud several times), and political economic explanation for his choices and the choices of those around him.

But this is not all. The autobiographical narrative itself makes up only the first and last thirds of the book; in its middle section, *Dusk* leaves its subject-in-history narrative to make several arguments about the present state of race relations that explore, in a way that would become influential only in the 1960s, the plausibility and advantages of a separate African American cooperative economy in the United States. This economy is plausible, he claims, because the essentially self-hating black middle class has a nationalist motivation in its inability to attain any significant amount of industrial, let alone financial, capital; its claims to being a "bourgeoisie" depend only on its professional status and its position as a merchant class for blacks. However, if the members of this class form purchasing cooperatives that will keep money within the black community, they may lay the foundations for a vibrant socialist economy that will eventually grow powerful enough to help shape the U.S. and/or Pan-African economy as a whole.

Finally, in the concluding section of *Dusk*, Du Bois speaks of the political and intellectual initiatives of which he is part in 1940, specifically initiatives for global decolonization and the study of socialism. Thus, the structure of the book, as a whole, places his personal account first within its field of local psychological motivation, which is then located in its national/racial context, and then located again more globally at the connected levels of racial colonialism and the international capitalist economy. It is the study of this last level that primarily occupies him at the moment of the writing, he says, and as a result he has decided that the struggle for global decolonization is the most fruitful place for him to work for the remainder of his life.

Dusk of Dawn is arguably the most complicated book of social theory Du Bois wrote and one of the significant works of Marxian theory in the mid-twentieth century. *See also*: Colonialism.

FURTHER READING

Du Bois, W.E.B. *Dusk of Dawn: An Essay toward an Autobiography of a Race Concept.* Millwood, NY: Kraus-Thomson Organization, 1975.

Kenneth Mostern

DYER ANTI-LYNCHING BILL

Following World War I, there was an alarming increase in the rate of lynching. However, in May 1919 the National Association for the Advancement of Colored People (NAACP) initiated the establishment of a program to combat intolerance and inequality. After meticulously gathering congressional support, Representative L. C. Dyer of Missouri introduced the Dyer Anti-Lynching Bill in the House. The proposal sought federal legislation against lynching. It specifically wanted to "Assure to persons within the jurisdiction of every state the equal protection of the law, and to punish the crime of lynching" (Franklin 486). The bill eventually passed the House, 230–119, over the objections of southern members of Congress. Passing the Senate, however, was much more difficult despite intense lobbying by civil rights groups.

Du Bois in his *Crisis* columns supported the bill's passage. In April 1922 Du Bois predicted that if the bill did not pass, it "will end these United States." His "Opinion" column in the same issue editorialized that the bill could be passed if the Republican Party really wanted it; if it does not, black voters should respond accordingly. By September 1922 Du Bois was still calling for the bill's passage. In 1923 after the bill had passed the House, his editorial in the "Opinion" column was devoted to the filibustering carried on by southerners in the Senate. After the defeat of the bill, African Americans, using the power of the ballot, began to fight those senators responsible for the bill's failure.

FURTHER READING

Franklin, John Hope. *From Slavery to Freedom: A History of African Americans.* New York: Alfred A. Knopf, 1994.
——. *From Slavery to Freedom: A History of African Americans.* New York: McGraw-Hill, 1997.

Courtney Young

E

EBOUE, FELIX (1884–1944)

Eboue was an African colonial officer and the governor-general of Chad from 1940 to 1944. Born in Cayenne, French Guiana, and educated in France, Eboue joined the France (French) Ministry of Colonies in 1908. While a colonial official in the Belgian Congo (1908–1917), Eboue developed a sensitivity to the plight of colonial peoples. On leave from the colonial service, Eboue was in Paris during the Second Pan-African Congress in 1921. It is not known whether he attended the conference, but black French colonial notables such as Blaise Diagne, Senegal's deputy, were in attendance. Because Eboue knew Diagne, it is probable that he was aware of the resolutions adopted.

Eboue held positions in numerous French possessions throughout the 1930s. He served as the secretary general in Martinique, 1932–1934, as an administrator in the Soudan [Sudan] colony, 1934–1936, and as governor of Guadeloupe, 1936–1938. His ascendancy to the position of governor-general of Chad, 1940–1944, marked his finest hour. Invaded and forced to surrender to the German occupation forces, France lay prostrate in 1940. The formation of the Vichy government heightened the crisis. Shrewdly, Eboue refused to support the Vichy government, declaring allegiance to the Free French government in exile under Charles de Gaulle. When Eboue died in a French hospital in Cairo, and his death was ignored by the British press, Du Bois took umbrage, stating, "It is discouraging to reflect that the death of a man whose timely and courageous action contributed to the security of the democracies in Central Africa could so easily be forgotten" (*Amsterdam News*, June 3, 1944). *See also*: Africa; Belgium and the Belgian Congo; France; Pan-Africanism.

FURTHER READING

Weinstein, Brian. *Eboue*. New York: Oxford University Press, 1972.

Stephen G. Hall

EDUCATIONAL PHILOSOPHY

Du Bois was the most influential African American intellectual in the first half of the twentieth century. As historian, sociologist, poet, novelist, journalist, and editor, Du Bois' ideas and ideals were circulated widely among the masses and elites within the African American community. Du Bois was also a pioneering educational sociologist, and his views on the educational objectives for black children and families dominated discussions of the most appropriate forms of schooling needed for the collective climb "up from slavery." As an educational administrator, Du Bois chaired university departments and organized and oversaw huge research projects, spanning decades. But it was in his role as educational philosopher that Du Bois made his greatest contribution to African American educational thought in the twentieth century. Du Bois relied upon his activities as an educator at various levels to serve as the experiential basis for his pragmatic philosophical approach to "The Education of Black Folk."

Education and Experience

The young Du Bois received his elementary and secondary schooling in Great Barrington, Massachusetts, where he was born in 1868. Upon graduation from high school in 1885, he enrolled at Fisk University in Nashville, Tennessee, where he was first introduced to "The Colored World Within." At Fisk he was quite impressed by the beauty, culture, and sophistication of his fellow students and faculty members. Du Bois' first teaching experience came during two summers while he was a Fisk undergraduate. He taught poor black children in rural Tennessee, and these experiences were important in developing his philosophical approach to African American education.

In the essay "The Meaning of Progress," in his classic work *The Souls of Black Folk* (1903), he recalled the families he met and lived with, the children he taught: "I loved my school, and the fine faith the children had in the wisdom of their teacher was truly marvelous. We read and spelled together, wrote a little, picked flowers, sang and listened to the stories of the world beyond the hill." Du Bois was acutely aware of the social and economic factors that limited the mental and material horizons for these black youth and himself and recognized that this reality spawned a "common consciousness . . . from a common hardship in poverty, poor land, and low wages; and above all from the sight of the Veil that hung between us and opportunity" (102).

Du Bois received a B.A. from Fisk University in 1888; he enrolled as a junior at Harvard College and received a second B.A., graduating cum laude in 1890. He went on to graduate school at Harvard in history with an M.A. degree in 1891. While at Harvard he studied with William James, Josiah Royce, and Charles Saunders Pierce and imbibed their version of "American Pragmatic philosophy." However, he also studied in Germany at the University of Berlin, where he was exposed to the works of German philosophers and social theorists, including George Hegel, Johann Fichte, Gustav von Schmoller, Adolph Wagner, and Max Weber.

Upon his return to the United States, the young Du Bois took his first collegiate teaching position at Wilberforce University in Xenia, Ohio. While there he put the finishing touches on his Ph.D. dissertation, "The Suppression of the African Slave Trade to the United States of America, 1638–1870," which was later (1896) published in the first volume in the prestigious Harvard Historical Studies. When Du Bois graduated from Harvard in June 1895, he was one of the best educated Americans in the United States, black or white.

At Wilberforce, where he remained for two years, Du Bois was a professor of Greek and Latin, but he also taught history, German, and English. Beginning in 1897 Du Bois taught at Atlanta University, where he remained until 1911 and returned to teach between 1935 and 1944. As editor of Atlanta University Studies from 1897 to 1911, which were considered the most scholarly assessment of African American life available at that time, Du Bois often focused on various aspects of African American schooling and its significance in the overall social development of the black population in the United States. The Atlanta University Studies not only examined the role of the "College Bred Negro" on the African American community as teacher and leader, but they also presented detailed information in 1901 and 1911 on "The Negro Common School." In both years Du Bois and his research staff concluded that "in many parts of the South Negroes are paying into the school fund in the way of taxes much more than they are receiving in actual appropriations for their [public] school facilities." As a result, African Americans themselves were making "heroic efforts to remedy these evils thru a widespread system of private self-supported schools."

Education and Leadership

At the turn of the century, when Booker T. Washington and other conservative black spokespersons echoed the sentiments of southern whites that African American children needed to be taught to work, Du Bois made it clear in the 1905 statement of purpose for the Niagara Movement that

[w]e believe in work. We ourselves are workers, but work is not necessarily education. Education is the development of power and ideal. We want our children trained as intelligent human beings [who] should be and will fight against any proposal to educate black boys and girls simply as servants and underlings, or simply for the use of other people. They have the right to know, to think, to aspire.

In his ideological debates with Booker T. Washington, who called for black political withdrawal in the South, agrarian capitalism, and industrial education, Du Bois often emphasized the fact that he did not oppose the expansion of industrial educational opportunities for black children. But he knew that the educational campaign that had been mounted by northern industrial philanthropists to introduce industrial training at all levels of black schooling, including colleges and universities, had as its objective the creation of a conservative black leadership group that would not challenge white supremacy and the racial status quo in the South. In his writings on the "Talented Tenth" and "The College Bred Negro," Du Bois was basically pragmatic in his approach, and he argued that African American leaders must be trained at the same levels as the leaders for other groups in American society. More important, he understood that the type of "Negro industrial education" provided at Hampton, Tuskegee, and other manual training schools and industrial institutes would not produce the kind of intelligent and independent leadership needed for African American social advancement.

In the 1920s the students at Hampton Institute rebelled against the Jim Crow segregation practiced on the campus and the poor quality of the industrial and academic programs. Students at Fisk, Howard, Lincoln, and Wilberforce mounted protests against the social and educational conditions on these campuses and Du Bois as editor of the National Association for the Advancement of Colored People's (NAACP's) *The Crisis* magazine, the most influential publication among African Americans nationally, championed their cause. Historian Raymond Wolters, in his book *The New Negro on Campus*, argued that "the spirit of W.E.B. Du Bois hovered over the Black college rebellions of the 1920s and . . . he published and celebrated collegiate protest throughout the land" (18).

At the same time, however, Du Bois was known to castigate black college students who were not taking full advantage of the educational opportunities being made available to them at great sacrifice and who came to college primarily to socialize, party, and have a good time. In 1930 in a commencement address at Howard University, Du Bois criticized the black college students for their acceptance of the "materialistic ethos" of U.S. society in general and among white college students in particular. "The average Negro undergraduate has swallowed hook, line, and sinker, the dead bait of the white undergraduate, who, born in an industrial machine does not have to think, and does not think." Du Bois believed that the predominating ideals of the college-educated African American should be "poverty, work, knowledge, and sacrifice." Unfortunately,

[o]ur college man today is, on the average, a man untouched by real culture. He deliberately surrenders to selfish and even silly ideals, swarming into semiprofessional athletics and Greek letter societies, and affecting to despise scholarship and the hard grind of study and research. The greatest meetings of the Negro college year like those of the white college year become vulgar exhibitions of liquor, extravagance, and fur coats. We have in our colleges a growing mass of stupidity and indifference.

In this speech, entitled "Education and Work" and later published in *The Education of Black People: Ten Critiques, 1906–1960 by W.E.B. Du Bois* (1973), he criticized the industrial institutes for failing to "impart the higher technique of the industrial process or of business organization" and the colleges and universities for failing to establish

that great and guiding ideal of group development and leadership, within a dominating and expanding culture . . . as the leading motif of the educated Negro. Its vocational work has been confined to the so-called learned professions, with only scant beginning of the imparting of the higher technique of industry and science.

And at a speech delivered at Fisk University in 1933, entitled "The Field and Function of the Negro College," also included in *The Education of Black People*, Du Bois outlined the social and intellectual purposes of the Negro college.

There can be no college for Negroes that is not a Negro college . . . [N]o matter how much we may dislike the statement, the American Negro problem is and must be the center of the Negro university. It has got to be. You are teaching Negroes. There is no use pretending that you are teaching Chinese or that you are teaching white Americans or that you are teaching citizens of the world. You are teaching American Negroes in 1933, and they are the objects of a caste system in the Republic of the United States of America and their life problem is primarily this problem of caste. Upon these foundations, therefore, your university must start and build.

Education and Jim Crow Segregation

The pragmatic approach to African American education that Du Bois exhibited in his criticism of the behavior of black college students and in his views on the objectives of African American higher education was also found in the principled position he took on the issue of "separate v. mixed schools" for black children. During the twenty-four years he served as editor of *The Crisis* magazine (1910–1934), Du Bois annually devoted entire issues to the topic of black education, often praising the work being carried out in the separate black public and private schools throughout the country. Although Du Bois was an officer of the NAACP, whose main objective was the destruction of those legal barriers to full integration of African Americans into the larger society on the basis of full equality, he was sometimes accused of supporting "Jim Crow education." For example, in 1923 Du Bois made it clear that he believed that "a 'Jim Crow' school system is the greatest possible menace to democracy and the greatest hindrance to our advance in the United States." At the same time, however, he pointed out in this statement: "We have separate schools in the South and in some cases in the North and these schools have done [and] are doing an excellent job. The teachers in them in most cases have been capable, self-sacrificing persons. I believe in these schools in the sense that without them we could not have gotten our present education."

In 1935, following his resignation from the editorship of *The Crisis* and the NAACP Board of Directors over what he considered was the organization's failure to put forward a viable program or economic strategy for African Americans suffering during the Great Depression, Du Bois published in the *Journal of Negro Education* one of his most controversial essays, "Does the Negro Need Separate Schools?" While some scholars have suggested that this essay reflected Du Bois' turn toward the separatist doctrines associated with his former ideological opponents, Booker T. Washington and Marcus Garvey, when the positions taken in this essay are compared with earlier statements on "Jim Crow education," there is a great deal of continuity that reflects the pragmatism that was the hallmark of Du Bois' educational philosophy throughout his life.

Du Bois presented his answer to the question he posed at the outset: "They are needed just so far as they are necessary for the proper education of the Negro race." Du Bois made it clear that he was dealing with the realities of black education in the 1930s.

If the public schools of Atlanta, Nashville, New Orleans, and Jacksonville were thrown open to all races tomorrow, the education that colored children would get in them would be worse than pitiable. It would not be education. And in the same way, there are many public school systems in the North where Negroes are admitted and tolerated, but they are not educated; they are crucified.

Du Bois in all of his educational writings made it clear that he advocated schooling that was in the best interest of the black child.

[A] separate Negro school, where children are treated like human beings, trained by teachers of their own race, who know what it means to be black in the year of salvation 1935, is infinitely better than making our boys and girls doormats to be spit and trampled upon and lied to by ignorant social climbers, whose sole claim to superiority is the ability to kick "niggers" when they are down. I say, too, that certain studies and discipline necessary for Negroes can seldom be found in white schools.

Du Bois made it clear that "theoretically the Negro needs neither segregated schools nor mixed schools. What he needs is Education." But he also understood there was "no magic" in either segregated or mixed schools, and "other things being equal, the mixed school is the broader, more natural basis for education of all youth. It gives wider contacts; it inspires confidence, and suppresses the inferiority complex. But other things are seldom equal, and in that case, Sympathy, Knowledge, and Truth, outweigh all that the mixed school can offer."

When Du Bois returned to teaching at Atlanta University in 1935, he continued his educational research and published numerous reports on the status of the black colleges and universities. In his newspaper columns in the 1940s and 1950s he often discussed various aspects of black education. It is interesting that during the early years of the campaigns for public school desegregation, Du Bois warned African American leaders that in opposing "Jim Crow education" they must be careful not to disparage and demean African American children and educators. In too many instances, however, this warning went unheeded, and by the 1960s, education researchers were suggesting in studies such as the Coleman Report (1965) that African American children could learn only in classrooms and schools that contain a substantial nonblack majority.

Throughout his long life W.E.B. Du Bois was a brilliant and uncompromising spokesperson for his race, and in his pronouncements and scholarly assessments of the status of black education, he always supported the pragmatic view that, regardless of the political or economic issues under debate at the time, what is best for the black child must always be reasserted and used to define policies and practices as African American parents and children move into the twenty-first century. *See also*: Fisk University; Garvey, Marcus; Hampton Intitute; Harvard; Howard University; *The Souls of Black Folk*; Tuskegee Institute; Washington, Booker T.; Wilberforce University.

FURTHER READING

The most complete listing of the educational writings of W.E.B. Du Bois may be found in the following.

Aptheker, Herbert, ed. *The Education of Black People: Ten Critiques, 1906–1960*. New York: Monthly Review Press, 1973.

Du Bois, W.E.B. "Does the Negro Need Separate Schools?" *Journal of Negro Education* 4 (July 1935): 328–335.

——. ed. *Report of the First Conference of Negro Land Grant Colleges for Coordinating a Program of Cooperative Social Studies*. Atlanta, GA: Atlanta University Press, 1943.

Du Bois, W.E.B., and A. G. Dill, eds. *The Atlanta University Publications (1897–1910.)* Reprint, New York: Arno Press, 1968.

Franklin, V. P. *Black Self-Determination: A Cultural History of African American Resistance*. Brooklyn, NY: Lawrence Hill Books, 1992.

——. *Living Our Stories, Telling Our Truths: Autobiography and the Making of the African American Intellectual Tradition*. New York: Charles Scribner's, 1995.

——. "W.E.B. Du Bois and the Education of Black Folk." *History of Education Quarterly* (Spring 1976): 111–118.

——. "Whatever Happened to the College Bred Negro?" *History of Education Quarterly* (Fall 1984): 411–418.

Lewis, David Levering. *W.E.B. Du Bois: The Biography of A Race, 1868–1919*. New York: Henry Holt, 1993.

Walden, David, ed. *W.E.B. Du Bois: The Crisis Writings*. Greenwich, CT: Fawcett Publications, 1972.

Wolters, Raymond. *New Negro on Campus*. Princeton, NJ: Princeton University Press, 1975.

V. P. Franklin

ENCYCLOPEDIA PROJECTS

In 1893, on his twenty-fifth birthday, while studying in Germany, Du Bois pledged in his journal "to make a name in science, to make a name in literature and thus to raise my race" (*Against* 29). That pledge encapsulates Du Bois' encyclopedic imagination—as in his analysis of race in "The Conservation of Races" (1897), in which he speaks of each of eight basic races contributing its "message" to the world, and in his famous statement of double consciousness: two warring ideas in one dark body, seeking to merge into "a better and truer self" in which neither of the older selves is lost. Thus, the movement of his mind from analysis to synthesis, from anatomy to a comprehensive, is seen. One could argue that throughout his life Du Bois was writing the encyclopedia of his race.

Over the course of his ninety-five years, Du Bois' encyclopedic vision sought expression in a number of ways. The sheer variety of genres in which he worked is an expression of his encyclopedism. In literature he produced novels, poetry, academic and journalistic essays, history, sociological treatises, short stories, pageants, speeches, editorials, autobiography, and reviews. In individual texts like *The Souls of Black Folk*, comprising essays, short fiction, poetry, and song fragments, he displays this encyclopedic impulse. As for making a name in science, during his years as professor of economics and history at Atlanta University, he took over editing of the two-year-old Atlanta Conference Studies, expanding their scope and mapping out a century-long project covering all aspects of African American life, amounting to, in Du Bois' own estimation, "a current encyclopaedia on the American Negro problems" (*Dusk* 599–601).

It is no surprise, then, that Du Bois involved himself with actual encyclopedias. Not only did he contribute individual articles to several encyclopedias; he was the primary force behind three separate attempts to publish an encyclopedia devoted to the history and culture of the African and African diasporic peoples. "As early as 1909," Du Bois writes in *Dusk of Dawn*, "I had planned an Encyclopedia Africana and secured on my board of advisers Sir Flinders Petrie, Sir Harry Johnston, Giuseppe Sergi, Dr. J. Deniker, William James, and Franz Boas; and on my proposed board of editors I had practically all the leading Negroes of the United States who were then inclined toward research" (790). That project, he goes on to say, was cut short by his duties in the newly established National Association for the Advancement of Colored People (NAACP) and by the onset of World War I. More important, perhaps, as David Levering Lewis notes, Du Bois was unable to secure funding from the General Education Board, the philanthropic combine that was more encouraging than useful for Du Bois' encyclopedia projects (379–380). Twice more in his life, he sought, with others, to produce an "Encyclopedia Africana." The first time was in 1932 when he was selected to edit the *Encyclopedia of the Negro* under the auspices of the Phelps Stokes Fund. And less than two years before his death in 1963, he became a citizen of Ghana and directed renewed work on an "Encyclopedia Africana" at the invitation of Kwame Nkrumah, leader of the fledgling African republic. In this instance, as before, the dream of the encyclopedia went unrealized.

Du Bois' first foray into the encyclopedia business was an article entitled "The Negro in America," published in the revived *Encyclopedia Americana* in 1904. In 1924, he was asked to submit an article for the *Standard Encyclopedia of the Alcohol Problem* on alcoholism among African blacks (*Papers* 14/95), and he wrote an article on "Miscegenation" for the 1936 *Encyclopedia Sexualis,* which for some reason never made it into publication. During its early preparatory stages, the *Encyclopedia of the Social Sciences* (published from 1930 to 1935) consulted with Du Bois on its list of African American contributors to the development of the social sciences (*Papers* 31/222), and in 1934, the editors accepted for inclusion his article on Booker T. Washington (*Papers* 42/238–245). His most important association with another encyclopedia, however, began in 1925 when he wrote the subsection "Negro Literature" for the article on American literature in the thirteenth edition of the *Encyclopaedia Britannica,* published in 1926.

Although Du Bois' research and writing for the various encyclopedias broke new ground for the genre, more important were his experiences in trying to get the articles and projects into print. His dealings with *Encyclopaedia Britannica* introduced him to some key issues that would plague him as editor of the *Encyclopedia of the Negro* project. *Britannica*'s publishing guidelines sought objectivity from the contributors stating, "Articles should be devoid of political, national, or personal bias" (*Papers* 15/288–289). Yet a firestorm of protest arose when the encyclopedia refused to capitalize the word "negro," as Du Bois and the many African American scholars he had recruited as contributors insisted. Had *Britannica* been even and consistent in its designation of the various races, there may not have been a problem. However, Charles G. Seligman's entry "Anthropology" discussed "hybrid" races with these designations: Chinese-white, Mongolian-white, and Japanese-white but negro-Amerind and Arab-negro.

Furthermore, Seligman declared the Arab-negro prominently Arab, based on the Arab-negro's admirable mental and moral qualities, and concluded that "the inferior stock [that is, the "negro" addition] may be said to have been improved by the mixture" (49). The encyclopedia editors were unhappy as well with some of Du Bois' ideas, demanding that he revise some of the conclusions regarding the contribution of African Americans to restoring the South to the Union. Du Bois responded with an ultimatum: Publish my article on the American black as is, or do not publish it. They did not.

Du Bois' most extensive and promising attempt to publish an encyclopedia on Africans and peoples of African descent came when he was named, not without controversy, editor of the *Encyclopedia of the Negro* project, sponsored by the Phelps-Stokes Fund. Over the thirteen years spent trying to make the *Encyclopedia of the Negro* a reality (1932–1945), Du Bois encountered in concrete ways the issues that had always faced African Americans struggling for equality in the United States. The first and perhaps the most important issue was the question of authority. It was as though, like slave narratives, an African American encyclopedia could not be self-authorizing. Instead, in the eyes of the financial sponsors a white presence was necessary to signal objectivity. From the point of view of the potential audience, the sponsors were probably right. For such a groundbreaking scholarly enterprise, the presence of acknowledged white scholars would ensure a more receptive white readership. However, the fact that the Phelps-Stokes Fund had been and still was a strong supporter of Tuskegee raised all the old questions about the role of whites in the uplift of African Americans. The presence on the encyclopedia's Executive Board of Thomas Jesse Jones, the Phelps-Stokes Fund's director of education, was especially irksome for Du Bois and others. Writing to another Board member Du Bois argued that to "contemplate a Negro encyclopedia dominated and controlled by Thomas Jesse Jones and Mr. [T. J.] Woofter . . . would be as inconceivable as a Catholic encyclopedia projected by Protestants" (*Correspondence* 1:477). Ultimately, after considering various editorial options, the Board went with Du Bois as editor along with "white and Negro scholars as his associates" (*Papers* 37, 507). Professor Robert E. Park, former ghost writer for Booker T. Washington, was the white section.

The question of authority was integrally linked to concerns about objectivity. After all, Du Bois had written in 1926 "that whatever art I have for writing has been used always for propaganda for gaining the right of black folk to love and enjoy" ("Criteria" 1000). In the context of a history of white propaganda against blacks, Du Bois' position was certainly understandable. In the context of a scholarly encyclopedia, such a stance prompted uneasiness on the part of white sponsors and scholars. One white scholar asked to participate, Donald Young of the Social Sciences Research Council, voiced his concern (although he exempted Du Bois from his worries): "My one question concerning the project has to do with the possibility of its scientific character being strictly maintained in spite of the pressure for eulogistic and reform emphasis which will be brought to bear" (*Papers* 45/130).

The worries about propaganda also masked a less frequently stated fear of incompetence. Even though he had earned Du Bois' confidence and deferred to Du Bois, Robert Parks had doubts about the capabilities of some of the black scholars involved. In early 1938 he told Du Bois of certain "experiments . . . designed to be exploratory merely." He assigned two projects to two potential African American contributors "to get some notion of how competent they, and other men, with the same intellectual background, were to write articles in the particular fields in which they have specialized." To be fair, Parks did conclude that "there were enough colored men to do most if not all the work" but that he felt the need to explore the issue goes to the heart of the need for the encyclopedia in the first place.

Along with the question of authority and its subissues of objectivity and competence, the international scope of the material, which was to cover not simply African America but Africa and dispersed African peoples wherever they were to be found, led to the question of identity. In an encyclopedia of African Americans, just who would qualify under the term? Park put the issue succinctly:

I foresee that anthropologists and sociologists also are going to have difficulty with any conception of the Negro, since as you propose to use the term, it designates not a race, in the strict sense, but a group of peoples, of diverse and mixed racial stocks, who because they have been identified with Africa have come to have common interests and a sense of sharing, somehow, in a common destiny. (*Papers* 47/973)

Later Park noted that "people in Brazil have a totally different conception of the Negro from that which prevails in the United States. They do not think of a man of mixed blood as one whose fate is bound up with the Negro in Africa or the United States. Those of mixed blood, at least, are Brazilians." His research in South Africa indicated that the Bantu, while concerned with African American progress, "did not think of themselves as Negroes" (*Papers* 49/402–404).

Du Bois' conception of race has generated much discussion. Anthony Appiah, for example, has referred to Du Bois' use of the term as the "illusion of race." For Du Bois, race, like the encyclopedia, was always an instrumental construct. As he puts it in "The Conservation of the Races," "We believe it is the duty of American Negroes, as a body, to maintain their race identity until this mission of the Negro is accomplished, and the ideal of human brotherhood has become a practical possibility." Unfortunately, the *Encyclopedia of the Negro*, one attempt to maintain race identity, never received the necessary financial backing to do its work. In 1945, after thirteen years of research and preparation, the best that Du Bois and Anson Phelps Stokes could do was release a "preparatory volume"—an outline of the project that included lists of the subjects and library resources of black studies, and a bibliography of bibliographies. The *Encyclopedia of the Negro* was finally the shadow of a dream in outline form.

By the time Du Bois joined Kwame Nkruma in Ghana in 1961 to organize and edit an Encyclopedia Africana, he had little time and energy left. He died having given almost two years of work to the project. In looking back at Du Bois' encyclopedia projects, it is interesting to note what Anson Phelps Stokes said to Du Bois early during their collaboration on the *Encyclopedia of the Negro*: "I have felt that possibly my major emphasis was on subjects, yours on contributors. Both are important, but at this stage before we have the Encyclopedia financed it seems to me that the most important emphasis should be on the analysis of the material" (*Papers* 44/876). What Stokes failed to realize was that for this project as for all encyclopedias Du Bois worked on "the material" *was* the contributors. His encyclopedic projects were acts of self and racial definition and of self and racial assertion. At least as important as what was said was who would speak. Sadly, this is one instance in Du Bois' great career when he was silenced. *See also: Dusk of Dawn.*

FURTHER READING

Appiah, Anthony. "The Uncompleted Argument: Du Bois and the Illusion of Race." In *Race, Writing, and Difference*, ed. Henry Louis Gates, Jr. Chicago: University of Chicago Press, 1985. 21–37.

Aptheker, Herbert, ed. *The Correspondence of W.E.B. Du Bois*. 3 vols. Amherst: University of Massachusetts Press, 1976.

Du Bois, W.E.B. "Booker T. Washington." In *Encyclopedia of the Social Sciences*. 1930–35.

———. "Celebrating His Twenty-fifth Birthday." In *Against Racism: Unpublished Essays, Pa-*

pers, Addresses, 1887–1961, ed. Herbert Aptheker. Amherst: University of Massachusetts Press, 1985. 26–29.

——. "The Conservation of the Races." In *Writings* 815–826.

——. "Criteria of Negro Art." In *Writings* 993–1002.

——. *Dusk of Dawn: An Essay toward an Autobiography of a Race Concept.* In *Writings* 549–802.

——. "The Negro in America." In *Encyclopedia Americana: A General Dictionary of the Arts and Sciences, Literature, History, Biography, Geography, Etc. of the World.* 1904.

——. "Negro Literature." In *Encyclopaedia Britannica.* 13th ed. 1926.

——. *The Papers of W.E.B. Du Bois.* Microfilming Corporation of America. (Microfilm).

Du Bois, W.E.B., and Guy B. Johnson. *Encyclopedia of the Negro: Preparatory Volume with Reference Lists and Reports.* New York: Phelps-Stokes Fund, 1946.

Lewis, David Levering. *W.E.B. Du Bois: Biography of a Race, 1868–1919.* New York: Henry Holt, 1993.

Seligman, Charles G. "Anthropology." In *Encyclopaedia Britannica.* 14th ed. 1929.

Mark S. Braley

ETHIOPIA

Located in the strategic area of the world, known as the Horn of Africa, Ethiopia is one of the largest and most populous countries in Africa. During its history, it has been influenced and even occasionally occupied by other nations; however, Ethiopia is one of the few countries in Africa or Asia never truly colonized.

Her history is virtually that of a continuous feudal monarchy, but it also includes wars with neighbors and colonial nations. Italian colonial influences expanded into Eritrea and Ethiopia in the last two decades of the nineteenth century, but Ethiopia defeated the Italian armies in 1896 at the battle of Aduwa. The routing of the Italians preserved Ethiopian independence, but in 1935 Italy again invaded Ethiopia.

Before the invasion, Du Bois had warned that Mussolini was "eyeing" Ethiopia. Throughout the Italian occupation, Du Bois participated in protests against Italy. Later, he blamed the increase in the arms race on European nonaction. Not only did he reproach Europe, but Du Bois also chided ex-President Herbert Hoover for ranting about "poor little Finland," while he had little to say about Italian aggression in Ethiopia.

In the 1950s, Ethiopia was still a source of concern for Du Bois. Writing in *Freedom*, he praises Haile Selassie's use of foreign capital to bring his country into the twentieth century. *See also*: Africa; Mussolini, Benito.

FURTHER READING

Carter, Boake. *Black Shirt, Black Skin.* Harrisburg, PA: Telegraph Press, 1935.

"Ethiopia: State Socialism under an Emperor." *Freedom* (February 2, 1955).

Mary Young

F

FAUSET, JESSIE REDMON (1882–1961)

Fauset's main connection with Du Bois was through her work on *The Crisis* magazine. This journal was started by Du Bois and served as the organ of the National Association for the Advancement of Colored People (NAACP). Fauset was the only person to hold the editor position formally. She became the literary editor of *The Crisis* in 1919 when the magazine was expanding its staff because it was at the high point of its circulation. Before Fauset became the editor, Du Bois appears to have maintained as strong an influence on the literary role of the magazine as he did on its editorial policy. The early *Crisis* announced its basic artistic criteria as literature set in black life but not so directly propagandistic that it ignored the principles of art.

During her tenure as literary editor of *The Crisis* (1919–1926), Fauset published many of the early voices of the Harlem Renaissance, including Jean Toomer, George Schuyler, Langston Hughes, and Claude McKay. She supported the works of the young writers, even if their direction ran counter to her own, and she was a prolific Harlem Renaissance novelist herself. Fauset wrote the following four books in less than ten years: *There Is Confusion* (1924), *Plum Bun* (1928), *The Chinaberry Tree* (1931), and *Comedy American Style* (1933).

In contrast with many writers of the Harlem School who portrayed the stark realities of inner-city life, Fauset, who came from a prominent Philadelphia family, dealt with the problems of the African American middle class. When Fauset resigned from *The Crisis* in 1926, Du Bois, the principal literary spirit of the journal, assumed the editorial responsibilities again. *See also*: Art and Literature; *The Crisis*; Cullen, Countee; Harlem Renaissance; McKay, Claude.

FURTHER READING

The Crisis (March 1912).

McLendon, Jacquelyn Y. *The Politics of Color in the Fiction of Jessie Fauset and Nella Larsen.* Charlottesville, VA: University Press of Virginia, 1995.

Laura de Luca

FEDERAL BUREAU OF INVESTIGATION

Congressional investigations in 1975 revealed that for many years the Federal Bureau of Investigation (FBI) had been engaged in actions, often illegal, to destroy groups or movements considered radical by J. Edgar Hoover. As early as 1919 the Bureau had institutionalized surveillance against African Americans preaching social change in that they called for civil rights. In the early 1920s Hoover decided that Marcus Garvey must be found guilty of a crime and sent to prison. In the process of accumulating the information necessary to do this, a major investigation of "the colored press" was launched.

As editor of *The Crisis*, the monthly magazine of the National Association for the Advancement of Colored People (NAACP), Du Bois came under the Bureau's scrutiny at this time. Thus began the FBI file entitled "W.E.B. Du Bois," which would continue to accumulate entries throughout the years. In her memoir *His Day Is Marching On* (1971), Shirley Graham Du Bois, his second wife, recalls it was well known that their home was watched by the FBI and that in 1961, before they moved to Ghana, the FBI came to the door and threatened them should they help Robert Williams, an activist from North Carolina wanted by the government.

After Du Bois joined the Communist Party in 1961, Du Bois clubs formed to discuss—and act upon—his works and ideas. The FBI responded by leaking information to the United States Information Agency (USIA) that it hoped would help discredit Du Bois, whom the FBI acknowledged was held in high regard in many of the emerging African nations. *See also*: Hoover, J. Edgar.

FURTHER READING

Du Bois, Shirley. *His Day is Marching On: A Memoir of W.E.B. Du Bois.* Philadelphia: Lippincott, 1971.

Scot Guenter

FISK UNIVERSITY

When his mother's death made it impossible for him to afford tuition at Harvard University, community leaders in Great Barrington, Massachusetts, collected enough money to send Du Bois to Fisk University (Tennessee) in 1885 at the age of seventeen. Opened in 1866, Fisk provided African Americans of both sexes with a liberal arts education built upon a "broad Christian foundation." In moving to Nashville, Du Bois became a member of a southern black community for the first time. Although appreciative of Fisk's faculty and mission, he always felt that the college's limited resources hindered his quest for a classical liberal education. After receiving his Bachelor of Arts (B.A.) degree in 1888, he elected to pursue a second bachelor's degree at Harvard (1890), his Master of Arts (M.A.) at Harvard (1891), and after a brief tenure at the University of Berlin, he received a Ph.D. in Sociology from Harvard. Throughout his life, Du Bois only supported black colleges that supported a liberal arts curriculum. In 1908, he criticized Fisk's president, James Merrill, for his decision to support industrial education. During the 1920s, he accused Fayette McKenzie of bowing to white southern demands that compromised the principle of black autonomy. In spite of these criticisms, on his seventieth birthday, Fisk awarded Du Bois with an honorary degree and granted him membership in the National Institute of Arts and Letters. *See also*: Educational Philosophy.

FURTHER READING

Editorial. *Fisk Herald* (November 1887).

Catherine M. Lewis

FRANCE

W.E.B. Du Bois first traveled to France in 1893 and returned in 1900 for the Paris Exposition Universelle, where he organized an American Negro Exhibit boasting African American progress after Emancipation. The young scholar had a deep admiration for French culture, and his display at the Exposition aimed to prove that people of African descent were on their way to joining Europeans at the table of modern civilization.

Under French colonial policy, Africans had access to education and administrative training. Compared to British, German, or Belgian colonies, French West Africa came closest to Du Bois' ideal of helping Africans to advance along European standards. At the 1918 Congress of Versailles, and at three Pan-African Congresses held in Paris in 1919, 1921, and 1923, he pled with French politicians to consider Africa in international deliberations after World War I.

Not until the Great Depression did Du Bois question the sincerity of French paternalism. As European imperialism grew increasingly exploitative during the 1930s, he recognized that French colonialism had "exactly the same object and methods as the fascism" that was sweeping Germany and Italy.

Du Bois returned to Paris for the 1949 World Peace Conference. The professor's speech at that massive demonstration against the Cold War stressed that imperialism, not communism, posed a threat to world peace and security. His statements, along with his endorsement of an international Peace Manifesto, proved the final straw that would break the U.S. government's tolerance for his radicalism.

In spite of his disdain for their government, Du Bois retained an admiration

for the achievements of French working people. In 1957, he advised Ghana's
new president Kwame Nkrumah to model Pan-African socialism upon French
welfare capitalism, as well as Soviet communism and Scandinavian social democracy. At the same time, he warned France's former colonies to resist neo-
colonialism under French capital. *See also*: Cold War; Nkrumah, Kwame;
Pan-Africanism.

FURTHER READING

People's Voice (July 26, 1947).

William Powell Jones

G

GANDHI, MOHANDAS (1869–1948)

Du Bois realized that the world wars of the twentieth century created a changing world in which people of color were increasingly freeing themselves from the domination of Europe and the United States. The most dramatic instance of such change came from India under the insurgent leadership of Mohandas Gandhi. Eulogizing Gandhi in 1948, Du Bois called him the "greatest man in the world" and noted the irony that a non-Christian was the only great world leader to truly exemplify the Christian doctrine of peace. Du Bois noted with awe that Gandhi had managed to bring freedom to more than 350 million Indians, with minimal bloodshed, by following the path of peace instead of war.

A contemporary of Gandhi's, Du Bois did not learn of him and his work in Africa until after World War I. On his own, Du Bois had struggled with the question of peace; as a young man he believed the only path to freedom for the world's people of color was through armed struggle. By the end of the nineteenth century, however, Du Bois signed a pledge never to participate in war. Although Du Bois found himself swept into the general fervor of wartime, the aftermath of World War I left him feeling more than ever that war would never cause peace. In this regard, Du Bois found much kinship with Gandhi, who had also supported World War I in the belief that it would be the "war to end all wars." Understanding World War I finally as a war for industrial profit, not freedom at all, Gandhi turned to passive resistance, inaction, and noncooperation as the means to force Britain to give India its freedom.

The parallels to the situation of African Americans were strong and clear to Du Bois, and he saw great possibilities in the use of Gandhi's principles to cause social and political equality. Writing in February 1957, Du Bois noted the use of passive resistance in the Montgomery bus boycott, which was still in effect, but he was also discouraged by the results. After many months of boycott, black workers were still encountering difficulty and Du Bois began to analyze why change remained elusive.

Passive resistance, Du Bois reasoned, would work only if used on civilized people, with whom nonviolence is the customary response to another who refuses to fight. Arguing that the American South is rife with pathological persons who cannot be reasoned with on racial issues, Du Bois saw the remedy for this ignorance in educating all children together so they would grow to adulthood with the recognition of each others' humanity. But he noted that nonviolence would never bring about peace since whites continued the tradition of teaching hate. As the civil rights era dawned, Du Bois wistfully looked to Gandhi's example for inspiration but saw little hope of his principles working in the United States unless the South was first civilized. *See also*: Africa; Asia; South Africa.

FURTHER READING

Bondurant, Joan V. *Conquest of Violence. The Gandhian Philosophy of Conflict.* Princeton, NJ: Princeton University Press, 1958.
"Mahatma Gandhi." The Amsterdam News (October 28, 1931).

Christy Rishoi

GARVEY, MARCUS (1887–1940)

Marcus Garvey led the United States' first mass Black Nationalist movement and became one of W.E.B. Du Bois' major political opponents and foils. Born in Jamaica in 1887, Garvey's father was descended from the Maroons, a group of escaped slaves who won autonomy from the British in 1739. After a brief career in Jamaican labor politics, Garvey became interested in the cause of blacks and traveled to Costa Rica, Panama, and eventually London in search of a following. In London he met with African nationalists who were mounting a critique of European colonialism. He also read Booker T. Washington's bible of black self-help *Up from Slavery* (1901). In 1914 Garvey returned to Jamaica and organized the United Negro Improvement Association (UNIA) in Kingston. Failing to find support in his native land, he moved his organization to New York in 1916, where he quickly took hold in the climate of social and political upheaval caused by the large migration of southern African Americans to the industrial North.

The UNIA grew rapidly among the manual laborers and industrial workers of Harlem's rapidly growing African American community; Garvey had found his constituency. He began publication of *Negro World*, which further articulated Garvey's great theme, that African Americans belonged to a distinguished race with a proud history and a bright future. By 1919 he claimed 2 million members for the UNIA and purchased Liberty Hall, a large auditorium in New York City.

Garvey also expressed his Black Nationalism in the business world. He believed that African Americans needed to open and patronize their own businesses, and to this end, in 1919 he established the Black Star shipping line. Garvey was a promotional genius. Bypassing the European American financial community, he took his enterprise directly to the African American community. Garvey's representatives sold small amounts of stock in the Black Star Line directly to working African Americans. In less than a year this practice had raised over $600,000. The line provided a morale boost for many African Americans searching for black advances in an era of racial setbacks, but Garvey proved sadly inexperienced in business practice, and the enterprise quickly began losing money. Despite his own devotion to the cause of racial advancement, Garvey was a poor judge of personnel, and a series of dishonest subordinates fleeced the line of hundreds of thousands of its stockholders' hard-earned dollars.

By 1921, the line was in dire financial straits, and in 1922, Garvey and his associates faced federal mail fraud charges. The Black Star Line had failed so rapidly that prosecutors took it as a scheme for fleecing investors. Garvey defended himself at his 1923 trial but was found guilty and sentenced to five years in federal prison. While incarcerated, however, he inaugurated a successor to his ill-fated line, the Black Cross Shipping Line, and organized an extensive project for black colonization in Liberia. The Black Cross Line failed when Black Star creditors successfully attached its assets for its predecessors' debts, and the colonization movement disintegrated before a combination of hostile colonial powers and a wary Liberian government. In 1927, President Calvin Coolidge commuted Garvey's sentence, but as a convicted felon, he was immediately deported to Jamaica. He struggled mightily to revive the moribund UNIA movement, eventually moving to London in 1934, but to no avail.

Marcus Garvey died in 1940 at the age of fifty-two.

Garvey's dramatic, self-aggrandizing style and racial chauvinism attracted criticism, and this condemnation intensified as the UNIA businesses failed and took thousands of black dollars with them. By the mid-1920s Garvey and Du Bois squared off in an Olympian rhetorical battle that masked basic divisions in the movement for black freedom. There were basic policy differences. Garvey sought to organize a back-to-Africa movement for his followers, and Du Bois reserved his support for Africans' struggles against colonialism. In the early 1920s Garvey turned away from a politics sympathetic to the international Left and toward a vision of "racial purity," whereas Du Bois explored the possibilities of international Left politics. Increasingly Garvey and his lieutenants portrayed the light-skinned highly educated Du Bois as a race traitor. When Garvey loudly proclaimed the Ku Klux Klan were "better friends of the race" than the National Association for the Advancement of Colored People (NAACP) due to their "honesty of purpose toward the Negro," Du Bois shot back with scathing and personal rebukes. There followed a volley of invective in which Du Bois stooped to calling Garvey a "demagogue" and his supporters "the lowest type of Negroes." The bitter attacks illustrated the growing diversity in the movement for black freedom in the United States. Where Booker T. Washington had appealed to southern African Americans living in the shadow of European American power and Du Bois spoke for upwardly mobile black professionals, Garvey now led the new urban dwellers. Where African Americans had once faced only a vision of racial accommodation, they now could choose between battling ideologies and leaders for black independence. *See also*: Washington, Booker T.

FURTHER READING

"Marcus Garvey." *The Crisis* (December 1920).
"Marcus Garvey." *The Crisis* (January 1921).

                                                                         Drew VandeCreek

GARVEY AND THE UNIA

Jamaican born Pan-African leader Marcus Garvey (1887–1940) brought his Universal Negro Improvement Association (UNIA) to Harlem (New York) during World War I. Garvey, heavily influenced by the "self-help" teachings of Booker T. Washington, came to the United States at a time when Du Bois and the National Association for the Advancement of Colored People (NAACP) were considered the major voice and organization for African Americans. Garvey's strong Pan-Africanist and separatist teachings, along racial lines, caused many members of the NAACP, both black and white, to view the UNIA as a hindrance to their agenda of racial solidarity in the United States.

Initially, tensions among Garvey and Du Bois were quite severe. Both wrote articles that not only attacked each other's political ideology but went so far as to stereotypically characterize one another on the basis of skin color. Du Bois felt that Garvey brought the ideology of *shade-ism* (colorism)—that was and continues to be very prevalent in Jamaica—to the plight of African Americans, whereas Garvey viewed Du Bois as part of the—European-created—light-skinned elite class among Africans throughout the diaspora. Despite their disagreement, Du Bois, in many articles in *The Crisis*, lauded Garvey's enthusiasm and determination but felt that his poor business management skills would eventually bring about the demise of the UNIA.

Even though Du Bois and Garvey differed in many respects, both believed in a liberated and self-sufficient Africa; and it is also ironic that Du Bois was able to actualize one of the major teachings of Garvey—repatriation back to the African continent.

FURTHER READING

"Marcus Garvey." *The Crisis* (December 1920).
"Marcus Garvey." *The Crisis* (January 1921).

                                                                         Muata Kamdibe

GEORGIA

W.E.B. Du Bois' first association with the state of Georgia occurred when he moved to Atlanta in 1897 to assume a teaching position with Atlanta University. Du Bois was appalled at the treatment of blacks in Atlanta and throughout the state of Georgia, particularly when compared to northern cities and states. He was shocked at the political system in place in Georgia whereby blacks were excluded from voting in the Democratic primary. This exclusion in essence prevented active black political participation in a one-party state such as Georgia. Years later, in 1950, he was still criticizing the antidemocratic county-unit system used in Georgia when writing about blacks residing in the state. Another situation that outraged Du Bois was the number of lynchings of blacks around Atlanta and throughout the state.

During the early Atlanta University years, the U.S. Department of Labor requested that Du Bois conduct a study entitled *The Negro Landholder in Georgia*, which was published in 1901. In this county-by-county study, Du Bois looked at black Georgia landowners, tenant farmers, and sharecroppers in an attempt to determine how "470,000 black freedmen and their children have in one of the former slave States gained possession of over a million acres of land in a generation." Du Bois also wrote of the black belt of Georgia, in particular Dougherty County, in the 1903 publication *The Souls of Black Folk*. Revealing that blacks still lived very much as they had under slavery with restrictions on job mobility, he also described how the character of blacks had to be "vouched for by some white man." He compared this treatment to the old Roman patronage system.

Du Bois was very concerned about the condition of black education within Georgia. Along with other prominent black Georgia educators, Du Bois signed *A Memorial to the Legislature of Georgia on Negro Common Schools* around 1900. In testimony before the U.S. House of Representative's Committee on Education in 1949, he maintained that the "discrimination between white and colored schools in Georgia is large and growing." As a possible solution, he suggested to Congress that the federal government establish guidelines regarding expenditures of educational funds. *See also*: Atlanta, Georgia; Atlanta University; *The Souls of Black Folk*.

FURTHER READING

Du Bois, W.E.B. *The Negro Landowner of Georgia, Bulletin of the Department of Labor*. Vol. VI. Washington, DC: Government Printing Office, 1901.

Mary Ellen Wilson

GERMANY

Throughout most of his life Du Bois maintained an affinity for things German. In his commencement oration at Fisk University in 1888, he professed admiration for the forceful, unifying leadership of Otto von Bismarck, chancellor of the first German Reich, in whom he saw the kind of model leadership African Americans required in the post-Reconstruction era. "He was my hero," he later wrote in his autobiography. "He had made a nation out of a mass of bickering people." Du Bois began studying German in his junior year at Fisk University and, encouraged by his professors at Harvard University, applied for graduate study at the Friedrich Wilhelm University at Berlin (a.k.a. the University of Berlin). His two years there allowed him to interact with not only renowned academics like Gustav Schmoller and Heinrich von Treitschke but also the common folk of cities and towns who did not carry the same racial baggage as European Americans; thus, he established friendships, experienced the love of a fraulein, and boarded in the homes of German families. Temporarily relieved of the crucible of American racism, he could view the world from a different perspective, entertain the tenets of Marx and Engels, and consider himself a freethinker and a socialist. But he also appreciated and participated in cultural life, regularly taking in museums, art galleries, and symphonies. Though he recognized the genius of jazz and blues, he developed a personal preference for the works of Brahms, Schumann, and Handel.

Du Bois returned to Germany on three occasions. In 1926 he visited Cologne, Frankfurt, and Berlin before traveling to the Soviet Union. In the summer of 1936, he observed firsthand the transformation of Germany into a fascist state. He reported on Hitler's adept use of radio and commented on Germany's brand of racism and anti-Semitism, which in *The Crisis* he compared to American racism. He viewed the ascendancy of Nazism, to a large extent, as the result of a conspiracy of vengeful capitalist states, the Great Depression, and a highly insecure middle class and frightened industrialists who were both intimidated and impressed by the strength and vision of the Nazis. On the other hand, some misinterpreted his apparent amazement at the "splendid accomplishment" of the German economic revolution and socialist state planning under Hitler.

The onset of World War II found Du Bois more actively anti-Nazi, particularly after Germany attacked Russia in 1941, which he believed was a blow to the promise of communism, that is, his assumption that Russia's experiment in "industrial democracy" represented hope for the modern world, whereas Germany's war for world domination would further degrade all races of color and subjugate the white working classes. His final visit to Germany in October 1958 with his second wife, Shirley Graham Du Bois, was at the invitation of the Communist-led government of the German Democratic Republic. On November 5, he received the degree of Doctor of Economics from his alma mater (renamed Humboldt University) sixty-four years after he had entered its gates. Fear that the Americans would seize his passport dissuaded him from crossing over into West Berlin. *See also*: Anti-Semitism.

FURTHER READING

The Autobiography of W.E.B. Du Bois. New York: International Pub., 1968.

Robert Fikes, Jr.

GILPIN, CHARLES SIDNEY (1878–1930)

Gilpin, an actor, was born in Richmond, Virginia, and began his acting career in 1913 with road companies. He managed a black theater company in Harlem (1916) and appeared in John Drinkwater's *Abraham Lincoln* (1919). Gilpin's greatest success was his creation of Brutus Jones, the lead role in Eugene O'Neill's (1888–1953) *The Emperor Jones.* Of his performance, Du Bois declared that Gilpin had "scored a great triumph." While praising Gilpin in *The Emperor Jones,* Du Bois chided the drama: "*The Emperor Jones* is the kind of play that should never be staged under any circumstances, regardless of theories, because it portrays the worst traits of the bad elements of both races" ("Negro Art").

In a 1924 *Crisis* article "The Negro and the American Stage," Du Bois observed that the customary role of blacks as buffoons or fools must give way for "the most dramatic group of people in the history of the United States is the American Negro." Unquestionably, he continues, "it would be very easy for a great artist so to interpret the history of our country as to make the plot turn entirely upon the black man." Du Bois stresses the "tremendously sensitive nature of the Black world and this often leads to a fear of true art, but it must come." It is for this he commends the efforts of Eugene O'Neill.

Du Bois supported Gilpin in his columns, as he did other performing artists. As early as 1920, Du Bois began offering his readers sketches of Gilpin's career. Gilpin faced blatant discrimination during his career, and Du Bois reported in *The Brownies' Book* (1921) of one such incident with Gilpin. Du Bois reported that Gilpin had "conducted himself with manliness and dignity when some grossly prejudiced people sought to bar him from being among the honored guests at a dinner of the Dramatic League in New York City."

Gilpin retired from the stage in 1926. *See also*: Art and Artists; *The Brownies' Book*; Drama.

FURTHER READING

"Opinion." *The Crisis* (February 1921).

Courtney Young

GREAT BARRINGTON, MASSACHUSETTS

Willie Du Bois, as he was known to his family and townspeople, was born in 1868 on a quiet side street in downtown Great Barrington, a small town nestled in a valley of the Berkshire mountains. As revealed in his many writings, the town, its scenery, denizens, and rural New England charms and sensibilities greatly affected him.

W.E.B. Du Bois' Great Barrington High School Class of 1894. Courtesy of Special Collections and Archives, W.E.B. Du Bois Library, University of Massachusetts Amherst.

Great Barrington afforded Du Bois an idyllic upbringing, "a boy's paradise," as he called the town in *Darkwater: Voices from Within the Veil* (1920). He climbed mountains, explored caves, swam during the summer in the Housatonic River, and skated on Lake Mansfield in the winter.

The town had fewer than three dozen black residents, but Du Bois—the only black boy in his elementary school—mingled and played with the white children, most of whom came from far more privileged homes. Relations between blacks and whites were tolerant and often warm, as he recalled, and rarely tense. Many of his mentors were white adults who did all they could to help advance the promising young Du Bois.

But with adolescence, and particularly after he entered high school, came the painful and indelible realization that race mattered. He admitted spending "some days of secret tears" as he began to understand that even in Great Barrington there were whites who thought blacks hopelessly inferior.

Still, he soon discovered sources of true comfort. Maria Baldwin, for one, was an African American teacher at Great Barrington High School, at whose home he would engage in intellectual debates. And Frank Hosmer, the high school's principal, arranged to cover the expense of Du Bois' textbooks and steered him into college preparatory courses that set him on the track for success.

The only black in a class of thirteen students, Du Bois graduated from Great Barrington High School with high honors in 1884. Though his family lacked the means to pay for college, four area Congregational churches contributed $25 each for four years to ensure he could afford Fisk University.

His love for Great Barrington and the Berkshires was unwavering, and he returned often in his adult life, eventually buying the property on Route 23 where his grandfather Othello's house once stood. He planned to restore the property and live there in his retirement, but in the end, he never retired.

FURTHER READING

Town of Great Barrington: Great Barrington, Massachusetts. Great Barrington Bi-Centennial 1761–1961, 1961.
"The Winds of Time." *The Chicago Defender* (February 3, 1945).

Tim Cebula

GREAT BRITAIN

In the eighteenth century Great Britain emerged as the leading colonial and maritime power. Led by Disraeli, Great Britain by the end of the nineteenth century was devoted to a system of imperialism based on new inventions such as the steamship and the machine gun. And with the support of much of the British public, the country maintained colonialism until well into the twentieth century.

As early as 1924 Du Bois predicted that the system of white supremacy that

Great Britain was establishing with the Germans in East Africa would "never succeed but it will cause endless bloodshed and misery before it falls" (*The Crisis*, February 1924). By 1940 Du Bois was pointing out that despite their stance on racial supremacy the British had no qualms about using people of color in their war efforts (*Phylon*, 1940).

During World War II, Du Bois accused Britain and the United States of anti-Semitism for failing to help Europe's Jews. In a 1944 issue of *Phylon* he saw "the power-politics now being pushed in Great Britain and America" as "a discouraging combination with Hitler's anti-Semitic program." Continuing his criticism of Britain's Jewish policy (*Amsterdam News*, September 18, 1943), Du Bois persisted in his condemnation of Britain and the United States for not aiding Jews during World War II. "The United States and Britain could help rescue the surviving 3,000,000 Jews but 'they stand dumb' because of the racism and anti-Semitism in those countries." When the question of a Jewish homeland arose, Du Bois was still supportive. He denounced Britain and the United States for "placing difficulties in the way of those Jews who wish to go to Palestine" (*Amsterdam News*, May 15, 1948).

With the establishment of the United Nations, Du Bois maintained the same critical stance on Britain, accusing Britain and the United States of attempting to maintain colonialism. Du Bois again censured British actions, writing in *The Chicago Defender* (1946) that "the first meeting of the United Nations showed Britain and the United States doing all it could . . . [at] preserving or extending colonial holdings."

However, Du Bois seemingly reserved his strongest criticism of Britain for Winston Churchill (British prime minister and historian). Commenting on Churchill's "Iron Curtain" speech, Du Bois wrote that it was "one of the most discouraging occurrences of modern times" (*The Chicago Defender*, August 3, 1946). Continuing, he accused Churchill of being wrong on every important social issue of the time; therefore, "If his policy [of defending 'free people'] is adopted by Britain and the United States, the result will be catastrophic for mankind."

With the opening of the Cold War following World War II, Du Bois considered it as stemming from America's desperate effort to revive colonial imperialism under their own control instead of Britain's. Throughout his career, Du Bois was critical of Britain, particularly because of its dominion over people of color. *See also*: Africa; Anti-Semitism; Cold War; Colonialism.

FURTHER READING

Peace Is Dangerous. New York: The National Guardian, 1957.

Mary Young

H

HAITI

The occupation of Haiti by the United States between 1915 and 1934 occasioned a continual stream of protests from blacks in the diaspora. Viewed as having underlying expansionist and racist implications, Haiti's occupation became emblematic of the excesses of Social Darwinism and the jingoistic Roosevelt corollary of 1904 that provided justification for intervention in any part of the Western Hemisphere by U.S. forces. Although black participation in foreign affairs and protest against U.S. foreign policies that were unjust was well established, the importance of Haiti as the first independent black republic in the Western Hemisphere made this issue particularly volatile. With the advent of the Progressive era (1895–1920), African Americans with the assistance of liberal European Americans formed the National Association for the Advancement of Colored People (NAACP). Its organ, *The Crisis*, edited by W.E.B. Du Bois, became, during the occupation years, an important forum for denouncing the U.S. policy toward Haiti.

Utilizing knowledge of world affairs and history, Du Bois, in the pages of *The Crisis*, evoked images of the Haitian Revolution of 1791—namely, the heroism of Toussiant L'Ouverture, the leader of the Haitian revolution and his successor Dessalines. During the first five years of the occupation, in an effort to inform the reading public about Haiti, numerous articles on Haiti's history and culture appeared in the magazine. In 1920, when James Weldon Johnson, Field Secretary of the NAACP, conducted a fact-finding mission to Haiti, his report was published in its entirety.

Furthermore, biographical sketches or comments by Haitian officials such as Dantes Bellegarde and Bishop John R. Hurst were also presented. Bellegarde served as Minister of Public Instruction, 1918–1921. He later served as Haitian Minister Plenipotentiary to Paris and as Haitian delegate to the second and third assemblies of the League of Nations. Bishop John R. Hurst was the leader of the Protestant Episcopal Church in Port-au-Prince. Moreover, Haitian short stories, poetry, and book reviews were also featured in the magazine.

The NAACP and *The Crisis* also exerted pressure on U.S. presidents to end the occupation of Haiti. Editorials were critical of the administrations of Woodrow Wilson (1913–1920) and Warren G. Harding (1921–1924) for their continuation of the occupation. In an editorial in 1921, Du Bois demanded Harding "free Haiti from the South and National City Bank." In addition to commissioning an investigation of conditions in Haiti in 1928, the magazine was also critical of the Hoover administration's (1928–1932) appointment of two separate commissions—one white and the other black—to study conditions in Haiti. The black commission was led by Robert R. Moton, successor to Booker T. Washington at Tuskegee Institute (Alabama). It was accorded second-class status and given limited responsibilities focusing primarily on education.

The centrality of Du Bois and *The Crisis* in providing publicity for Haiti's plight is summed up in a 1931 letter from Stenio Vincent, leader of the Patriotic Front. Although a public affirmation of *The Crisis*' role, this campaign was valuable not only to Haiti but to all diasporan blacks in the interwar years. *See also*: Bellegarde, Dantes; *The Crisis*; Johnson, James Weldon; Moton, Robert Russa; National Association for the Advancement of Colored People (NAACP).

FURTHER READING

The Amsterdam News (September 30, 1944).
Dayan, Joan. *Haiti, History, and the Gods*. University of California Press, 1998.

Stephen G. Hall

HALL, GUS (1910–2000)

Gus Hall, a longtime leader of the Communist Party in the United States, received an important letter from Du Bois dated October 1, 1961. At the age of ninety-three, Du Bois applied for membership in the Communist Party. Du Bois reached this decision after choosing to accept President Nkrumah's invitation to reside in Ghana and supervise research on a monumental study, the *Encyclopedia Africana*.

In his application letter to Party Secretary Hall, Du Bois summarized his commitment to socialism developed as a student in Berlin, his political strategies from Woodrow Wilson through the New Deal, the lessons he learned from travel in Communist lands, and the disillusionment the Cold War engendered. He stated "a firm conclusion: Capitalism cannot reform itself; it is doomed to self-destruction." He defined communism as "the effort to give all men what they need and to ask of each the best they can contribute" and predicted it would triumph in the long run. He ended the letter with a ten-point plan for the American Communist Party: public ownership of resources and capital; public control of transportation and communication; abolition of poverty; no labor exploitation; socialized medicine; free education; job training; discipline; freedom; and no dogmatic religion.

Hall read the letter to the National Board of the Communist Party on October 12, 1961, where it was warmly received. In a letter of reply, Hall quoted the 1906 Address to the Country of the Niagara Movement, which he hailed as prophetic. He also recognized Du Bois as "the acknowledged Dean of American letters and most eminent living American scholar" and praised his heroism and courage in joining the Communist Party at a time when the McCarran Act and Smith Act were legalizing persecution and the denial of the basic civil rights of party members. *See also*: Cold War; Socialism/Communism.

FURTHER READING

Hall, Gus. *Fighting Racism: Selected Writing.* International Pub., 1985.

Scot Guenter

HAMPTON INSTITUTE

A frequent opponent of Booker T. Washington, Hampton Institute's favorite son, Du Bois was often critical of the institution itself. He believed Hampton used a system that encouraged industrial education at the expense of the liberal arts. Du Bois believed this form of education tacitly approved of the racial hierarchy in the South.

Hampton was founded in 1868 by Samuel Chapman Armstrong, a Northern soldier who opened the school as part of a general wave of Northern interest in educating Southern Blacks. It made its name as the alma mater of the first two presidents of Tuskegee Institute (Alabama)—Washington, the de facto leader of African Americans, and Robert Russa Moton. Washington attended in the 1880s and popularized the school in *Up from Slavery*, his autobiography. In the book, he details the method of industrial education that remained a staple of the curriculum into the 1920s and beyond.

Because of its attachment to Washington's philosophy, and its continued leadership by European Americans, Du Bois often chastised Hampton for its educational focus, although he spent more time criticizing Washington and Moton, its products. He criticized Hampton's president in the 1920s, James E. Gregg, for his subservience to European American pressure after efforts to segregate audience members at Hampton performances in 1925. He also bemoaned the fact both Hampton and Tuskegee were among the biggest recipients of European American largesse.

Finally, as Hampton changed, so did Du Bois' attitude. He sided with students when they struck in 1927, and he criticized parents and alumni who disagreed with the student stand. Later, as Hampton joined other black institutions in becoming more progressive, Du Bois lauded the change. *See also*: Moton, Robert Russa; Tuskeegee Institute; Washington, Booker T.

FURTHER READING

Armstrong, Mary F. *Hampton and Its Students*. Freeport, NY: Books for Libraries Press, 1971.
The Crisis (December 1927).

Jonathan Silverman

HARLEM RENAISSANCE

Du Bois was very much involved with the artistic movement among black writers and artists known as the Harlem Renaissance. The Harlem Renaissance provided a challenge for Du Bois to refine his views on African American art and literature and brought into focus many of the dualities in Du Bois' own philosophy on the conflicts between a segregationist and assimilationist viewpoint on race, the question of art as propaganda, and the notion of blacks writing for two audiences, one black and one white.

Du Bois was very busy during these years. He continued to work as director of Publication and Research for the National Association for the Advancement of Colored People (NAACP) that he helped found in 1909. He was the editor of *The Crisis*, the most influential African American magazine at the time, which encouraged and published many writers and artists of the Harlem Renaissance. Du Bois was instrumental in creating the Pan-African Conferences that he attended in 1921, 1923, and 1927, and he visited Russia in 1926. Also, in 1926 he organized the most successful theater company of the Harlem Renaissance, the Krigwa Players. With Augustus Dill and Jessie Fauset he created a model for a black children's magazine, *The Brownies' Book*, which first appeared in 1920. Two major works were published during this time, *The Gift of Black Folk* (1924) and *Dark Princess* (1928). Both works were considered part of the background for the Harlem Renaissance.

Du Bois and Alain Locke were supporters of many writers during the Harlem Renaissance. The publication of Langston Hughes' poem in the 1921 issue of *The Crisis* might be considered the first herald of a modern movement in African American arts. As editor of *The Crisis* he encouraged black writers such as Jessie Fauset, Countee Cullen, Langston Hughes, Jean Toomer, and Claude McKay. On *Crisis* covers he proudly introduced black painters. Aaron Douglas was the magazine's art editor and a frequent contributor.

The New Negro (1925), an anthology of African American literature and art edited by Alain Locke, contained an article by Du Bois entitled "The Black Man Brings His Gifts." But as the decade wore on he became more disillusioned with the direction of the Renaissance. He pronounced it both a success and a failure as he became more conscious of the two audiences for literature by blacks, one within the community and one outside. He tried to assure the white world that he was satisfied with the Renaissance, yet for the African American audience he suggested the movement had failed because it was too exotic and not sufficiently positive about black life. In particular he disapproved of Claude McKay's novel *Home to Harlem* (1928), implying that it was crude and it would give the outside world the wrong impression of black life. However, many other artists were criticized by Du Bois along the same lines, and the debate was rooted in ideas that Du Bois shared with Alexander Crummell about developing a scholarly and refined elite (10 percent) of blacks who would lead other blacks to liberation. Du Bois' concept of the Talented Tenth ran counter to the Harlem Renaissance's more egalitarian sense of the pure and primitive powers of black life in all of its aspects.

In 1934 Du Bois resigned as editor of *The Crisis* and from his leadership role in the NAACP. The years of the Harlem Renaissance proved to be a fruitful and exciting decade and a half in Du Bois' long, productive life. *See also*: Art and Literature; *The Brownies' Book*; *The Crisis*; *Dark Princess*; Drama; Fauset, Jessie Redmon; Locke, Alain; Pan-Africanism; Talented Tenth.

FURTHER READING

The Crisis (June 1928).
Lewis, David Levering. *When Harlem Was in Vogue*. New York: Knopf, 1981.

Stephen Soitos

HART, ALBERT BUSHNELL (1854–1943)

In the fall of 1890 Du Bois entered Harvard University to study history. Socially, his time at the esteemed institution was affected by the racism of the period; however, his years at Harvard were intellectually stimulating. This period, the 1890s, was Harvard's golden age characterized by scholars such as George Santayana, William James, and Josiah Royce; Du Bois was especially influenced by Albert Bushnell Hart, one of the fathers of the new discipline, sociology.

In addition to sociology, Hart, historian and author, focused on the development of government in the United States. He was born in Clarksville, Pennsylvania, and graduated from Harvard in 1880. After further study in Germany, he began teaching at Harvard. A prolific scholar, Hart wrote many books about American history and government, including *Formation of the Union* (1892), *Foundations of American Foreign Policy* (1901), and *Essentials of American History* (1905). In the December 1909 issue of *The Horizon* Du Bois reviewed positively Hart's *Southern South*.

Of their relationship Du Bois wrote that while he was at Harvard, Hart, along with William James and Josiah Royce, deeply impressed him. The three men made him a friend and welcomed him into their homes (*The Crisis*, October 1926).

Upon Hart's death, Du Bois wrote: "[His death] removes a man who tolerated no discrimination on the grounds of race" (*Amsterdam News*, July 3, 1942). *See also*: Harvard.

FURTHER READING

The Amsterdam News (July 3, 1943).
"As the Crow Flies." *Amsterdam News* (July 3, 1942).
"Opinion." *The Crisis* (October 1926).

Courtney Young

HARVARD

> I did not find better teachers at Harvard, but teachers better known, who had had wider facilities for gaining knowledge and had a broader atmosphere for approaching truth.
>
> *Autobiography*, 13.

This was the manner in which W.E.B. Du Bois described his experience at Harvard. What was true of Harvard in Du Bois' time is true today. By his own account, Du Bois' experience at Harvard was positive, although it was one limited by race. Du Bois chose not to fraternize with his European American peers beyond what was absolutely necessary. This distancing was a deliberate choice on his part as it was a reflection of the social mores of the times, since he built a shell around himself rather than risk the disappointment of social exclusion. The one exception was his competing for membership in the Glee Club. Despite his good singing voice and his love for music, he was rejected solely because of his race. He himself said that he chose to work within the boundaries of race, and yet he reaped the full rewards of the intellectual life at Harvard and all that a Harvard education meant.

Du Bois had very good and occasionally very close relationships with several well-known faculty members; notably among them were William James and Albert Bushnell Hart. It appears that he was fully supported and sometimes befriended and mentored by many distinguished faculty at Harvard.

He described himself as a "somewhat selfish and self-centered 'grind' with a chip on my shoulder and a sharp tongue" (*Autobiography*, 139). As often happens, this probably was protective covering for his natural shyness and his fear and resentment of being excluded from the full range of collegial association and, to some extent, a recognition of this racist atmosphere and other racial experiences in his life. Despite that attitude and the circumstances that fostered it, Du Bois was one of six speakers at his graduation ceremony from Harvard. He was the first black awarded the Ph.D. by Harvard. Additionally, he won several prestigious scholarships, among them the Price Greenleaf and the Mathews Scholarships. To that point, they were based on "whiteness." While at Harvard, his academic record was sufficiently impressive to earn a fellowship (from the Slater Fund for the Education of Negroes) that enabled him to pursue graduate study in Germany. This opportunity came only after extended and forceful correspondence with ex-president Rutherford B. Hayes, who was chair of the Fund and, initially, would have denied Du Bois the Fellowship.

Du Bois saw the breaking of the color line in several traditions at Harvard, one of which was the election of a black student as class orator, a position always held by a scion of one of the great New England families. This was the result of a "conspiracy" by students who were not members of that reigning social clique but in which Du Bois apparently had no part. It was at Harvard that he began his scholarly writing and his first incursions into the field of sociology, a discipline not yet recognized by Harvard and upon which his work would eventually have a profound effect. His determination to study philosophy was weakened by admonitions against such pursuit by William James himself, since one could make a living at philosophy only with great difficulty. Even then, his writings brought him much attention, especially his master's thesis on the subject of the enforcement of the Slave Laws. He presented it as a paper at the 1891 meeting of the American Historical Association. The paper was later published and widely acclaimed. After his return from Germany, he resumed his Ph.D. studies at Harvard. His dissertation topic was an expanded version of his earlier thesis, and the dissertation itself was subsequently published by Harvard in 1896—*The Suppression of the African Slave Trade*—as the first book in the Harvard Historical Series. It was a landmark study and has remained a classic work.

His social life, however, was quite lively, due in part to the fact that by this time he accepted the fact of racial segregation and found solace, so to speak, in the company of "colored friends." Having had the experience at Fisk before coming to Harvard, he was prepared for the racial divisions in a way in which he would not have been had he gone straight to Harvard from his Great Barrington high school experience. During his Harvard years, he met and was often a guest in the home of Josephine St. Pierre Ruffin, who was herself a crusader of note. He met and became friends with Monroe Trotter, although the friendship was not an enduring one because the temperaments of the two men were so different and Du Bois could not condone Trotter's fiery behavior. Trotter would often erupt in public over some racial injustice and was jailed for heckling Booker T. Washington during a speech in Boston. In this social circle, he met Maud Cuney, to whom he later became engaged but did not marry.

Throughout his career, Du Bois carried the mantle of "a Harvard man" with pride. But he did not flinch in his criticism of that institution when he felt such criticism was called for, as during the turmoil that surrounded Roscoe Conkling Bruce's protest regarding Harvard's treatment of his (Bruce's) son by excluding him from on-campus housing when he was a first-year student. At that time, Du Bois was most eloquent in his condemnation of such behavior. There is some irony in the fact that Du Bois' stay at Harvard overlapped that of James B. Conant, who later became president of the institution. Their experiences were very dissimilar. Yet the Harvard years shaped him and marked him as the intellectual giant that he was. *See also*: Hart, Albert Bushnell; Slater Fund; Trotter, William Monroe.

FURTHER READING

Du Bois, W.E.B. *The Autobiography of W.E.B. Du Bois: A Soliloquy on Viewing My Life from the Last Decade of Its First Century.* New York: International Publishers, 1968.
——. *The Correspondence of W.E.B. Du Bois, Vols. I and II.* Herbert Aptheker, ed. Amherst: University of Massachusetts Press, 1973–1978.
Sollars, Werner, et al. *Blacks at Harvard: A Documentary History of the African-American Experience at Harvard and Radcliff.* New York: New York University Press, 1993.

Yvonne Williams

HAYES, ROLAND (1887–1976)

Hayes, the first African American concert star, was a tenor born in Curryville, Georgia, on the same plantation where his mother had been a slave. His formal education ended at the sixth grade, but his talent earned him admission to Fisk University (Tennessee). While on a tour with the Fisk Jubilee Singers in 1911, he decided to settle in Boston to study voice. Later, he studied in London with Sir George Henschel, the first conductor of the Boston Symphony. Since professional management would not handle a black classical performer, Hayes became his own concert promoter. Noted for his singing of spirituals, he sang within the Boston, New York, and other leading orchestras. In 1923, with Pierre Mantas and the Boston Symphony, he became the first black artist to appear with a major international orchestra.

Du Bois' praise for Hayes reflected the regard Du Bois had for him. In a May 1920 *Crisis* article, Du Bois described a Hayes concert as "an hour to live for." Later, in 1927, again Du Bois praised Hayes and his impact upon the thousands of European Americans who heard him. After waiting for the audience to become quiet before his concert, Du Bois wrote (*The Crisis*, July 1929) that Roland Hayes should continue teaching European Americans manners.

Despite his talent and fame, Hayes still performed in a racist society. In 1942 racists in Georgia physically assaulted him. Du Bois reported "that no one had been arrested for this outrage." Later, Du Bois stated that "the attack on Roland Hayes in Rome, Georgia illustrates the small southern town where racism is most deeply embedded. One solution is flight, but running away never won a battle. . . . Even if I can say nothing helpful, I can at least keep my mouth shut" (*The Amsterdam News*, 1942). *See also*: Art and Artists; Fisk University.

FURTHER READING

Helm, MacKinley. *Angel Mo' and Her Son, Ronald Hayes.* Boston: Little, Brown, and Company, 1942.

Mary Young

HITLER, ADOLF

Since his student days at Fisk University, Du Bois remained an engaged observer of social and political developments in Germany. Although he admired the strong leadership style displayed by Otto von Bismarck, he also recognized that dark, disturbing side of the German national character that was quite susceptible to beguiling notions of racial superiority and servile acquiescence to authority. While a student at the University of Berlin, he wrote of the martial influence of Prussia and compared the boundless optimism of a freedom-loving America with the German's "restlessly pessimistic state found on obedience" (*The Amsterdam News*, August 15, 1942). He would later conclude that these character flaws—combined with the catastrophes of defeat in World War I and the aftermath of reparations, unemployment, political turmoil, the social dislocation caused by postwar hyperinflation, and the Great Depression—gave rise to the consummate demagogue: Adolf Hitler.

To Du Bois, the ascendancy of Hitler was but the latest manifestation of the effects of twisted racial theories carried forward from the nineteenth century when Europeans needed to justify their grab for colonial possessions. He believed France, Britain, and the United States had conspired to isolate and impoverish Germany, which ultimately played into Hitler's hands as he exploited the bitterness of a defeated nation for his own gain. Du Bois also blamed the former World War I adversaries for having derailed Germany's course toward socialism, leaving it to wander into the evil abyss of fascism. Du Bois abhorred Hitler's "national socialism"—which blended capitalism, socialism, and nationalism, all superintended by an oppressive state apparatus—and he decried racism (particularly anti-Semitism), the subordination of organized labor, intimidation of the middle class, and male chauvinism, all of which he described as other hallmarks of "Hitlerism." Du Bois repeatedly acknowledged that Germany had spectacularly rebounded in the 1930s under the Nazis; and that he expressed a degree of admiration for the economic miracle and social stability wrought by state planning under Hitler prompted the unwarranted criticism that he harbored sympathies for the fascist regime.

On his third trip to Germany in 1936, which lasted five months, Du Bois had the opportunity to witness firsthand German progress under Hitler. In dispatches to the *Pittsburgh Courier* he reported that Hitler had erected a tyrannical state replete with domestic spies and informers, a feared police force, and an increasingly formidable military. He saw in Hitler's petit bourgeois German-Austrian background the basis for his popular appeal and argued that Hitler's common man experiences as an artisan, war veteran, and worker who allegedly had to confront the economic interest of Jews made him a leader with whom many Germans identified, and this translated into votes. Du Bois described an anxious citizenry who clung to the Fuhrer's promise of a brighter future and who were too frightened and insecure to do anything other than shout, "Heil Hitler." He was impressed with Hitler's use of radio to sway the masses and the crucial role of propaganda in sustaining the Nazi Revolution. *See also*: Anti-Semitism; Germany.

FURTHER READING

"Neurope: Hitler's New World Order." *Journal of Negro Education* (July 1941).

Robert Fikes, Jr.

HOOVER, J. EDGAR (1895–1972)

J. Edgar Hoover began work for the Bureau of Investigation during World War I, participating in the Palmer Raids, where he began a lifelong commitment to ruthlessly seeking out and destroying suspected Communists. By 1924 he had risen to director of the Bureau of Investigation (it would add the *Federal* to the front of its name in 1934), and for almost half a century, he used his incredible power as FBI chief to stifle the civil rights of those he opposed and thwart and destroy political enemies.

In a revealing biography, historian Anthony Summers (*Official and Confidential: The Secret Life of J. Edgar Hoover*, 1993) asserts that just as his alleged secret homosexuality drove Hoover to strike out at suspected gays, a prevalent rumor that he was of mixed racial background only increased his hostility toward African Americans. Leaders in the black community had been targeted as early as 1919 when he went after Marcus Garvey. Because of the liberal and progressive social, political, and cultural agendas advanced by Du Bois, he became a subject of FBI investigations in the early 1920s.

Hoover saw himself in the tradition of a southern gentleman and believed any change from Jim Crow sensibilities would endanger U.S. society. In having his agents track, hound, and in some cases threaten Du Bois over the years, he placed Du Bois in a category that included two other African American leaders whom Hoover hated even more than he did Marcus Garvey: Paul Robeson, whom he had harassed for more than three decades; and Martin Luther King, against whom he personally directed a massive investigative and slur campaign beginning in 1963. *See also*: Federal Bureau of Investigation; Garvey, Marcus; Robeson, Paul.

FURTHER READING

Summers, Anthony. *Official and Confidential: The Secret Life of J. Edgar Hoover*. New York: G. P. Putnam's Sons, 1993.

Scot Guenter

HOPE, JOHN (1868–1936)

One of the foremost African Americans of the twentieth century, John Hope, a graduate of Brown University (1894), became the president of two black colleges, Atlanta Baptist College (later Morehouse College) (1906) and Atlanta University (1929). Largely responsible for elevating Atlanta University from a second-rate college into a consortium of colleges offering a wide variety of liberal arts education, Hope's interest in racial advancement and his educa-

tional interests endeared him to his erstwhile colleague and longtime friend
W.E.B. Du Bois. Du Bois met Hope when he joined the faculty of Atlanta
University in 1897 as a professor of economics and history. Both men were
opposed to Booker T. Washington's program of vocational and industrial education as well as his stranglehold on educational funds from largely European
American philanthropies. Less vocal than Du Bois on the Washington question, due to his tenuous position as president of a liberal arts college, Hope,
nevertheless, criticized Washington's program in private whenever the opportunity arose.

The founding of the Niagara Movement, an all black protest group that
opposed Washington's program of racial accommodation coupled with vocational education, in 1905 by W.E.B. Du Bois also received the support of John
Hope. Actually, Hope was the only college president, black or white, to attend
the organization's first meeting at Niagara Falls. During the Atlanta Riot of
1906, Du Bois produced his famous "Litany of Atlanta," while Hope patiently
continued to build Morehouse College. In 1909, at the founding meeting of
what would become the National Association for the Advancement of Colored
People (NAACP), Hope supported Du Bois by attending. He would later serve
as a member of the advisory board of the NAACP. Throughout his career,
Du Bois was supportive of Hope's aspirations for both Morehouse College
and later Atlanta University. As with other issues, Du Bois publicized Hope's
work in *The Crisis*. In 1929, when plans for a graduate school were initiated at
Atlanta University, Du Bois praised the talents and foresight of Hope. He went
further to say that "*The Crisis* knows no better man to lead a graduate school
than John Hope" (June 1929).

In the 1930s, Hope appointed Du Bois as guest lecturer in the Economics
and Sociology Departments. Then Du Bois resumed his former position as
professor of sociology. It was during his time at Atlanta University that he
finished his opus, *Black Reconstruction in America, 1860–1880: An Essay toward a
History of the Part which Black Folk Played in the Attempt to Reconstruct Democracy in
America* (1935). John Hope's death in 1936 elicited an outpouring of sorrow
from students, faculty, and notables from around the world. He praised Hope's
identification with the cause of African Americans and education. Du Bois
concluded that Hope's work was eminently more successful than that of
Booker T. Washington and that the world had lost a truly great educator. *See
also*: Atlanta University; Niagara Movement; Washington, Booker T.

FURTHER READING

Davis, Leroy. *A Clashing of the Soul: John Hope and the Dilemma of African American Leadership
    and Black Higher Education in the Early 20th Century.* Athens: University of Georgia
    Press, 1998.
"A Forum of Fact and Opinion." *The Pittsburgh Courier* (March 28, 1936).
Summers, Anthony. *Official and Confidential: The Secret Life of J. Edgar Hoover.* New York:
    G. P. Putnam's Sons, 1993.

Stephen G. Hall

HOWARD UNIVERSITY

As one of the first black universities in the United States, Howard University was founded by the Freedmen's Bureau in Washington, D.C. in 1867. It functioned along with Fisk and Atlanta University to educate and train teachers, ministers, and black professionals as leaders. While Du Bois rarely served in any official capacity with Howard University, he closely followed the developments at Howard and provided a continuous commentary on it in periodicals like *The Crisis.*

By the beginning of the twentieth century, Howard was already distinguishing itself from the type of vocational institution that Booker T. Washington was promoting at the Tuskegee Institute founded in 1881. Du Bois also rejected these vocational training schools as limiting black students from studying subjects offered by the standard curriculum of European American universities.

At the turn of the century, Du Bois and other black intellectuals publicly rejected Washington's ideas on blacks in politics, education, society, and economics. Du Bois' *The Souls of Black Folk* (1903) called for black leadership by the "Talented Tenth," a group of black intellectuals to guide African Americans in their own liberation. All of these developments shaped the kind of institution that Howard University was becoming in the early part of the twentieth century.

Howard provided black intellectuals with an arena for teaching that they could not have been offered at European American universities. Du Bois' call for "the Talented Tenth" coincided with a growing percentage of black faculty at Howard. While Du Bois was never a faculty member there, many of his "disciples" were. Du Bois' disciples considered themselves members of the Talented Tenth and dedicated their lives to teaching, writing, and scholarship in academic institutions.

Du Bois gave addresses at Howard during their Semi-Centennial celebration in 1917 and again in 1935 at a Howard student conference to strike against war and fascism. Du Bois intervened on behalf of Fisk Univertisty students during their strike in 1925 against poor conditions at the institution by asking the president and trustees of Howard University to admit them as students. After deliberations between the Howard administration and faculty, Du Bois, then chairman of the Executive Committee of the intercollegiate Fisk Clubs, was informed by Howard's President Durkee that the Fisk students would be admitted in 1945. Professor E. Franklin Frazier appointed Du Bois as a Special Lecturer and Consultant at Howard to a project that studied the economic and social problems of African Americans. Du Bois gave lectures to faculty and students about how to improve teaching in the social sciences.

In 1958, Du Bois was to give an address at Howard University when the Deputy Commander of the Veterans of Foreign Wars tried to prevent him from speaking. Du Bois was suspected of being a Communist for his support of several Soviet policies. A longtime supporter of academic freedom, President

Johnson read about this and intervened by arranging for Du Bois' lecture to be held at Rankin Chapel on March 31, 1958. *See also*: Fisk University; *The Souls of Black Folk*; Talented Tenth; Washington, Booker T.

FURTHER READING

Dyson, Walter. *The Founding of Howard University.* Washington, DC: Howard University Press, 1921.
"Opinion." *The Crisis* (August 1925).

Amy Bowles

HUNTON, ALPHAEUS (1903–1970)

Hunton was born in Atlanta, Georgia, in 1903. After the infamous race riot in Atlanta in 1906, his family moved to Brooklyn, New York. After graduating with an M.A. from Harvard, Hunton began teaching at Howard University in 1926. Hunton's socialist views were strengthened by his Marxist dissertation adviser, Edward Berry.

Hunton's support of leftist labor activity began as an officeholder in Local 440 of the American Federation of Labor (AFL). In 1938, Hunton wrote in the *American Teacher* that he supported the merger with the leftist Congress of Industrial Organizations (CIO).

In January 1937, the Council on African Affairs (CAA) was founded, and Hunton, Paul Robeson, and Du Bois worked together for many years in the CAA to fight against and support the end to colonialism in Africa. As a trustee of the Civil Rights Congress Bail Fund, Hunton was imprisoned in 1951, and Du Bois led the protest against this McCarthyite injustice. After his release, Hunton was able to finish his great work, *Decision in Africa* (1957), which described how the West had plundered Africa over the centuries. Du Bois' preface remarks noted, "This book, with its . . . deep knowledge of Africa . . . is invaluable."

In 1959, Hunton attended the transforming All African People's Conference in Ghana, and with the invitation of President Sekou Toure of Guinea, he took up residence in Guinea in 1960. Soon after, Dr. Du Bois invited Hunton to Ghana to work on the *Encyclopedia Africana*. After Nkrumah was deposed by a coup in 1964, Hunton was deported. Later, President Kenneth Kaunda of Zambia invited Hunton to be his guest in Zambia. Alphaeus Hunton died in Zambia on January 13, 1970. *See also*: Council on African Affairs.

FURTHER READING

The Autobiography of W.E.B. Du Bois. New York: International Pub., 1968, pp. 343–360.

Malik Simba

I

INTEGRATION VERSUS SEGREGATION

Du Bois' analysis of whether African Americans should attempt to integrate with European Americans to become full social and political participants in the United States or organize autonomously among themselves is generally viewed as having three phases. In Du Bois' period of greatest direct political influence, between *The Souls of Black Folk* (1903) and the Great Depression, he was an integrationist whose politics were consistent with the National Association for the Advancement of Colored People (NAACP), the organization for which he worked. During the 1930s, however, he grew frustrated with the inability of that organization to effect substantive change. Therefore, he began to identify that inability with the limitations of organizations reliant on European American capital for funding. As a result, during the 1930s and culminating with the publication of *Dusk of Dawn* (1940), he developed a program for the autonomous work of a black middle class that identified blacks working among themselves as the agents of political change. Then, during the 1940s, as his deepest involvement moved to international movements for decolonization, world peace, and socialism, he found himself Red-baited by black middle-class organizations and increasingly in alliance with predominantly white leftist organizations and U.S. communism. At this point he abandoned separatism as a political program. Without question, it is Du Bois' arguments for civil rights and integration during the early period that are most often read. As a result, the later positions are sometimes dealt with as the result of personal frustrations rather than intellectual considerations, somehow not authentically Du Boisian. Even among those who take the positions of the later Du Bois most seriously, these positions are usually interpreted as dramatic breaks from his earlier position.

While this simple narrative is accurate in many ways, it leaves out many important considerations that may alter the significance of its parts. First, during the earliest phase, when Du Bois advocated integration politics, he was always acutely aware of issues of black cultural autonomy. Consequently, he invented many concepts that have been most influential for the description of this autonomy. Undoubtedly, his early integrationist period was the time when he was most likely to speak imprudently of separate biological races or culturally autonomous civilizations. Thus, in *The Souls of Black Folk*, he directly challenged Booker T. Washington's acceptance of segregation as appropriate politics and stated, famously, "I sit with Shakespeare and he winces not." He also writes of "the unifying ideal of Race" and the resulting special project that blacks, as a race, were to achieve. Washington was to be challenged not because he advocated the creation and expansion of black industrial schools, something Du Bois also supported, but because he argued that Negroes should have no other choices of schools and therefore were to be permanently subordinated. Actually, his earliest explanations of the program of the NAACP, like the one under the heading "NAACP" in the second issue of *The Crisis* (December 1910), said nothing at all about "integration" but instead stressed the fight for "manhood rights" and the elimination of prejudice. Even when, two issues later (February 1911), he argues forcefully against those who believe that Negro rights can be brought about in a situation of segregation, he *agrees* with the statement "The Negro does not desire racial intermingling. All he wants is a square deal before the law." He goes on to argue that a "square deal" requires the right to intermingle, so there is no question that Du Bois is advocating integration; but integration is not the good in itself but always requires a further explanation of its necessity.

During the 1930s, when Du Bois advocated autonomist politics (which, he insists in *Dusk of Dawn*, is not *nationalism*), he is engaged in intense study of Marxism and the evolutionary socialism that he had advocated since the first decade of the twentieth century. This advocacy becomes the priority of his politics. During this period he was particularly insistent about the biological, cultural, and intellectual hybridity of African Americans, indeed, building his entire theory of race in *Dusk* by first showing that, biologically, he is primarily European but then going on to show that the major events of his life were determined by his being *recognized* as "African," despite his biological heritage. In this analysis, it is precisely because race is a social construction, a political metaphor, and not an intrinsic feature of an individual that *politics* is precisely the field in which black autonomy is necessary. Intellectually, blacks needed to be internationalistic. Du Bois suggests that autonomist politics will be a stage in causing the eventual socialist revolution in the United States, at which point integration would necessarily be achieved. For all that, politically, in the United States during the 1930s, Du Bois felt that African Americans could only trust themselves.

Finally, in his last period, Du Bois discovered that the largest groups of Americans who agreed with his analysis of the need for Third World decolonization and national autonomy for people of color were white Communists, fellow travelers, and independent socialists, whose advocacy of the Leninist analysis of imperialism converged with Du Boisian politics in this period. In this context, the argument for Pan-African autonomy made most sense within an interracial movement, and as at all other points in his life, Du Bois did not hesitate to work with those whose political analysis matched his.

All of this corresponds, in Du Bois' writing, with the gradual shift in his self-understanding between himself as African American and himself as Pan-African. When focusing on U.S. politics, integration makes sense; when links between people of African descent become the primary concern, integration becomes less relevant, since the problem for Africans is never integration with the colonizer but independence from the colonizer. He never maintained that full independence was possible for African Americans in the same way it was for Africans, but he did for a period maintain that certain aspects of the model of decolonization–specifically, the formation of a communal economy–could be adapted by African Americans.

Seen through the lens of the 1903 Du Bois, the question of integration versus separation is central to understanding his political and social theories. However, set against his entire life's work, the question of integration versus separation begins to seem considerably less significant. Du Bois' goal for blacks was always rights first as "Americans," then as "humans." Ultimately he came to understand that the particular strategy for achieving those rights–integration or separation–depended more on the regional, national, or global context of the analysis than it did on any particular political principle. *See also*: Colonialism; *Dusk of Dawn*: Lenin, V. I.

FURTHER READING

Du Bois, W.E.B. *Dusk of Dawn: An Essay toward an Autobiography of a Race Concept*. 1940. Reprint, New Brunswick, NJ: Transaction, 1983.

——. *The Souls of Black Folk*. 1903. Reprint, New York: Modern Library, 1996.

Marable, Manning. *W.E.B. Du Bois: Black Radical Democrat*. Boston: Twayne Publishers, 1986.

Walden, David, ed. *W.E.B. Du Bois*: The Crisis *Writings*. Greenwich, CT: Fawcett Publications, 1972.

Kenneth Mostern

IRELAND AND THE IRISH

Since Jonathan Swift's (1667–1745) "A Modest Proposal" (1729), pundits have been trying to answer the Irish question. Du Bois is no exception. Considering the virulent antiblack attitude of the Irish, Du Bois' stance is revealing.

As more Irish immigrated to the United States, friction between the Irish and blacks grew in direct proportion to their proximity. Frequently forced to live in overlapping slum neighborhoods and compete for the same low-status jobs, hostility was inevitable. In New York City, Irish and blacks lived together in the "tenderloin" district. Shortly before the New York City draft riots (1863) began, 3,000 dockworkers went on strike for higher wages. Blacks, with official police protection, took their places. Thus, when the government began recruiting the Irish draftees who could not afford to pay others to be "stand-in" recruits, they turned on blacks. Understanding that the government was sending them to fight a war that would free even more blacks, the Irish resisted conscription and began to riot. Subsequently, later events grew into Irish-black antagonism.

Acknowledging the oppression shared by the two groups, Du Bois championed the Irish cause despite their antiblack stance. Seeking to explain the source of Irish-black hostility (*The Crisis*, August 1916) he wrote:

It happened unfortunately that the first Irish immigration to the United States took place as the free Negroes of the North were making their most impressive forward movement. Irishmen and black men came therefore, in bitter industrial competition in such cities as Boston, New York and Philadelphia. Riots and street fights ensued. Irishmen hanged Negroes during the draft riots in New York City, and drove them off the streets of Philadelphia.

Du Bois insisted, "All this is past. Now Black people in the United States should sympathize with the rebellious Irish for their suffering under British rule is like our suffering." He concluded, "The recent Irish revolt may have been foolish, but would to God some of us had sense enough to be fools!"

Continuing to compare Irish oppression with black oppression, Du Bois denounced British tyranny in Ireland. "The Irish people in the United States have often led in attacking blacks . . . this does not make less our desire for Irish freedom. . . . It is the Oppressed who have continually been used to cow and kill the Oppressed in the interest of the Universal Oppressor" (*The Crisis*, March 1921). With his public support of the Irish, Du Bois was subjected to much criticism. Many letters chastised him, accusing him of not having given weight to the traditional Irish American hostility to blacks. To such censure, Du Bois responded that he was aware of the animosity, but the knowledge was irrelevant to his argument: "The realities of racism and colonialism of the British empire and the justice of the cause of Irish national liberation."

Despite criticism Du Bois maintained his support of the Irish liberation struggle. "The real question of Ireland today is how much of the island is going to be allowed to govern itself and how much of it the industrial interests of Ulster are going to be able to keep as part of England, and as a center of English power" (*The Crisis*, January 1922). However, he suggested that Ireland should accept half a loaf, but it must keep before its eyes the real goal, namely, entire unity. *See also*: Great Britain.

FURTHER READING

"Opinion." *The Crisis* (February 1922).
"Opinion." *The Crisis* (March 1920).

Mary Young

J

JAPAN

The surprisingly competent performance of Japan's military forces in the Russo-Japanese War (1904–1905) announced Japan's status as a major world power. To Du Bois, Japan represented hope for the masses of colored people in Asia, Africa, and Latin America who endured the racism and the bullying of Europe and the United States. Though he lived to regret his prediction in 1922, following the Washington Naval Conference, that Japan, along with China, would form a solid coalition to resist the "aggressions of the whites," he continued to view Japan as a counterbalance to Western imperialism up until World War II. To Du Bois, native populations residing in the colonial holdings of the greedy, rapacious Western nations could only look to Japan and the Soviet Union to provide models for economic reform and to champion their struggle against oppression. Despite its growing militarism and embracing of the capitalist system, he saw Japan as a formidable rival of what he believed was a quasi-conspiratorial alliance, composed primarily of the United States, Great Britain and France, that wished to keep it from extending its influence into their imperial spheres. He conveniently disregarded Japan's obvious expansionist designs in Asia because, he reasoned, Japanese control in the region would certainly be more benevolent, uplifting, and humane than what had been experienced under the region's white interlopers.

Du Bois argued that in the interwar period in which the major powers labored to rebuild the global economy, and in the wake of World War I and the Great Depression, the West continued to shun Japan partly out of racism and partly because it feared having to compete against such a robust nation. The denial of raw materials for its dynamic industries, he believed, encouraged Japan to resort to territorial acquisition as a means to ensure its survival. In 1937, on the last leg of a momentous round-the-world tour, Du Bois visited the puppet state of Manchuria, which Japan had invaded six years earlier.

Dismissing criticism of the imperialistic nature of its dominance of the Chinese inhabitants, he portrayed Japanese rule in Manchuria as enlightened and beneficent in his dispatch to the *Pittsburgh Courier*. Furthermore, he felt that Japan's conquest of Manchuria would have a somewhat benign outcome because of Japan's alleged close racial kinship with the people of northeastern China. From there he journeyed to Nagasaki, Yokohama, Kobe, Kyoto, and Tokyo, where he was treated like a foreign dignitary by extremely hospitable officials and the press. He responded to such unaccustomed attention with unrestrained praise for Japan's modern-day achievements. At a press conference in Tokyo, he speculated once more that it was white American racism in the form of anti-Japanese immigration sentiment that helped western and southern congressmen to strike a deal to kill antilynching legislation supported by the National Association for the Advancement of Colored People (NAACP). Du Bois also had the opportunity to meet the young author who was translating *The Souls of Black Folk* into Japanese. Upon leaving the island nation, he reported to his African American audience back home: "It is above all a country of colored people run by colored people for colored people. . . . Without exception, Japanese with whom I talked classed themselves with the Chinese, Indians, and Negroes as folk standing over against the white world" (*The Crisis*, April 1922). Such wishful thinking and naivete faded by the midpoint of World War II.

As World War II drew near, Du Bois continued to insist that it was President Franklin D. Roosevelt's trusted advisers—particularly War Secretary Harry L. Stimson, Secretary of State Cordell Hull, and Ambassador to Japan Joseph Grew—who were propelling the United States toward a showdown with Japan. He thought that Japan would limit its expansion into Asia and that it did not covet other Asian territories. He held the hope that if Japan could somehow purge its ruling elite of fascists and imperialists, it could potentially inspire and lead the world's darker races in their quest for freedom, independence, and add democracy. Finally, he recoiled at the prospect of African American troops battling another colored race to preserve white hegemony. The "unwise and ill-considered" attack on Pearl Harbor and the rapid conquests in Asia made by the Japanese forced him to review his thinking and, temporarily at least, tone down his criticism of U.S. foreign policy. Instead, he wondered aloud how the United States would manage the disposition of former colonial territories recaptured from Japan.

Despite his suspicions regarding the motivations of the Allies in prosecuting the war with Japan, Du Bois welcomed that nation's capitulation in August 1945. On the other hand, he regretted the loss of Japan as the only viable colored model of a powerful industrial state worthy of emulation by the other colored peoples of the world. In articles in *The Chicago Defender* he conceded that Japanese dominion over other Asiatic peoples was no less brutal and reprehensible than life under Western colonial masters. He asserted that Japanese trusts and industrialists exploited Asian peasants during the war and that as imperial masters the Japanese established a caste system in their conquered territories based on Japanese racial supremacy. He warned, however, that the United States should not extend its occupation or engage in the repression of Japanese citizens. With the global struggle concluded, Du Bois reiterated his prewar stance that it was largely American greed and racism that precipitated armed conflict with Japan. He directed his harshest criticism at President Harry S. Truman, whom he ranked with Adolf Hitler as one of the greatest mass murderers of modern times, for his seemingly unrepentant use of the atomic bomb on Japanese cities. Though Japan had initially championed the call for "Asia for the Asians," Du Bois was confident that the idea would reach fruition in the postwar world as the clamor for freedom would push the weakened Western empires to decolonize. A defeated, humiliated, and later reconstructed Japan hardly commanded Du Bois' attention in the Cold War era, and he rarely commented on developments in that nation after 1945. *See also*: Asia.

FURTHER READING

"The White Masters of the World." *The World and Africa*. New York: Viking Press, 1947.
"The Winds of Time." *The Chicago Defender* (September 5, 1945).

Robert Fikes, Jr.

JESUS CHRIST

Throughout his adult life W.E.B. Du Bois remained ambivalent about Jesus Christ. He praised the ethical principles of Jesus' teaching but balked at the dogma concerning Jesus that he felt that the Christian church tried to enforce on its adherents. Undoubtedly Du Bois' education at Harvard and the University of Berlin encouraged his separation of the historical Jesus from the church's appropriation of Christ. Consequently, although reared in the Congregationalist tradition, by the age of thirty, he had rejected the Christian church while continuing to champion the principles of Jesus.

In particular, Du Bois appreciated Jesus' identification with the marginalized of society. If Christ came to the United States today, he argued in 1906, one of Jesus' first deeds would be to align himself with the African American. Why? Because "Jesus Christ was a laborer and Black men are laborers. He was poor and we are poor; He was despised; He was persecuted and crucified, and we are mobbed and lynched." Moreover, Jesus stood for an "attitude of humility, a desire for peace ... mercy and charity toward fellow men, willingness to suffer persecution for right ideals" (*The Crisis*, 1913).

The African American church, Du Bois believed, advanced such attitudes, desires, dispositions, and ideals by transcending the contrived sacred-secular dichotomy of Western culture and introducing Jesus' ethics into "every line of human endeavor." The European American church, on the other hand, played the "deliberate hypocrite and systematic liar." Although it preached

"Come unto me all ye that labor" and "Whosoever will may come," the white church intentionally excluded African Americans from the invitation (*The Crisis*, October 1913). Du Bois also railed against a white church that lamented Jesus' crucifixion, but tortured African Americans in unrelenting daily life. "Here you are," Du Bois argued in 1929, "a great white nation with a magnificent Plan of Salvation (*The Crisis*, November 1929). You have an ethical code far beyond anything the world ever knew. You are the followers of the Golden Rule and of the meek and lowly Jesus. [But] you do not try to follow your own religion because you know when your religion comes up against the race problem that religion has absolutely nothing to do with your attitude toward Negroes." Thus Du Bois warned that the church that professed to follow Jesus Christ but failed to serve as an advocate for justice "merits the denial of the Master—'I never knew you' " (*The Crisis*, May 1917).

Although Du Bois sounded like many Christian radicals throughout history, he did not see Jesus or his message as particularly unique. In his commencement address at Fisk University in 1938, for example, Du Bois asserted that one's religious affiliation (e.g., Protestant, Catholic, Muslim) need not matter. The "word of life could be found in Jeremiah, Shakespeare, Jesus, Confucius, Buddha, and John Brown" (*Trek*, April 5, 1946). He could even include Jesus with V. I. Lenin in his list of rebels standing for economic and social freedom of the masses.

Finally, when planning for his funeral, he requested that those officiating not stress religion, the afterlife, or Jesus Christ. Instead, Du Bois remained true to his sense of purpose. He wanted the focus on the needs of peoples of African descent and visions of future progress, for "we are here to work hard for a better world and not merely 'to submit ourselves to Jesus Christ' " ("The Religion of the Negro").

FURTHER READING

"The Religion of the Negro." *New World* (December 1900).

Richard C. Goode

JIM CROW

During his long life, Du Bois saw many changes take place in the social conditions of black Americans and wrote often on segregation and Jim Crow. As was true with his position on most major issues, his views on Jim Crow evolved, and he avoided taking a simplistic view. His stand on segregation was to become a major source of conflict with the National Association for the Advancement of Colored People (NAACP) and its executive director, Walter White, and led to his first break with the organization in 1934.

Du Bois' personal animus toward Jim Crow was stoked in 1900 as he boarded an evening train for Savannah, Georgia, and was denied an overnight berth. Forced to sit upright all night in the dirty, crowded Jim Crow car, just behind the engine, Du Bois' outrage led him to file a formal protest with the Southern Railway Company. Segregated public facilities continued to provoke his wrath long after he tempered his stand on segregation.

In the early years of the NAACP, Du Bois was an ardent and vociferous opponent of segregation. Recognizing the compulsory separation of races as a thinly veiled substitute for slavery, Du Bois argued that the argument for segregation in schools and public institutions was an argument against democracy. While he admitted that separate school systems did allow more black children to stay in school longer, he declared that segregation made for poorer schools because facilities were grossly inequitable. Further, black enterprises struggled valiantly to succeed, but the odds were clearly against them when they lacked access to the same kind of training and education afforded to whites.

Race discrimination caused blacks to blame themselves, turning external hatred into virulent self-hate that stood in the way of progress. But Du Bois also noted that where racial hatred is so bitter and illogical that segregated society becomes necessary, blacks must make the best of the circumstances, turning disadvantage to advantage whenever possible. But in 1913, he was adamant that no advantages of segregation could ever compensate for depriving a group of people of equal opportunity, education, and self-determination.

Writing in *The Crisis* in 1910, Du Bois opposed segregation unequivocally, and he called for blacks and whites alike to resist segregation in all forms but particularly in schools. He believed that segregation in schools resulted in class and racial tension and deprived all children of the great lesson that a person's character cannot be determined by the color of his skin.

In 1923, Du Bois acknowledged the terrible paradox of the imperative to oppose Jim Crow education and the seemingly contradictory need to respect the efforts of black teachers in black schools who labored under terrible disadvantages. That paradox was responsible for passionate difference of opinion and community dissension among blacks. But Du Bois argued that since race sentiment remained what it was, it was impossible to advocate for school desegregation. In places where schools were mixed, black children were not educated—they were ignored, maltreated, and abused. Du Bois realized that the only thing worse than segregation for blacks was ignorance, and so he applauded a growing program in New York City in which black students in mixed schools received guidance and mentoring. This movement sought to eliminate prejudiced teachers in the schools and to encourage black students to continue into high school.

As the years passed, however, Du Bois came to the conclusion that a degree of voluntary segregation was inevitable, but he no longer saw it as entirely negative. In his last years as editor of the *The Crisis*, he moderated his earlier stand on segregation, arguing that blacks must not just accept the situation, as Booker T. Washington advocated, but rather that blacks needed to concentrate on making their segregated institutions competitive to expose the irrationality of Jim Crow laws. Noting in 1934 that segregation often went hand in hand with discrimination in the United States, he also pointed out that the two are not necessarily synonymous. Furthermore, he argued that it was not necessary to oppose segregation unless discrimination was involved. He no longer believed it was in the best interests of racial uplift for one or two individuals to insist, for instance, on membership in a white church where they were clearly unwanted. Far better to do as the free blacks of Philadelphia did in 1792, when they were told to sit in the balcony after enjoying the freedom of sitting anywhere they chose. Some of those free blacks founded the African Methodist Episcopal Church that in 1934 boasted 750,000 members and a very powerful national organization. As Du Bois saw it, internal organization was the inevitable answer to compulsory segregation.

It would be another twenty years before the Supreme Court *Brown v. Board of Education, Topeka, Kansas* decision would vindicate Du Bois' goals and approach. However, throughout that time he steadfastly believed that the best way for blacks to achieve in American society was to attend to their own institutions, as opposed to always pleading for white society to treat them with dignity and respect. *See also*: Integration versus Segregation; National Association for the Advancement of Colored People (NAACP); Racism.

FURTHER READING

"The Passing of Jim Crow." *Independent* (July 14, 1917).
Woodward, C. Vann. *The Strange Career of Jim Crow*. New York: Oxford University Press, 1974.

Christy Rishoi

JOHNSON, JAMES WELDON (1871–1938)

A talented and prolific writer, who Du Bois first met when the former returned to Atlanta University in 1904 to receive an honorary Master of Arts degree, and diplomat, serving as U.S. consul in Venezuela, Nicaragua, and the Azores, growing out of his activities with the New York Colored Republican Club, Johnson was at one time associated with Booker T. Washington and the Tuskegee Machine. This would be of some concern to Mary White Ovington and others who thought him too reactionary on questions of labor when he was being considered for the post of field secretary of the National Association for the Advancement of Colored People (NAACP) after John Hope, Du Bois' first choice, declined the offer. He was proposed for this post by board member Joel Spingarn, who had been quite impressed with Johnson at the Amenia Conference in August 1916.

In his new post, which he accepted in mid-December, Johnson worked tirelessly, traveling throughout the United States to organize new branches and revive old or lapsed local branches, following his appointment. He would also serve as acting executive secretary following the U.S. entry into World War

I until early 1918. In that same year, he led an NAACP delegation to Washington to meet with President Woodrow Wilson and present him with a petition requesting commutation of the death sentences of five black soldiers arising out of the Houston Riot of the previous year. He would go on to characterize 1919 as the year of the "Red Summer" because of continuing racial violence in cities throughout the country.

In 1920, following the resignation of John Shillady, an act that revealed a leadership crisis that had been brewing for some time, Johnson was appointed permanent executive secretary of the national organization. During his tenure with the NAACP, he left in 1930 to take a teaching post at Fisk University in Nashville, Tennessee, to resume his writing. Johnson did something that few others up to his appointment had done, and that was impress on the organization by force of his personality his vision of where he wanted the NAACP to go and what he wanted it to do.

Johnson was particularly instrumental in lobbying the Congress to support the Dyer Anti-Lynching Bill and guiding the organization in court challenges to benefit African Americans. One of his reports detailing the conditions of the U.S. occupation of Haiti resulted in a Senate investigation. Clearly, his activities made the NAACP a formidable force in the pursuit of civil rights that could not be easily ignored.

Contending that the creative arts paralleled and supported political activism, Johnson, along with Du Bois, Walter White, Jessie Fauset, and several white writers, critics, and publishers, worked to establish, by regularly including their productions in the pages of *The Crisis*, a receptive audience for the black poets, novelists, artists, and musicians that would collectively be known as the Harlem Renaissance. In his last autobiography published in 1968, Du Bois would revive a minor controversy surrounding Johnson's resignation, writing that he had been forced out by White, who had been brought into the organization in 1917. Perhaps some of this revisionist history was occasioned by Du Bois' own difficulties with White in that four years later he was forced to resign. *See also*: Amenia Conference; Dyer Anti-Lynching Bill; Fauset, Jessie Redmon; Fisk University; Haiti; Hope, John; National Association for the Advancement of Colored People (NAACP).

FURTHER READING

Du Bois, W.E.B. *The Autobiography of W.E.B. Du Bois*. New York: International Publishers, 1968.

William M. King

JOURNAL OF NEGRO EDUCATION

Founded at Howard University in 1932 and published quarterly, Du Bois appears to have used this serial as a vehicle for advancing some of the ideas that would lead to his break with the National Association for the Advance-

ment of Colored People (NAACP) in 1934. For example, the commencement
address that he gave at Howard University in June 1930 on the topic of education and work argued that neither the industrial ideas of the late Booker
T. Washington nor the liberal education ideas he advanced coevally, by themselves, had succeeded in addressing the training needs of blacks. Therefore,
he recommended a specific program that would grow out of a reassessment of
black needs, not the imposition of an "American" endeavor thereupon. In
short, he hinted at a separatist program not unlike that advocated by Garvey
that would be more fully developed in a succeeding series of articles that
appeared in the *Journal* throughout the depression. In the article titled "Does
the Negro Need Separate Schools?"—which appeared in the July 1935 edition—
Du Bois makes the point that the reality of racism in the United States may
require black people to develop specific curricula and press for their own
schools to ensure that their talents and dreams will not be frittered away by
schooling not designed to serve their needs. "Social Planning for the Negro,
Past and Present," in the January 1936 edition, simultaneously rejects the program of the Communist Party, USA, as it was then being articulated. *See also*:
Educational Philosophy; Howard University.

FURTHER READING

"The Future of Wilberforce University." *Journal of Negro Education* (October 1940).
"Have Negroes Taken Advantage of Educational Opportunities Offered by Friends."
    Journal of Negro Education (April 1938).

                                                              William M. King

K

KU KLUX KLAN

A series of secret organizations with the general aim of suppression of African American political and civil rights, the Ku Klux Klan has appeared in three distinct incarnations from Reconstruction to the present. Most broadly, the Klan can be viewed as a manifestation of the U.S. nativist and antiblack sentiment as reflected in the nineteenth century, for instance, by the anti-Irish "Know Nothing" Party and by antiabolitionist and antiblack violence. The first Ku Klux Klan was founded in Pulaski, Tennessee, in 1866 by six Confederate veterans. Originally a club similar to contemporary social fraternities, the Klan quickly expanded its membership and purpose to seek the overthrow of Reconstruction and the reassertion of white supremacy in the region. The Klan and other similar groups spread throughout the South, employing violence against people, both blacks and white Republicans, and property before federal intervention in 1871 and 1872 brought an effective end to the organization.

In the twentieth century, the Ku Klux Klan was founded in 1915 at Stone Mountain, Georgia, by William J. Simmons, a onetime preacher, teacher, and insurance salesperson. Drawing his ideas about the organization less on its Reconstruction-era predecessor than on the florid depictions of the Invisible Empire in the novels of Thomas W. Dixon, Jr., and D. W. Griffith's film *The Birth of a Nation* (1915), Simmons found that his organization had an appeal far beyond the South. The Klan gained a broad following in the 1920s as many Americans feared that the New Era brought unwelcome changes to their lives; among the perceived threats that the Klan exploited were post–World War I economic and political uncertainties, immigration, the black migration to northern cities, and the widespread belief that American values and 100 percent Americanism were under assault by the forces of modernism. Far more centrally organized than the original Klan, the 1920s version was planned similar to such fraternal lodges as the Elks and the Masons. The Klan appealed not only to the era's prejudices but to its love of fraternal ceremony, with its robes, insignia, and dizzying array of high-sounding titles and orders. Displaying more inclusive bigotry than the first Klan, this new incarnation was not only antiblack but deeply suspicious of Jews, Catholics, Asians, and the use of alcohol. By 1924 the Klan claimed a membership of nearly 3 million—urban and rural, midwestern and southern—and began to flex its considerable political muscle, winning political office in such states as Indiana and Oregon. The second Klan faded around the time of World War II, beset by poor financial management and legal and political scandal among its national leadership.

With postwar anticommunism and the rise of the civil rights movement the Klan appeared yet again, this time mainly in the South. While this incarnation would gain much notoriety, especially through campaigns of violence in the 1960s, the third Klan never gained either the power or the membership claimed by the 1920s Klan. Throughout his long public career, Du Bois challenged the assumptions of each of these groups, disputing the Reconstruction Klan's characterization of the postbellum South in *Black Reconstruction* (1935), answering Imperial Wizard Hiram Wesley Evans in the pages of the *North American Review* in 1926, and exhorting Americans to forego the reflexive anticommunism that fueled the twentieth-century Klans. While discrete organizations, each of the Klans resorted to violence, terror, and intimidation while claiming to defend traditional political and moral values. *See also: The Birth of a Nation*; Integration versus Segregation; Jim Crow; Racism.

FURTHER READING

Du Bois, W.E.B. *Black Reconstruction in America, 1860–1880.* New York: Harcourt Brace, 1935.

Trent Watts

L

LA FOLLETTE, ROBERT (1855–1925)

Politician and reformer, La Follette was born in Primrose, Wisconsin. After graduating from the University of Wisconsin in 1879, he was admitted to the bar. With his intelligence, urbanity, charm, and an ambitious wife, Belle Case (1859–1921), the first woman graduate in law from the University of Wisconsin, La Follette soon entered politics. He served the state of Wisconsin as district attorney of Dane County (1880, 1882), and he was a member of the U.S. House of Representatives from 1885 to 1891. After his failed bid for reelection in 1891, he returned to private practice, where he developed his own political program.

His plan became nationally known as the "Wisconsin idea." It advocated direct primaries, equalization of tax rates, and regulation of railroads. Because of his political ideas, he amassed a statewide following that elected him governor three times, 1900, 1902, and 1904. From 1906 to 1925 he served as U.S. senator. In 1911 La Follette helped organize the National Progressive Republican League. As La Follette's popularity and movement grew, Theodore Roosevelt found this new party attractive, and in 1912 Roosevelt assumed leadership of the Progressive Party.

While not always agreeing with La Follette's proposals, Du Bois endorsed La Follette's 1924 platform. However, while endorsing La Follette, Du Bois excoriated him for "avoiding direct reference to black people" (*The Crisis*, August 1924). But Du Bois declared that he would vote for La Follette. In 1936 Du Bois noted La Follette's efforts in attempting to transform political history.

FURTHER READING

The Crisis. (August 1924).
Maxwell, Robert S., ed. *La Follette*. Englewood Cliffs, NJ: Prentice Hall, 1969.
"The Shape of Fear." *North American Review* (June 1926).

Mary Young

LENIN, V. I. (1870–1924)

There is surprisingly little direct reference by Du Bois about V. I. Lenin. Even late in Du Bois' life when, working as a Commintern fellow traveler in the fight against imperialism, about which Du Boisian and Leninist theories converge, Du Bois rarely mentions Lenin by name, while mentioning the Soviet Union all the time. There is no reason to believe that Lenin is a direct influence on Du Bois with regard to imperialism, since Du Bois began to theorize imperialism in many of the same terms as Lenin by 1915, two years before Lenin's famous work appeared in Russian. On the other hand, Du Bois' work was a source, however minor, for Lenin, who refers to Du Bois–penned U.S. government reports on southern agriculture in his *Capitalism and Agriculture in the United States*, noting their "remarkably detailed descriptions . . . unavailable . . . in any other country." Otherwise, Du Bois refers to Lenin in passing perhaps half a dozen times in his writing. Aptheker (in his annotated bibliography of Du Bois) finds this so conspicuous that he notes a number of places where Du Bois could have referred to Lenin. In *The Crisis* (June 1932) Du Bois provides a list for African Americans who are interested in studying specific works of socialist political economy that includes Marx–but does not include Lenin.

Because of this relative overlap, any analysis of the relationship between Du Bois and Lenin primarily consists of the direct comparison between Du Bois' May 1915 essay "The African Roots of the War," published in the *Atlantic Monthly*, which contains a thesis extremely close to Lenin's, and Lenin's pamphlet *Imperialism: The Highest Stage of Capitalism*. Additionally, there is the question of Du Bois' analysis of the Russian Revolution and the USSR, which is frequent throughout his writings, and of the Communist Party, USA (CPUSA), which is somewhat less frequent, though of great importance.

In "The African Roots of the War," Du Bois argues that to explain modern colonialism in Africa the economic needs of Europe must be viewed as central. He dates modern colonialism to 1884 with the scramble for territorial rule during and after the Berlin Conference, and asks why all of a sudden, at this point, a new form of racial domination comes into being, stating that "the answer to this riddle we shall find in the economic changes in Europe." These economic changes are the disappearance of social mobility in Europe and the emergence of workers' movements that must be placated through reduced exploitation at home and increased investment for exploitation abroad; already existing color prejudice, a habit created during the slave trade, made it clear where this exploitation would be possible. As more and more industrial peace at home relied on a greater concentration of investment abroad, war over spaces in which this investment could take place is inevitable. Thus, "the world invest[s] in color prejudice and the scramble to control the places where this investment occurs necessarily leads to war."

Lenin's remarkably similar analysis starts from a different place. He also argues that the world war is caused by imperialism, but he explains imperialism first as the emergence of capital concentration; this capital, in order to continue to reproduce, needs constantly expanding markets that the home country is unable to provide. It, therefore, must look to the colonial world. In finding these markets, Lenin agrees with Du Bois that big capital is able to buy off a segment of the home country's most privileged proletariat, the "labor aristocracy," who will then actively support the expansion of imperialism at the expense of the international workers' movement. Nationalism and chauvinism among workers results from this.

For Du Bois, imperialism requires race prejudice among the workers from the beginning, as part of a legacy of superexploitation that began hundreds of years earlier with the slave trade; for Lenin, imperialism is a necessary outgrowth of national capitalisms, a "higher" stage of capitalism based on its natural progress, also over hundreds of years. Similarly, if we compare the subjective points of view of their analyses, we expose their different audiences. Du Bois states that "we pay for industrial peace at home by having much costlier wars abroad"–"we" speaking for those in the metropole; when Lenin states that "social chauvinism is the utter betrayal of socialism," the people addressed are primarily the world proletariat. However different the beginnings of these arguments, it is easy to see that they are closely related. They will converge in the anti-imperialist practice of the International Left between World War I and the period of decolonization in the 1950s and the 1960s, with Du Bois and a significant group of Pan-Africanists becoming increasingly interested in Marxian economic analysis and the International Left moving definitively toward an understanding of antiracism and the autonomy of the capitalist periphery as central to Marxist political practice.

Though he rarely referred to either Lenin's writings or his existence as a politician, Du Bois saw the USSR as an economic model from the early 1920s on, using exactly the same language writing about the country in 1922 and 1947: Russia is the most "hopeful phenomenon" in the world. He did not deny or endorse political repression there, but he consistently saw it as a minor issue in light of what he viewed as the more substantive shift in the control of the economy, to the newly educated workers, that he believed was happening. It is on the basis of this shift that he wished Russia judged. On the other hand, it is possible to see his persistent criticisms of the CPUSA between the 1920s and the 1940s as critiques of Leninism, if not Lenin, since he saw the actions of the Communist Party as damaging to the potential political activities of blacks and the form of the Party as irrelevant at best to the U.S. situation; still, in 1961, he joined the CPUSA before departing for Ghana. *See also*: Russian Revolution and the Soviet Union.

FURTHER READING

Aptheker, Herbert, ed. *Writings by W.E.B. Du Bois in Periodicals Edited by Others.* Vol. 2, 1910–1934. Millwood, NY: Kraus-Thomson Organization, 1982.

Du Bois, W.E.B. "The African Roots of the War." *Atlantic Monthly* (May 1915): 707–714. Reprinted in Herbert Aptheker, ed. *Writings by W.E.B. Du Bois in Periodicals Edited by Others*. Vol. 2, 1910–1934. Millwood, NY: Kraus-Thomson Organization, 1982.

———. "Revolution." In *Dusk of Dawn: An Essay toward an Autobiography of a Race Concept*. New York: Harcourt Brace, 1940. New Brunswick, NJ: Transaction Publishers, 1983.

Lenin, V. I. *Imperialism: The Highest Stage of Capitalism, A Popular Outline*. 1917. New York: International Publishers, 1939.

Lewis, David Levering. *W.E.B. Du Bois: Biography of a Race, 1868–1919*. New York: Henry Holt, 1993.

Lindberg, Kathryne V. "W.E.B. Du Bois' *Dusk of Dawn* and James Yates' *Mississippi to Madrid*, or 'What Goes Around Comes Around in Autobiography.' " *Massachusetts Review* 35.2 (Summer 1994): 283–308.

Kenneth Mostern

LIBERIA

Liberia became independent in 1847, following Haiti as the second of only two black republics in the world. Nineteenth-century black nationalists wished to make Liberia a center of civilization and Christianization in Africa. In 1920, the Universal Negro Improvement Association (UNIA) revived and modernized this interest. Marcus Garvey and other UNIA officials wanted to develop the country through agricultural communes and export facilities and use it to exemplify the achievements that the black race was capable of. As Liberia was already sovereign with a nominally black nationalist leadership, Garveyites anticipated success. The interests of Garveyites and the Liberian elite, however, did not always converge. Liberian officials worried, for example, about how British and French imperialists in neighboring colonies would receive Garveyism. They also feared the potential the powerful UNIA had to disrupt local politics. For its part, the UNIA found reports of Liberian decadence and despotism disheartening. In spite of mutual misgivings, plans began for a land concession for UNIA-sponsored emigrants.

In December 1923, President Calvin Coolidge appointed Du Bois to represent the United States at the inauguration of Liberian president C. B. King. Du Bois received the rank of envoy extraordinary and minister plenipotentiary. As Du Bois was known to strongly disagree with Garvey's program, the appointment sent a clear message to Monrovia about the U.S. position. Du Bois went to Liberia from the Third Pan-African Congress. He remained there for a month and lyrically described this first visit to Africa in his autobiography, *Dusk of Dawn*.

Du Bois' address at the inauguration stresses the close historic ties between the United States and Liberia. He reiterated the U.S. traditional stance of stewardship and protection over the black republic. While in Liberia, Du Bois toured with an official from the Firestone Rubber Company, which was seeking rubber concessions, and he endorsed U.S. corporate investment in the country. Foreign creditors in the spring of 1924 began to pressure Monrovia, suggesting that its indebtedness might require customs control or other incursions on Liberian sovereignty. In April 1924 President King allowed Firestone to lease 1 million acres for ninety-nine years in exchange for a $5 million loan to the state. The deal was a coup for Firestone and the United States; the British empire had until then monopolized rubber plantation acreage worldwide. The Firestone site was the same as that first promised to the UNIA. Garveyites knew nothing of this, however, and continued planning to bring in black settlers. When in June 1924 authorities at the port of Monrovia refused to let an advance party of UNIA technicians and administrators debark, they knew they had failed.

Du Bois subsequently denied any role in aborting Garveyism in Liberia. He claimed he had never mentioned Garvey to Liberian officials. His association with the U.S. government as its official representative, his known opposition to Garvey, and his endorsement of the Firestone concession nevertheless implicate him, if indirectly, in the demise of the UNIA's colonization project. *See also: Dusk of Dawn*; Garvey, Marcus; Garvey and the UNIA; Great Britain.

FURTHER READING

Du Bois, W.E.B. *Dusk of Dawn: An Essay toward an Autobiography of a Race Concept.* New York: Schocken Books, 1968.

Brenda Gayle Plummer

LOCKE, ALAIN (1885–1954)

Alain Leroy Locke was a teacher and the foremost philosopher on Howard University's faculty from 1912 to 1953. He was more widely known for his literary work and contributions to the black aesthetic than for his contributions to philosophy. Alain Locke's editorship of the *Survey Graphic* yielded an issue devoted to the "New Negro," "Harlem, Mecca of the New Negro" (1925). In December 1925, Locke expanded the original issue into a book entitled *The New Negro*, featuring the work of Countee Cullen, Charles S. Johnson, James Weldon Johnson, Arthur Schomburg, Walter White, and W.E.B. Du Bois.

In a review for *The New Negro* that appeared in *The Crisis* (January 1926), Du Bois offered a laudatory assessment of the work. He noted that the book was a very important contribution on the "present state and culture among American Negroes." Moreover, Locke's selections and editing were above reproach; the marriage of concepts of art and propaganda was significant. Pleased with this important opus, Du Bois continued to review Locke's work favorably in *The Crisis*. A January 1928 review of *Plays of Negro Life*, coedited with Montgomery Gregory, elicits a similar assessment. Again, acknowledging the importance of culture, Du Bois notes the importance of playwrights and actors in cultural construction during the 1920s.

Operating in different locales, Locke in Washington, D.C. and Du Bois in New York City, the two maintained an uneven relationship. In 1927, when Locke and three other professors were dismissed by Howard University's Board of Trustees, Du Bois protested to Howard trustee Jesse Moorland. With the advent of the 1930s, the Great Depression, and the New Deal, the opportunity arose for significant interaction between Locke and Du Bois. Long interested in exploring the linkages between race and culture, Locke sponsored a conference at Howard University entitled "Problems, Programs and Philosophies of Minority Groups" (1935). Along with several noted leftist scholars, Locke invited Du Bois. In addition to presenting at the conference, Locke asked Du Bois to contribute to a series of booklets on education. Du Bois' booklet entitled *The Negro and Social Reconstruction* was a caustic appraisal of the New Deal. He also included a section titled the "Basic American Negro Creed." Applying a Marxist analysis to economic conditions in the United States, Du Bois concluded that the redistribution of wealth utilizing a socialistic model was the paramount priority for blacks.

Locke's assessment of the New Deal was the direct antithesis of Du Bois'. Locke felt that Du Bois' position was somewhat extreme, although he agreed in the main with his proposals. Because the study was sponsored by the Carnegie Institute, Du Bois' "The Negro and Social Reconstruction" was never published. Although Du Bois did not blame Locke for the rejection of his manuscript, the views of the two men became more widely divergent in the 1940s and 1950s. Locke remained dedicated to integration, whereas Du Bois moved further toward socialistic and ultimately communistic approaches to solving the race problem. *See also*: Art and Literature; Harlem Renaissance; Howard University.

FURTHER READING

Harris, Leonard, ed. *Philosophy of Alain Locke: Harlem Renaissance and Beyond.* Philadelphia: Temple University Press, 1991.

Stephen G. Hall

LOGAN, RAYFORD W. (1897–1982)

W.E.B. Du Bois' intellect had a tremendous impact on black Americans during the early 1920s. He was considered a leader for most African Americans including Rayford W. Logan. Logan grew up in Washington, D.C. during the early 1900s. He went on to become a prolific scholar–activist; and he was considered a leading Pan-Africanist and black historian. Much of Logan's scholarship focused on African-diasporian history with emphasis on the United States and the Caribbean. He was of the "new school" of black historians that advanced research and writing in black history.

The relationship between Du Bois and Logan can be described as positive and effectual. Du Bois, as the older of the two, identified a sharp intellect and promising scholar in Logan. Du Bois respected Logan and his critical analysis concerning the social conditions of African Americans. Throughout Du Bois' professional career, he would often cite and acknowledge the intellectualism and research of Logan. This is illustrated by Du Bois' column "As the Crow Flies" in the *Amsterdam News* (January, 10 1942) that acknowledged Logan's book *The Diplomatic Relations of the United States and Haiti* as one of the premier works of the year. In a *Chicago Globe* (June 3, 1950) column, Du Bois acknowledged Logan's 1948 volume *The African Mandates in World Politics* as a key source in examining international policy toward Africa. Again, Du Bois cites the merit and importance of Logan's career production as instrumental to the publication of Du Bois' book *The World and Africa* (1947).

During the early 1920s, Du Bois and Logan worked fervently on the development and function of the Pan-African Congress. Du Bois received a great deal of assistance from the young scholar Logan in the organization of the Second Pan-African Congress meeting in 1921. Logan, as secretary to the Congress, translated the statutes from French into English. His role in the organizational scheme for this meeting was critical, because of the consistent discourse and interpretative analysis between Anglophone and Francophone Africans.

Moreover, Logan continued to work with Du Bois in the organization and planning of the Third Pan-African Congress, in 1923. During the preparatory stages of this Congress, Logan differed with the interpretative Pan-Africanist ideology of Du Bois. Allegedly, this dissension was over money. Nevertheless, after this brief misunderstanding, the two scholars continued to work as colleagues, forging their Pan-Africanist philosophies. In 1945, Du Bois was accompanied by Logan in attending the United Nations Conference on International Organizations.

Du Bois and Logan worked on several joint research projects, for example, *The Encyclopedia of the Negro: Preparatory Volume with Reference Lists and Reports* (1944). Logan was also a contributor to *An Appeal to the World. A Statement on the Denial of Human Rights to Minorities in the Case of Citizens of Negro Descent in the United States of America and an Appeal to the United Nations for Redress* (1947). To this work, Logan contributed a chapter, "The United Nations and the Rights of Minorities." In addition, Du Bois contributed an essay, "My Evolving Program for Negro Freedom," in Logan's edited volume *What the Negro Wants* (1944).

Logan introduced Du Bois at ceremonial events in which he was honored, such as "The 10th Annual Graduate Students Conference at Howard University in 1947." Logan said about Du Bois, "[V]oice and pen have never been stilled in his relentless struggle." Logan was also present at the Seventieth Birthday convocation of Morehouse College, Spelman College, and Atlanta University, where he delivered an opening address and presented a "bust of Du Bois to Atlanta University, which now faces the main reading room in the library." The scholarly-interpersonal relationship between Du Bois and Logan exhibited goodwill and cordiality.

FURTHER READING

Janken, Kenneth. *Rayford W. Logan and the Dilemma of the African-American Intellectual.* Amherst: University of Massachusetts Press, 1993.

Logan, Rayford. *The African Mandates in World Politics.* Washington: Public Affairs Press, 1948.

——. *Diplomatic Relations of the United States and Haiti.* Chapel Hill: University of North Carolina Press, 1941.

James L. Conyers, Jr.

M

McCARTHYISM

Thursday, February 9, 1950, while addressing a Republican women's club in Wheeling, West Virginia, Joseph R. McCarthy, the junior senator from Wisconsin, waved a sheet of paper, telling the gathering that it was a list of fifty-seven "known Communists" working in the State Department. Although the paper was blank, his actions at that meeting, along with subsequent allegations on his part, initiated a pogrom of sorts that before it was over would cost many people their jobs and sully the reputations of uncounted others. What made his "witch-hunts" possible was a climate of fear in the country—a climate whose immediate origins lay in the political instability that grew out of the depression of the 1930s and the creation by the Congress of, first, a Special Committee to Investigate Un-American Activities and Propaganda in the House of Representatives and, second, its replacement in 1945 by the House Committee on Un-American Activities.

Throughout this period until the beginning of McCarthy's downfall during his investigation in 1954 of supposed subversion in the U.S. Army, anyone who advocated peace or coexistence with the Soviet Union became an object of special attention for the forces of Truth, Justice, and the American Way. Throughout the McCarthy era, Du Bois continued his critique of U.S. foreign and domestic policy.

Although he was acquitted because the government was unable to prove its contention, his treatment by the authorities gave him even more reason to intensify his activities in the cause of peace while it increased his bitterness toward the United States as a less-than-democratic society. *See also*: Socialism/Communism.

FURTHER READING

Schrecker, Ellen. *The Age of McCarthyism*. Boston: Bedford Books, 1994.

William M. King

McKAY, CLAUDE (1890–1948)

Although Du Bois admired McKay's poetry and published his work in *The Crisis*, he disagreed vehemently with McKay on political matters. As one of the editors of *The Liberator*, McKay criticized Du Bois for failing to understand the significance of the Russian Revolution. McKay believed similar means could improve the situation of American blacks. As he saw it, African Americans suffered discrimination primarily due to their lowly status as workers. As a result, race prejudice was merely an outgrowth of the worker's plight that would disappear with a proletariat revolution.

In spite of the Third International's commitment to emancipate workers of all races, Du Bois remained skeptical that the proletariat revolution would solve the problem of the color line in the United States. He understood McKay's temptation to believe that if blacks supported the working-class agenda, the working class would return that support. Nevertheless, noting the discrimination practiced by trade labor unions in the United States and by American Socialists, Du Bois wondered why McKay would expect reasoned thinking on the race question from unschooled white workers when that could not be had from educated whites. Du Bois believed the socialist critique of the worker's status was sound but that it would be necessary to convince white workers that people of color are human and suffer the same conditions. He cautioned further that the agenda for social and political equality for African Americans must not be subsumed under the larger category of worker emancipation. *See also*: Art and Literature; Harlem Renaissance; Socialism/Communism.

FURTHER READING

McKay, Claude. *A Long Way from Home: An Autobiography*. New York: Harcourt, Brace and World, 1970.

Christy Rishoi

MANLINESS

In "A Philosophy for 1913," Du Bois declared: "I will be a man and know myself to be one, even among those who secretly and openly deny my manhood, and I shall persistently and unwaveringly seek by every possible method to compel all men to treat me as I treat them" (*The Crisis*, January 1913). From being denied the vote, to lynching and terror, and through a range of more subtle and pernicious racism, the harsh reality of African American life required a political philosophy to inspire and challenge. A key aspect of Du Bois' early political thought was the reconstruction of the meanings of race and manliness. Through the assertion of manhood, African Americans could be empowered.

"Race" and "manliness" were concepts constructed by white Americans in ways that oppressed African Americans. In his early thinking, Du Bois believed these powerful concepts could be infused with new meanings and turned back on the dominant society. Through his speeches and writings, Du Bois constructed and articulated a workable politics to unite and motivate the African American community.

Race would be embraced to positive ends. At the end of the nineteenth century Du Bois stated: "[T]he fact still remains that the full, complete Negro message of the whole Negro race has not yet been given to the world" ("The Conservation of Races"). The meanings white America invested in racial difference were recast by Du Bois: Yes, race existed, but the African American was a gift to the world. He sought to empower both sides of the unique dual identity of the African American: being black and being American. Equally, Du Bois did not—at this stage—reject the fundamental promise of America. African Americans, even more than white Americans, were "of" America, the product of its history.

As Du Bois grappled with conceiving an effective race politics in the face of racial realities, manliness became essential. He wanted to reassert African American manhood even as whites tried to emasculate them. The "Jim Crow" system was a direct assault on this manhood. Du Bois railed against the public opinion behind the order to sit in a separate train car. Such public opinion was denying him less his right to sit in a particular train car, than his very manhood ("An Open Letter to the Southern People" in Aptheker 1–4).

To assert one's manhood was to assert one's power as an African American, and race pride was essential. "It is race pride that fights for freedom," wrote Du Bois. "It is the man ashamed of his blood who weakly submits and smiles" (*The Crisis*, March 1912). Manhood was not something innate but had to be earned and asserted. "More and more manly assertion" was needed to win political rights, and this included protest ("The Social Effects of Emancipation," *Survey*, February 1, 1913). And nothing less than manhood could be given. Political power, manhood rights, and freedom were intimately linked. "We are men, we will be treated as men," he declared angrily, and "we will not be satisfied to take one jot or tittle less than our full manhood rights" ("Niagara Address of 1906" in Aptheker, *A Documentary History* 902–910).

Manhood and manhood suffrage went hand in hand: "[V]oting is necessary to modern manhood," wrote Du Bois (*The Souls of Black Folk* 55). Du Bois' Niagara Movement, organized in 1905, recognized the crucial importance of the vote. With the "right to vote goes everything: freedom, manhood, the honor of your wives, the chastity of your daughters, the right to work, and the chance to rise, and let no man listen to those who deny this" (*Dusk of Dawn* 90). African Americans must aspire to full citizenship. Not to struggle for such rights was wrong: "[T]he man that supinely sits down and gives up the rights of manhood or even goes so far as actually to protest that he doesn't want them," he admonished, "such men do not deserve American citizenship" ("Lecture in Baltimore," 1903). Education was one means to this manhood. Education and training could facilitate race pride and manhood—the result should "be neither a psychologist nor a brickmason, but a man" (*The Souls of Black Folk* 86).

Du Bois' views of African American power through manhood did not fail to recognize the power of African American women. On the contrary, he idealized them. They were more powerful than their men and were closest to fulfilling the possibilities of the race. "I honor the women of my race," wrote Du Bois (*Darkwater* 185). They were also the protectors of the race: It was critical not to be "further burdening the overburdened but by honoring motherhood, even when the sneaking father shirks his duty" (*Darkwater* 185). Du Bois' greatest desire was to see African American men fulfill their potential, for the legacy of slavery had been the destruction of African American manhood.

Participation in World War I seemed to offer African Americans the opportunity to show their courage and loyalty to the United States. Du Bois was to be cruelly disappointed. The war did not deliver the hoped-for benefits and recognition, and Du Bois' faith in progress, civilization, and American ideals was fatally challenged. In fact, the African American community faced even greater race oppression—many lynchings and race riots occurred throughout 1918 and 1919, and the postwar period did not deliver the expected progress for African Americans.

As the war shattered many of the tenets that underpinned people's beliefs in their world, Du Bois was to turn to new explanations and means to effect political empowerment for African Americans. Du Bois turned to socialism for solutions: It stood "for the rights of men in America without regard to race and color" ("Speech to Forum on Current Events at the Rand School," 1929 in Foner, 357). His faith in the working class reflected the changing economic realities of African American life, and socialism offered a unity beyond race. Disillusionment and the realities of the post–World War II world eventually led to Du Bois turning to Africa itself. He became a citizen of Ghana in 1963.

Race and manliness, central tenets of W.E.B. Du Bois' early political thinking, were not the solutions to African American oppression. The ideals of the nineteenth century could not be a sufficient means to achieve power and combat the racism of U.S. society: These ideals had already been corrupted and used as weapons of oppression by a dominant society and could not be salvaged. *See also*: Jim Crow; Race Riots; Socialism/Communism; Women's Rights.

FURTHER READING

Aptheker, Herbert, ed. *Against Racism: Unpublished Essays, Papers, Addresses, 1887–1961.* Amherst: University of Massachusetts Press, 1985.
——. *A Documentary History of the Negro People, 1910–1932.* Secaucus, NJ: The Citadel Press, 1973.
"The Conservation of Races 1897." American Negro Academy Occasional Papers no. 2 (1892).

Du Bois, W.E.B. *Darkwater: Voices from Within the Veil.* New York: Harcourt, Brace and Howe, 1920. New York: AMS Press, 1969.

——. *Dusk of Dawn: An Essay toward an Autobiography of a Race Concept.* New York: Harcourt Brace, 1940.

——. *The Souls of Black Folk.* Chicago: A. C. McClurg & Co., 1903.

Foner, Philip S., ed. *W.E.B. Du Bois Speaks: Speeches and Addresses, 1890–1919.* New York: Pathfinder Press, 1970.

Moon, Henry Lee, ed. *The Emerging Thought of W.E.B. Du Bois: Essays and Editorials from The Crisis.* New York: Simon and Schuster, 1972.

Weinberg, Meyer, ed. *W.E.B. Du Bois: A Reader.* New York: Harper and Row Publishers, 1970.

Amanda Laugesen

MAO ZEDONG (1893–1976)

Du Bois expressed great admiration for Mao Zedong, the leader and founder of the Chinese Communist nation, and what Du Bois termed the miracle of the People's Republic of China. Having led the fight against the Chinese Nationalists led by Chiang Kai-shek for many years, Mao Zedong and his fellow Communists finally assumed leadership in China in 1949. Du Bois had journeyed to pre-Communist China in 1936 and commented, in his *Autobiography*, that he heard nothing of the 6,000-mile Long March led by Mao and others. Du Bois thought this quite odd.

Upon traveling to Communist China in 1959 Du Bois was greeted as a national hero. In fact, his ninety-first birthday, which was celebrated on this trip, was proclaimed a national holiday. On this visit, he spent four hours with Mao and met with other Chinese officials such as Chou En-lai. Du Bois believed that Mao and other Communists were successful as leaders because they had led by example, "by starving and fighting." One of Mao's characteristics was great patience, Du Bois asserted in the *National Guardian* (June 8, 1959). Du Bois observed that Chairman Mao had been able to convince ordinary Chinese that they were the "real nation," not the elites. In his conversations with Mao, Du Bois was impressed that the Communist people did not fear war. China, Chairman Mao related to Du Bois, would have no difficulty defending itself.

When Du Bois died in Ghana in 1963, one of the many messages of condolence cabled to Shirley Graham, Du Bois' widow, was sent by Mao Zedong. In that communication, Mao gave great praise to Du Bois (Lewis 10). *See also*: Asia; China.

FURTHER READING

The Autobiography of W.E.B. Du Bois. New York: International Pub., 1968.

Lewis, David Levering. *W.E.B. Du Bois: Biography of a Race, 1868–1919.* New York: Henry Holt, 1993.

Mary Ellen Wilson

MARCANTONIO, VITO (1902–1954)

Marcantonio was born in a poverty-stricken area of New York City's East Harlem, a district then composed of an ethnically diverse population. In 1925, he graduated from New York University's School of Law and became a clerk in Fiorello La Guardia's Law office.

With La Guardia as his mentor, Marcantonio entered politics. In 1934 he succeeded La Guardia as East Harlem's Republican representative. Except one term—1936 to 1938—Marcantonio represented the district until 1951.

From 1937 on, Marcantonio adapted views akin to those of the political positions of the U.S. Communist Party, but he consistently denied being a Communist. By 1946 he was openly critical of the administration's foreign policy. Because of his outspoken criticism and his alleged Communist sympathies, the Federal Bureau of Investigation (FBI) put Marcantonio under surveillance. Du Bois championed Marcantonio and his efforts to hold the U.S. government accountable. In a *Chicago Globe* article (June 24, 1950), Du Bois protested the efforts of "all political parties against Representative Vito Marcantonio to drive him out of Congress." Du Bois' admiration for him continued until Marcantonio's death in 1954. According to Du Bois, Marcantonio was a "politician in the finest sense." Du Bois also relied heavily on Marcantonio's skill as an attorney after he was indicted, then put on trial in 1951.

FURTHER READING

Waltzer, Kenneth. "The FBI, Congressman Vito Marcantonio, and the American Labor Party." In *Beyond the Hiss Case. The FBI, Congress, and the Cold War*, ed. Athan C. Theoharis. Philadelphia: Temple University Press, 1982.

Alle Parker

MARRIAGE AND RACE

For Du Bois, marriage was a sacred covenant not to be interfered with by the state. Governmental interference was "impudent dictation in [a] purely personal matter" (*The Independent*, 1910). In 1913 Du Bois observed in an editorial (*The Crisis*, February 1913) that recently there had been a "proliferation of state legislations . . . enact[ing] laws forbidding intermarriage."

Du Bois was opposed to such laws—"Not because we are anxious to marry white men's sisters, but because we are determined that white men shall let our sisters alone" (*The Crisis*, November 1913). Several northern and western states had voted down such measures, and Du Bois exulted, though he was still opposed to such marriages. Moreover, in an essay entitled "The Social Equality of Whites and Blacks" (*The Crisis*, 1920), he strongly advised against such unions because the intent was to build a strong black race.

Du Bois, again, voiced an opinion on intermarriage when a white reader expressed interest in his views after reading *The Souls of Black Folk* (*The Crisis*, March 1926). Du Bois replied, "No race is permanent, but marriage within one's own group has the best chance for success . . . marriage outside it is a matter for the people themselves to decide and no one else's business." *See also*: Birth Control.

FURTHER READING

Du Bois, W.E.B. "Again Social Equality." *The Crisis* (March 1920).
—— "The Social Equality of Blacks and Whites." *The Crisis* (November 1920).

Kathryn Rhoads

MARX, KARL (1818–1883)

During his academic training, Du Bois had limited exposure to Karl Marx. At Fisk, for example, he noted that Marx was never mentioned. Even at Harvard and the University of Berlin, Du Bois never read the writings of Marx. Instead, Marx was formally dismissed for his unrealized predictions and questionable theories on economic/human relations. However while in Berlin, Du Bois marveled at the German students' ability to recite Marx "for hours." This introduction to Marxist thought through a Socialist club enlightened Du Bois to the universal plight of the proletariat. To quote Du Bois, "I had left America thinking black people were the most downtrodden, exploited, and oppressed people in the world (*Autobiography*, 168). In that club I learned of millions of others." Moreover, his early travels through Europe, particularly Bohemia, Hungary, and Poland, further confirmed the existence of an even larger pool of exploited workers. In essence, Du Bois' informal education and personal experiences in Europe became a key element in his radicalism and scholarship later in life.

It is not at all clear at what point Du Bois began to read Marx in earnest, although the best estimate is shortly after World War I. Yet Aptheker (1978) suggested that as early as 1907 Du Bois' public addresses appeared influenced by a Marxist perspective. Furthermore, Marable identified Du Bois' analysis in "The African Roots of the War" (1915) as "the first tentative step toward Marxism-Leninism" (Marable, 94). The seeming discrepancy is resolved when one considers Du Bois' reading of American socialists such as John Spargo and Jack London during his early years at Atlanta University (1897–1900). Without a doubt, Du Bois' six-week visit to the Soviet Union in 1926 inspired him to become a more serious student of Marxist thought and to incorporate his firsthand knowledge of social conflict theory and methods into his work.

The issue of Du Bois' first reading of Marx is imperative because he was often attacked by his contemporaries for a superficial review of Marx's writings and erroneous applications of his philosophy. In actuality, Du Bois' work, especially from the 1930s on, shows a keen understanding of Marx to the extent that his critique resulted in modifications consistent with Du Bois' morality and social reality.

Although Du Bois praised Marx as one of the greatest intellectuals of his time, two issues were central to his departure from pure Marxism: the inevitability of a violent revolution and the insufficient explanation of racial strife in the twentieth century. For example, Du Bois began "Marxism and the Negro Problem" (*The Crisis*, March 1933) equating Marx's *Capital* with the Bible in a category of "great books of truth." However, after Du Bois analyzed global and national class formations due to capitalist exploitation, he concluded that racial nepotism among whites irrespective of class hindered proletariat solidarity across racial lines. Even American Socialists and Communists deemed progressive and liberal had problems with the race question. Therefore, Du Bois had difficulty envisioning the overthrow of capitalism in the United States any time in the immediate future. No doubt, these same concerns were raised when Du Bois taught his course on "Karl Marx and the Negro" at Atlanta University (1933).

Though Karl Marx had a substantial influence on Du Bois, Du Bois refrained from identifying himself as a Marxist. Beyond scholarly exercises, his revisionist intellectualism was a means to an end. Still Du Bois' life work was an affirmation of Marx's statement "until now philosophers have only explained the world, our task is to change it" (Marx 201). *See also*: Aptheker, Herbert; Atlanta University; Germany; Socialism/Communism.

FURTHER READING

Marable, Manning. *W.E.B. Du Bois. Black Radical Democrat.* Boston: Twayne Pub., 1986.
Marx, Karl. "Theses on Feuerbach." In *Collected Works of Karl Marx and Friedrich Engels, 1845–47.* New York: International Publishers, 1976.

Shawn R. Donaldson

MILITARY

TO THE COLORED SOLDIERS OF THE UNITED STATES ARMY
  Hello, boys, what are you doing over here? Fighting the Germans? Why? . . . Do you enjoy the same rights as the white people do in America, the land of freedom and democracy, or are you rather not treated over there as second class citizens?

The Crisis, March 1919

This propaganda, dropped from a German balloon on September 3, 1918, depicts the difficult decision blacks in the United States have often faced. Is a country so obviously racist worth dying for? Besides fighting racism at home and in the ranks, black soldiers had to prove to white Americans that they are even qualified to wear a uniform. Du Bois was acutely aware of this problem, and as editor of *The Crisis*, his views were closely scrutinized by the black community, who saw the service as a way to increase civil rights, and also by the government, who wanted a complacent, efficient, and segregated army with white officers.

At the beginning of the war, Du Bois wrote essays linking the war with the color line. He did not believe that the Allies were "saints," nor the Germans "ogres," but he did find the German attitude toward race "indefensible" (*The Crisis*, June 1916). Throughout the war, he voiced great support for the French, whom he believed the champions of equal rights due to their Senegalese troops and comforting attitude toward blacks in the U.S. armed forces. After making the argument the blacks should join the military, Du Bois called for immediate changes, both at home and in the ranks. Du Bois believed the war provided an opportunity for blacks to earn respect and necessary skills either through fighting or through work on the home front.

As the war progressed Du Bois came under fire for seeming to subordinate the fight for civil rights to the war, as suggested by "Close Ranks," an editorial written in July 1918, in which Du Bois said, "Let us, while this war lasts, forget our special grievances and close our ranks shoulder to shoulder with our own White fellow citizens and the allied nations that are fighting for Democracy" (*The Crisis*, July 1918). The black community was highly critical. Indeed, the Washington Branch of the National Association for the Advancement of Colored People (NAACP) passed a resolution condemning the editorial, and William H. Wilson of Washington said that in "no issue since our entrance into the war am I able to find so supine a surrender—temporary though it may be to the rights of man" (*The Crisis*, July 1918). When it was announced that Du Bois had been offered a captaincy in the Military Intelligence Bureau, some went as far as calling him a traitor to the civil rights struggle.

In response, Du Bois countered these criticisms and explained his views more clearly. The "*first* duty of an American," he said, "is to win the war and that to this all else is secondary." Also, "have we black men for one moment hesitated to do our full duty in this war because we thought the country was not doing its full duty to us? . . . *The Crisis* says, *first* your country, and *then* your rights!" (*The Crisis*, July 1918). He celebrated the black role in the military from the Revolutionary War to the Spanish-American War and argued that although blacks had not received equal rights, they have certainly made advances. Additionally, he said many advances had been made since the beginning of the present war itself.

Although Du Bois hated the egregious injustices committed against African Americans, he believed in the ideals of the country. He argued that only through valor abroad could blacks gain rights at home. His words to black soldiers returning from the Great War clearly show his struggle and the position they so often find themselves in. "*We return. We return from fighting. We return fighting*" (*The Crisis*, April 1919). *See also*: National Association for the Advancement of Colored People (NAACP).

FURTHER READING

Du Bois, W.E.B. "The Black Man in the Revolution of 1914–1918." *The Crisis* (May 1924).
"Returning Soldiers." *The Crisis* (May 1919).

Alphine Jefferson

MILLER, KELLY (1919–1943)

An essayist, educator, and intellectual, Kelly Miller was an important and seminal contributor to black intellectual life in the early twentieth century. As intellectuals, Miller and Du Bois moved in similar circles. The men were among the fourteen called by Alexander Crummell, to form the American Negro Academy, an intellectual clearinghouse, in 1897. In his 1903 opus *The Souls of Black Folk*, in an essay entitled "Of the Wings of Atlanta," Miller was cited as an important component of racial leadership. Initially, Miller was critical of Booker T. Washington's program of industrial and vocational emphasis. Later, Miller vacillated and adopted a conciliatory stance toward Booker T. Washington. By 1904, Miller was refusing to oppose Washington's educational plans. Du Bois criticized him for this position.

Although Du Bois displayed a cautious attitude toward Miller, Miller played a prominent role in the affairs of the National Association for the Advancement of Colored People (NAACP). He served as a contributing editor for *The Crisis*, where several of his books were reviewed. In 1925, Miller wrote a laudatory review of the NAACP's progress for the fifteenth annual report. In exchange for these comments, Du Bois rallied to Miller's aid when Howard University's European American president, J. Stanley Durkee, arbitrarily demoted him from the position of dean of the College of Arts and Sciences to dean of the Junior College (1919–1925). Du Bois maintained cordial relations with Miller for the remainder of his life. *See also*: Howard University; National Association for the Advancement of Colored People (NAACP); *The Souls of Black Folk*; Washington, Booker T.

FURTHER READING

"Possibilities of the Negro. The Advance Guard of the Race." *Booklovers* Magazine (July 1903).

Stephen G. Hall

MOTON, ROBERT RUSSA (1867–1940)

Born in Amelia County, Virginia, Moton attended Hampton Institute and read law. Upon the death of Booker T. Washington (1915), Moton was appointed principal of Tuskegee Institute. As Washington's successor, Moton was the subject of much commentary by Du Bois. As early as 1916, Du Bois in "An Open Letter to Robert Russa Moton," writes that "he [Du Bois] hopes to see that Institution [Tuskegee] carrying forth the best of its work but also that Tuskegee agrees with Charles Summer that 'Equality of Rights Is the First of Rights' " (*The Crisis*, July 1916).

In subsequent articles, Du Bois often wrote glowingly of Moton. In an "Opinion" column (*The Crisis*, June 1923), Du Bois mentions a hospital that was being built for black veterans in Tuskegee. The European American majority was demanding an all-white medical staff because African Americans were inefficient. The Ku Klux Klan (KKK) had demanded that Dr. Moton sign a statement in support of this position. Moton had refused and invited them to "take vengeance on him if they must."

Later, in the September 1924 edition of *The Crisis*, Du Bois gave unstinted praise to Tuskegee and Moton on the decisive victory of its hospital that "was achieved in the face of great difficulty despite the KKK and all the Bourbonry." Throughout the succeeding years Du Bois continued his praise of Moton.

In 1940 Du Bois wrote revealingly of his relationship with Moton: "I do not think in my judgment of him I had been wrong, although I had not seen the whole picture. I do think that my criticism and that of other Negroes helped him to find a stronger and more tenable platform. But in any case Robert Moton was a great and good man who suffered for a noble cause" (*Phylon*). *See also*: Hampton Institute; Tuskegee Institute.

FURTHER READING

Moton, Robert Russa. *Finding a Way Out: An Autobiography*. Garden City, NY: Double-
    day, Page, and Company, 1920.
"Moton of Hampton and Tuskegee." *A Chronicle of Race Relation*, 1940. *Phylon* 1, no. 4
    (1940): 344–351.

                                                                          Mary Young

MUSSOLINI, BENITO (1883–1945)

An Italian dictator, Mussolini began his professional career as a school-teacher. Politically, he soon became associated with the Irredentist Movement. This movement was devoted to the recovery and union to Italy of all Italian-speaking districts then subject to other countries. Though a member of the Irredentist Movement, Mussolini soon switched to socialism. He advanced quickly within the party, becoming a member of the executive committee.

However, World War I confronted Mussolini with a major dilemma. He appreciated the revolutionary possibilities the war presented. But unlike most Italian Socialists, he advocated Italian participation in the war. In 1914 he founded the newspaper *Il popolo d'Italia* and was expelled from the Socialist Party.

After the war, he attempted to exploit the dissatisfaction in the country, and in 1919, he founded the Fasci di Combattimento ("Fighting Leagues"). After defeat in several elections, in November 1922, Mussolini, the founder of fascism, was appointed prime minister, answerable only to the king.

Sharing Hitler's expansionist policies, in 1935 Mussolini launched an attack on Ethiopia, despite League of Nations sanctions. With the invasion of Ethiopia, Du Bois entered the debate. Before the Italian aggression (1934), Du Bois had warned that Mussolini was "eyeing" Ethiopia, writing that "the crime of Mussolini in Ethiopia is colossal." Calling the 1935 invasion "the rape of Ethiopia," Du Bois noted that the only objection came from the Soviet Union (*The Pittsburgh Courier*, May 6, 1936). Thus, Du Bois' encounter with Mussolini—the embodiment of fascism—was another step on his path to the Communist Party. *See also*: Ethiopia; Hitler.

FURTHER READING

Hoyt, Edwin Palmer. *Mussolini's Empire: The Rise and Fall of the Fascist Vision.* New York: John Wiley and Sons, 1994.

Mary Young

NATIONAL ASSOCIATION FOR THE ADVANCEMENT OF COLORED PEOPLE (NAACP)

The NAACP grew out of the Niagara Movement and out of an interracial conference in 1909 to discuss the status of African Americans. Du Bois and other highly educated and upper-class African Americans initiated the Niagara Movement to create a forum for black intellectuals to debate routes toward racial equality. The movement quickly dissipated as the group became absorbed by other larger black organizations like the NAACP. Those involved in the interracial conference were black radicals dissatisfied with the agenda of Booker T. Washington and white Socialists or Progressives also discouraged with the degenerating status of black Americans. W.E.B. Du Bois, Ida Wells-Barnett, and William Monroe Trotter were among the most vocal blacks at the conference. The agenda at this interracial conference laid the foundation for the NAACP's strategy that involved the legal enforcement of African Americans' constitutional rights. The early agenda laid out by Du Bois was to secure the civil rights of African Americans by forcing the legal system to uphold the Fourteenth Amendment, equal education opportunities, and voting rights.

Du Bois became progressively outraged with the disfranchisement of blacks between 1890 and 1910 by the former slave states. These Jim Crow laws functioned to segregate the railroads, streetcars, and public facilities. The "legal caste system," as Du Bois called it, based on race and color, led him to abandon his teaching position at Atlanta University in 1910 and to accept a position with the NAACP as the director of Publications and Research in 1911. Du Bois, along with others, officially incorporated the NAACP.

The NAACP provided Du Bois with the opportunity to reach a broader audience. He was appointed editor of *The Crisis*, the NAACP's magazine. The editorship of *The Crisis* would prove his most important post. In *The Crisis*, Du

NAACP, San Diego organizing committee, 1917. Courtesy of Special Collections and Archives, W.E.B. Du Bois Library, University of Massachusetts Amherst.

Bois closely followed the development of the NAACP and provided important validation and support for its agenda. His agenda, however, far exceeded that of the NAACP's constitutional emancipation of African Americans. Du Bois promoted a viewpoint that encouraged black ownership and control over their own organizations. Du Bois began to espouse socialism out of his concern for impoverished blacks. His long-term goals clearly went beyond that of the NAACP, and this tension, which lasted almost a quarter of a century, would only be resolved through his resignation from the organization. In the end, Du Bois refused to be limited by the vision of the NAACP that he believed did not go far enough toward a radical revision of U.S. society to the benefit of African Americans.

Du Bois expressed his difficulties with negotiating his ideas within the confines of the NAACP's agenda. He was always sensitive to the fact that *The Crisis* belonged to the NAACP and was supposed to function essentially as propaganda for the organization. These tensions arose repeatedly and usually involved Du Bois' attempt to expand the scope of the magazine to include concerns other than U.S. legal issues about African American civil rights. For example, Du Bois' interest in Pan-Africanism around 1920 went beyond what the NAACP thought appropriate for its publication. Du Bois felt progressively confined by the limitations placed on the expression of his own broadening agenda.

By the early 1930s, the depression had created a desperate economic situation for African Americans. Du Bois became increasingly frustrated with the NAACP's unwillingness to reorganize its agenda to meet these new economic circumstances. By now he had abandoned his vision for the black business elite and instead advocated an economic separatist strategy for African Americans. Through Du Bois' extensive knowledge of socialism, he drew from the theories of nineteenth-century utopian socialists and adapted them to envision a twentieth-century black cooperative economy. The NAACP was opposed to his conception and particularly to his endorsement of segregation. Du Bois began to challenge and even reject the policies of the NAACP in its own publication, *The Crisis*. While Du Bois was criticizing the NAACP for its elitism and lack of concern for the black masses, the NAACP wanted to debate the issue of segregation.

Du Bois' rebuttal was that the NAACP had in the past selectively endorsed segregation when it clearly benefited black Americans. For example, during World War I, the NAACP had fought for a segregated officers' training camp so that blacks could receive their commissions. Du Bois' argument was that segregation did not necessarily mean discrimination and that it was the latter that historically the NAACP had opposed, not the former.

The NAACP's response was forceful reiteration of the old platform and specifically a denunciation of segregation and racial separatism of any kind. Du Bois published a few of these rebuttals in *The Crisis* in January 1934. Most notably, he published the statement by the new executive secretary, Walter

White, who had been the assistant to the previous secretary, James Weldon Johnson. Du Bois disliked and distrusted Walter White as an egotistical and unpredictable man. Soon after publishing White's remarks, Du Bois resigned from the NAACP. It had become clear that these arguments were not leading to any type of mutual resolution, and he returned to his teaching position at Atlanta University.

Du Bois' legacy at the NAACP did eventually lead to a dramatic rethinking of its role in the black community. In 1935, the NAACP convened to discuss its plans and decided that it must set up an economic plan in addition to its mission of civil and political equality. This economic plan eventually led to its alliance with labor unions and the Congress of Industrial Organizations. *See also: The Crisis*; Jim Crow; Johnson, James Weldon; Niagara Movement; Socialism/Communism; Trotter, William Monroe.

FURTHER READING

Aptheker, Herbert. *Annotated Bibliography of the Published Writings of W.E.B. Du Bois.* Millwood, NY: Kraus-Thomson Organization, 1973.

Du Bois, W.E.B. *The Autobiography of W.E.B. Du Bois: A Soliloquy on Viewing My Life from the Last Decade of Its First Century.* New York: International Publishers, 1968.

Lewis, David. *W.E.B. Du Bois: Biography of a Race.* New York: A John Macrae Book, Henry Holt Company, 1993.

Meier, August, ed. *Black Protest Thought in the Twentieth Century.* New York: Macmillan Publishing Company, 1971.

Amy Bowles

NATIONAL URBAN LEAGUE

As a founding member of the National Association for the Advancement of Colored People (NAACP), Du Bois had a favorable opinion of the National Urban League, whose aims, background, and journal mirrored his organization. Black and white leaders founded the interracial group in 1910 to aid African Americans in urban environments.

Like the NAACP, the Urban League assumed that African Americans belonged anywhere they wanted to live. It too had supporters of both races and published an organ, *Opportunity*, dedicated to improving black lives. It, too, had chapters all over the country. Early in its history, leaders of the Urban League and the NAACP met—Du Bois was part of the meeting—to ensure that the work of the groups would not overlap.

The League became more important during and after the Great Migration, which brought more than a million African Americans to the urban North. It took on the responsibility for investigating urban conditions, tried to secure jobs for African Americans, and through *Opportunity*, encouraged black scholarship and expression.

Du Bois praised the Urban League's mission several times in his writings. In 1914, he gave a brief history of the League; ten years later he happily noted the presence of *Opportunity*, which, like *The Crisis*, offered prizes to black writers and artists. In 1941, he lauded it for bringing pressure on white authorities for additional jobs ("A Chronicle of Race Relations").

With similar ideals, the NAACP and the National Urban League served as protectors and champions for African Americans during Du Bois' lifetime. As a leader who spent his life striving for black equality, Du Bois admired the work of the National Urban League. *See also*: National Association for the Advancement of Colored People (NAACP).

FURTHER READING

Aptheker, Herbert, ed. "First Meeting of Persons Interested in the Welfare of Negroes in New York." *Against Racism*. Amherst, MA: University of Massachusetts Press, 1985.
"A Chronicle of Race Relations." *Phylon* (1941).
"National League on Urban Conditions Among Negroes." *The Crisis* (September 1914).

Jonathan Silverman

NIAGARA MOVEMENT

Contemporary opposition to the leadership of Booker T. Washington and his allies at the Tuskegee Institute crystallized in 1905 with the founding of the Niagara Movement by a group of militant African Americans. In response to a call issued by Du Bois, twenty-nine delegates drawn from fourteen states gathered in a hotel in Fort Erie, Ontario, in July. Within the context of Washington's domination of economic and political leadership of black America (1903–1910), the Niagara Movement, originally Du Bois' brainchild, explicitly rejected the politics of racial accommodation in favor of militant political agitation. Placing the responsibility for the problem of the color line firmly on the shoulders of whites, Du Bois and other Niagara members urged blacks to seek full assimilation. This was to be achieved through freedom of speech, universal suffrage, eradication of caste distinctions based upon racial origins, education, equal employment opportunities, and constant protest activities to secure black rights.

Membership in the Niagara Movement did not reflect a true cross section of all the social groups that constituted black society at the turn of the century. A vast majority came from the ranks of college-educated professional men or the older middle to upper-class blacks who favored immediate integration. Dr. C. E. Bentley of Chicago, lawyers Clement Morgan and Frederick L. McGhee of St. Paul, and ministers Sutton E. Gregg of Nashville, Reverdy Ransom of New York, and George Freeman Bragg of Baltimore typified this element of the movement. Other members included J.R.L. Diggs, president of Kentucky State College, newspaper editor J. Max Barber (responsible for editing *The Voice of the Negro*), and a sprinkling of other educators. The Niagara Movement reported a maximum of approximately 400 members before its decline in 1908. However, Du Bois stood out as the guiding force of a new organization formed

Niagara Movement, 1905. Courtesy of Special Collections and Archives, W.E.B. Du Bois Library, University of Massachusetts Amherst.

specifically to combat Washington's centering of race interests at Tuskegee. Under Du Bois' influence, the Niagara Movement urged blacks to dispense with the ideology of racial accommodation and to turn, instead, toward collective action in testing disenfranchisement laws in the courts. The 1906 convention of the movement held in New York was further evidence of growing northern dissatisfaction with Washington's southern-style leadership. Delegates, outraged by the Atlanta Race Riot, vigorously condemned ballot restrictions, Jim Crow laws, and mob violence against blacks. White journalist Ray Stannard Baker noted the organization as an important example of black efforts to prevent racial discrimination and segregation through political agitation and political influence (*Horizon* 1908).

Almost immediately after its formal incorporation in January 1906 in Washington, D.C., the Niagara Movement was susceptible to the powerful control of Tuskegee, whose leaders still exerted influence in political and economic circles. Two agents sent by Washington to the Buffalo area infiltrated the meeting. Washington also ensured that the National Negro Press Bureau was ordered to halt or suppress any coverage of the new group's activities. Du Bois, conscious of Washington's virtual monopoly of the black press, moved quickly to establish *The Moon* (first published in Memphis in 1906) and *The Horizon* (published in Washington, D.C., 1907–1910) as unofficial organs of the Niagara Movement. Du Bois, with Henry H. Pace as the managing editor, edited the first issue of *The Moon*. Circulation numbered below 500. Few black middle-class intellectuals were prepared to back a magazine that heavily satirized Washington and his allies, and the enterprise collapsed by July 1906.

The second Niagara conference, held in August 1906 at Harpers Ferry, reported on the group's nationwide activities since its founding. Reform efforts included protests at the opening of the racist play *The Clansmen* and aiding the placing of a black on the New Chicago Charter Committee. In Massachusetts, members successfully defeated local legislation that would have introduced racial segregation in railroad cars. In Georgia, Du Bois and others participated in an Equal Rights Convention held in Macon in February 1906. Beyond agitation, the Niagara Movement achieved very little. At its Boston convention in 1907, Du Bois found gratification simply in its continued survival. Despite Washington's assaults on its activities, it had aided the Brownsville soldiers and won a segregation case in which the claimant was awarded one cent in damages. In March 1907, Niagara members helped create a formal committee to cooperate with the National Negro American Political League, an organization in which Trotter was to play a leading role. This event, however, signaled a weakening of Niagara's identity and raised Washington's hopes that the radicals who joined in 1905 could be merged into either the National Negro Business League or the Afro-American Council, where he exerted considerable influence.

The Niagara Movement failed to acquire a mass following among black

Americans. The organization's members could not function as chief ideological spokespersons for the race. Some members had worked closely with Washington prior to joining. For example, Minnesota attorney Frederick McGhee had been a supporter of the Tuskegee leader while serving on the Afro-American Council's legislative committee. Those members not of Du Bois' "Talented Tenth" in terms of educational background, such as high school graduates, were far more radical than the former J. Max Barber and the Reverend J. Milton Waldron and also of a more socialist persuasion. Niagara's instability was most evident in the amount raised in its first two years, $1,300. Many members were behind in payment of their dues, but most tragic of all, *The Horizon* consistently lost money, unable to attract adequate advertising revenue. By 1908, many local branches had ceased to hold regular meetings. Members reportedly drifted into other organizations. Tensions between Du Bois and Trotter had surfaced in the August 1907 conference held in Boston. Du Bois' inexperience as a political leader was a major factor in the decline of the Niagara Movement.

Yet Du Bois had been a pioneer in significantly expanding anti-Bookerite organized protests aimed at securing what he regarded as the necessary full emancipation of black Americans. Despite the Tuskegee Machine's harsh suppression of the Niagara Movement's last meeting in Oberlin (Ohio) in 1908 through effective collaboration with white newspapers, the radicals who had originally met in Fort Erie ultimately sent a strong message to the nation: Black Americans were prepared to jeopardize their lives in the aggressive pursuit of racial equality and constitutional liberty. The Niagara experiment not only institutionalized opposition to Washington's leadership but also served as the model for future militant black protest in the twentieth century. *See also*: National Association for the Advancement of Colored People (NAACP); Race Riots; Talented Tenth; Trotter, William Monroe; Villard, Oswald Garrison; Washington, Booker T.

FURTHER READING

Green, Dan S., and Edwin D. Driver, eds. *W.E.B. Du Bois on Sociology and the Black Community*. Chicago: University of Illinois Press, 1980.

Lewis, David Levering, ed. *W.E.B. Du Bois: A Reader*. New York: Henry Holt, 1995.

Marable, Manning. *W.E.B. Du Bois: Black Radical Democrat*. Boston: Twayne Publishers, 1986.

Meier, August. *Negro Thought in America, 1880–1915*. Ann Arbor: University of Michigan Press, 1973.

White, John. *Black Leadership in America from Booker T. Washington to Jesse Jackson*. London: Longman Publishers, 1990.

Nahfiza Ahmed

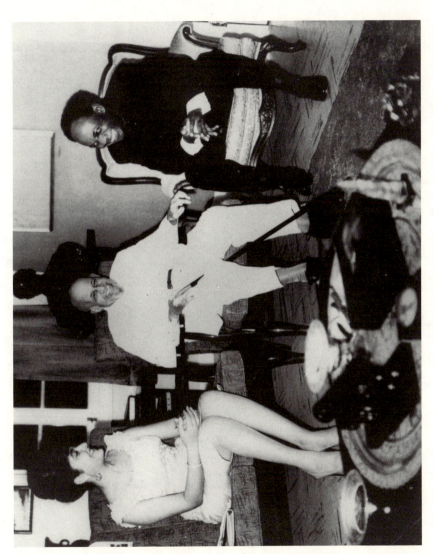

In Accra, Ghana, with Nkrumah and wife on W.E.B. Du Bois' ninety-fifth birthday, February 23, 1963. Courtesy of Special Collections and Archives, W.E.B. Du Bois Library, University of Massachusetts Amherst.

NKRUMAH, KWAME (1909–1972)

> Nkrumah was shabby, kindly, but earnest. . . . I did not then dream that Nkrumah had the stamina and patience for [the] task [of] becoming president.
>
> *The World and Africa*, 292.

These were the words that Du Bois used to describe the future president of the first independent African nation. Du Bois first met a young Kwame Nkrumah in 1945, at the Fifth Pan-African Congress in England, where Du Bois served as cochair. After the conference officially ended, a committee was established to devise practical plans that African nations could use in fighting colonialism. Du Bois was selected to preside over the committee, and Nkrumah served as secretary.

This committee served as the beginning of a mentor-mentee relationship and a close friendship that lasted until Du Bois' repatriation to Africa. Du Bois kept in contact with Nkrumah and wrote many articles describing Nkrumah's plight in the Gold Coast's (Ghana) struggle for independence. On the day of Ghana's independence in 1957, Du Bois personally telegraphed a letter of congratulations to Nkrumah and warned about the pitfalls of capitalism. He also advised Nkrumah to establish a Pan-African socialism that "will refuse to be *exploited* by people of other continents for their own benefit and not for the benefit of Africa" (*Freedom*, September 19, 1960).

Du Bois became a Ghanaian citizen and served as executive editor of the *Encyclopedia Africana* in Nkrumah's Ghana until his death in 1963. *See also*: Africa.

FURTHER READING

Assensoh, A. B. *African Political Leadership: Jomo Kenyatta, Kwame Nkrumah and Julius K. Nyerere*. Malabar, FL: Krieger Publishing Company, 1998.

Du Bois, W.E.B. *The World and Africa: An Inquiry into the Part Which Africa Has Played in World History*. New York: Viking Press, 1947.

Muata Kamdibe

O

ORIENTALISM

Du Bois' lifelong body of writings on Asia constitutes a strategic intervention in the tradition of Western scholarship known as Orientalism, one meant to challenge and undermine what Du Bois perceived to be its legacy of colonialism, imperialism, racism, and in the twentieth century, anticommunism.

Du Bois entered the formal tradition of Western Orientalism with his famous 1900 proclamation, "The problem of the twentieth century is the problem of the color line." The description of a national and global racial divide between blacks and whites, East and West—what Du Bois called more explicitly in 1915 "The World Problem of the Color Line"—was a direct challenge to nineteenth-century racist eugenics theorists like Count Arthur de Gobineau, cited by Edward Said in his classic 1978 work *Orientalism* as a pioneer of white supremacist thought (8, 99, 150). Gobineau's 1853 volume *Essai sur l'Inegalite des races Humaines* provided a segregated hierarchy and taxonomy of the "three basic races"—Aryan, Semitic, Negroid—to demonstrate that "[d]ifferent civilizations are in mutual repulsion" (Said, 274). Like other nineteenth-century Orientalists, Gobineau's Manichean worldview erected and preserved a mythic political, biological, and cultural "color line" between whites, Asians, and blacks. In his early work "The Star of Ethiopia: A Pageant of Negro History," Du Bois posited a countergenealogy, one central to contemporary Afrocentric debates, fancifully describing the ancient mingling of Asian and Egyptian cultures as a historical starting point of black liberation (*Pamphlets* 206). In the face of Orientalist theories of race, eliminating the "color line" after 1900 for Du Bois demanded recognition of patterns of miscegenation between the black and Asian worlds.

Du Bois' rival and nemesis among early twentieth-century Orientalists was Lothrop Stoddard, the primary American proponent of nineteenth-century Eu-

ropean racist ideologies. Stoddard's own formal career as an Orientalist began
with his 1922 book *The New World of Islam*, published the same year as his
polemic *The Rising Tide of Color*, where Gobineau is cited. There and elsewhere,
Stoddard uses Du Bois' "color line" trope ironically as a description of both
global combat between white supremacy and the colored world and of World
War I as a "disgenic" white civil war threatening to dilute white racial superiority. The battle between Stoddard and Du Bois over the color line and racist
ideology culminated in a public debate between them in March 1929 at the
Chicago Coliseum on the question "Shall the Negro Be Encouraged to Seek
Cultural Equality?"

Yet Du Bois' most complex and important answer to Stoddard's Orientalism
may be found in his novel published one year earlier, *Dark Princess*. The book's
romantic coupling of a black pullman porter and a beautiful Indian princess,
a coupling that produces a child who will be "Messenger and Messiah to all
the Darker Worlds" (311), was not only an attack on eugenics claims of "colored" inferiority but a utopian critique of Orientalist anti-Bolshevism after the
1917 Russian Revolution. In *The Revolt against Civilization* (1922) Stoddard had
imagined Lenin's Russia as both Asiatic terror and the potential igniter of
yellow peril throughout India, China, and Japan. In Du Bois' novel, representatives from Japan, China, India, Egypt, and black America, fueled by Soviet
proletarianism and support for minority nationalisms, conspire to assault white
political world control by destabilizing the biological, political, economic, and
geographic color line.

The novel is thus a pivotal test in Du Bois' lifelong attempts to create and
sustain a counterdiscourse, what might be called an "Afro-Orientalism," that
would deconstruct the binary logic of Orientalist East-West discourse as a tool
of white supremacy while increasingly positioning "Asia" at the center of world
efforts at national self-determination and liberation. This intellectual task
moved Du Bois past thinking about race in black/white terms and toward the
comprehension of what he called in *Dark Princess* a "color line within a color
line" (22), that is, an appreciation of international caste and caste relationships.
Du Bois demonstrated the symbiotic nature of this shift as early as 1933 when
he simultaneously published the essay "Color Caste in the United States" (*The
Crisis*, March 1933) and voiced support for a tenuous alliance of Japan and
Ethiopia. Du Bois' internationalist analysis also reflected the impulse developed
through his debates with Stoddard to interpret "civilization" and culture as the
manifestation of racial types—hence Du Bois' upside-down interpretation of the
Western Renaissance as "that new light with which Asia and Africa illumined
the Dark Ages of Europe" (*World* 18). Du Bois' Afro-Orientalism even moved
him to speculate that ancient Asia preempted and superseded European claims
to culture. "China is eternal," he wrote in his 1932 newspaper column "As the
Crow Flies." "She was civilized when Englishmen wore tails. She cannot be
killed. She cannot be enslaved. She cannot be conquered. Before civilization
was, China is" (Aptheker 330). Such rhetoric, verging on traditional Oriental-

ism's enthusiasm for "vitalism" in racial cultures, occasionally led Du Bois into aberrant political judgments, as in his defense of early Japanese interventions in China as "exceptional as a form of colonialism devoid of racism" (Aptheker 396).

Yet Du Bois also adamantly interpreted World War II, postwar Western aggression in the Cold War, and American and European hostility toward African and Asian decolonization as a deliberate refitting of earlier Orientalism's ideological themes, white supremacy and anti-Bolshevism. In response, Du Bois viewed the defeat of French and Dutch colonial rule, Indian liberation in 1947, the Chinese Communist Revolution of 1949, and the Bandung Conference of Afro-Asia States in 1955 as events in a geographical and ideological remapping, returning China and Africa and Asian socialist and nationalist movements to the center of the geopolitical world. Indeed, Du Bois' characterization of the immediate postwar era as "a morning when the sunlight is streaming from the East" finds echo in Mao Zedong's more famous revolutionary declaration that "the east wind shall prevail over the west wind" ("Crow" 80). This geographical inversion of the East/West, Communist/anti-Communist axis underscored Du Bois' attempts to provide himself and self-liberating African and Asian nations and peoples a "third way" beyond bipolar racism and anticommunism. Du Bois' 1959 visit to China after renewal of his passport and his glowing accounts of what was a period of strife in China's revolution may be counted as a climactic point in his quest for a revolutionary Afro-Orientalism. That Du Bois' embrace of Maoism and Communist Party membership coincided with his exile to Ghana reflected the logical last step in a geographical and intellectual migration in which the "East" came home to rest beyond the sphere of Occidental domination and control.

Fully understanding Du Bois' challenge to traditional Orientalist thought and ideology recasts not only his own career but the genealogy of African American intellectuals in the twentieth century. Langston Hughes, Paul Robeson, Richard Wright, Robert Williams, the Black Panther Party, and James Boggs all wrote sympathetically about Asia and communism after Du Bois' example. Like Du Bois, each of these writers implicitly or explicitly rejected traditional Orientalism's bipolar political and racial thinking. Robeson's study of African languages and Chinese and his support for China's liberation, for example, moved him to write that "the cultures of the East and of Africa are so close that they certainly have common heritage" (*World* 15). Similarly, Du Bois' leadership in the study and appreciation of early twentieth-century Asian socialism and national liberation movements inspired a generation of African and Afro-Caribbean friends and colleagues toward an Afro-Orientalist perspective, including George Padmore, Eric Williams, Kwame Nkrumah, C.L.R. James, Leopold Senghor, and Aime Cesaire.

Like their American counterparts, these intellectuals predicted and constructed the postwar affiliations not only of black and Asian intellectuals but of Asian and African decolonizing countries. Their anticolonial efforts in the

1940s, 1950s, and 1960s were premised on formal "Afro-Asian" solidarity, especially between China and decolonizing African countries, that repudiated, directly and indirectly, Eurocentric domination, white supremacist ideology, anti-Bolshevism, in short, the entire legacy of Orientalist thought. Finally, Du Bois' lifelong attempts to elucidate and demonstrate the historical intersection of black culture with world culture—"The Greeks, inspired by Asia, turned toward Africa for learning, and the Romans in turn learned of Greece and Egypt," he wrote in *The World and Africa* in 1947 (105)—can help us understand how contemporary debates about Afrocentrism, up to and including Martin Bernal's *Black Athena: The Afro-Asiatic Roots of Greek Civilization*, continue an Afro-Orientalist tradition spawned by, though rarely credited to, W.E.B. Du Bois. *See also*: Africa; Bandung Conference; China; Cold War; *Dark Princess*; Japan; Robeson, Paul.

FURTHER READING

Aptheker, Herbert. *Annotated Bibliography of the Published Writings of W.E.B. Du Bois*. Millwood, NY: Kraus-Thomson, 1973.

Biddiss, Michael D. *Father of Racist Ideology: The Social and Political Thought of Count Gobineau*. New York: Weybright and Talley, 1970.

Du Bois, W.E.B. "As the Crow Flies." *The Crisis* 34 (1932): 80.

——. *Dark Princess: A Romance*. New York: Harcourt, Brace and Co., 1928. Jackson: University Press of Mississippi, 1995.

——. *Pamphlets and Leaflets*. Ed. Herbert Aptheker. White Plains, NY: Kraus-Thomson Organization, 1986.

——. *The World and Africa: An Inquiry into the Part Which Africa Has Played in World History*. New York: Viking Press, 1947.

Said, Edward. *Orientalism*. New York: Vintage Books, 1978.

Stoddard, Lothrop. *The New World of Islam*. New York: Charles Scribner's Sons, 1922.

——. *The Revolt against Civilization: The Menace of the Under Man*. New York: Charles Scribner's Sons, 1922.

——. *The Rising Tide of Color against White World-Supremacy*. New York: Charles Scribner's Sons, 1922.

Bill Mullen

OVINGTON, MARY WHITE (1865–1951)

Ovington was born in Brooklyn, New York, on April 11, 1865, three days before Abraham Lincoln's assassination. Her abolitionist parents and Unitarian upbringing shaped her beliefs in social reform and women's rights. Attending the Harvard Annex (later Radcliffe College, 1888–1891) also motivated her to devote herself to social reforms.

A speech by Booker T. Washington (1903) awakened her to the continuing plight of African Americans, and she made the achievement of racial equality her life's work. In 1904 she began a study of the housing and employment problems of New York's black population that resulted in *Half a Man: The*

Status of the Negro in New York (1911) and to close associations with prominent African Americans, particularly Du Bois.

Ovington was among the European Americans who helped found the National Association for the Advancement of Colored People (NAACP) in 1909. She held a variety of positions within the organization for four years, including chairperson (1919–1932). Besides helping organize the Association and establish its policies during these formative years, she played an invaluable role in mediating between often conflicting personalities in the movement. Although she had been a Socialist since 1905, and spoke against war and colonialism and for women's rights, she was essentially a moderate whose main goal was racial integration. She wrote a syndicated newspaper column in the 1920s and several books dealing with issues of race.

Du Bois frequently reviewed her books in *The Crisis*. He recommended *Hazel* "to colored children almost as heartily as to white" (*The Crisis*, January 1914). Later he referred to her *Portraits in Color* (*The Crisis*, March 1927) as "an honest and moving piece of work" (*The Crisis*, 1927). Enthusiastically recommending *Zeke* (1931), Du Bois wrote that it is a "clean, interesting, fine piece of work that somewhat older Black children will find especially delightful" (*The Crisis*, December 1931).

Not only did she write fiction for children; her autobiography, *The Walls Came Tumbling Down* (1947), includes a history of the NAACP. Ovington's other writings also include a collection of short biographies of black leaders. She died on July 15, 1951, in Newton Highlands, Massachusetts. *See also*: National Association for the Advancement of Colored People (NAACP); Washington, Booker T.; Women's Rights.

FURTHER READING

Luker, Ralph E. *Black and White Sat Down Together: The Reminiscences of an NAACP Founder.* New York: Feminist Press, 1996.

Malaika Horne

P

PAN-AFRICANISM

W.E.B. Du Bois is often seen as the father of Pan-Africanism. This honor is bestowed upon him because of his central role in organizing five Pan-African Congresses and sustaining the movement for over a quarter century, from 1919 to 1945. However, Pan-African thinking and initiatives began soon after the start of the Atlantic slave trade. Du Bois' efforts to institutionalize and broaden the reach of the movement were a further manifestation of the vision and action of men like Edward Blyden, Martin Delaney, Alexander Crummell, Henry Sylvester Williams, and Bishop Henry Turner.

Through his involvement in the movement, Du Bois served many roles: committee chair, secretary, coordinator, and international president. At the 1900 Pan-African Conference, organized by Williams, Du Bois was the chair for the "Address to the Nations of the World" Committee. He was also elected as the U.S. vice president to the Pan-African Association, which was founded at this meeting. However, he never used this position to further the cause of the organization within the United States, nor did he mention his position in the organization in his writings. For Du Bois, "This meeting had no deep roots in Africa" (Du Bois, *World and Africa* 8). Yet Williams' 1900 conference had about the same degree of affiliation with Africa as Du Bois' 1919 Congress. So it is not clear why Du Bois said this. He later said that the Pan-Africanist movement died until the 1919 Congress in Paris. This is almost true, although Williams and Bishop Walters did attempt to institutionalize the movement by establishing headquarters for the Pan-African Association in London and the West Indies and by publishing the short-lived journal *The Pan African*.

Du Bois saw himself as a scientist. In part, his involvement in Pan-Africanism developed out of his desire to study scientifically and document the experiences of Africans in North America. In fact, Du Bois' attendance at

Pan-African Congress, Belgium, 1921. Courtesy of Special Collections and Archives, W.E.B. Du Bois Library, University of Massachusetts Amherst.

the 1900 Pan-African Conference in London does not appear to be a result of his interest in Pan-Africanism as a movement at this time in his life. Rather, he was in Paris to present a sociological paper on the "American Negro" at the Paris Exposition, for which he won a gold medal. DeMarco argues that "Du Bois' emphasis on Pan Africanism was quite weak in 1900" (DeMarco 35).

DeMarco was correct. Du Bois was a young man. He was still developing his ideas as evidenced in *The Conservation of Races* (1897). Here Du Bois articulates his earliest thoughts on Pan-Africanism. He writes that "Negro people ... must soon come to realize that if they are to take their just place in the van [*sic*] of Pan-Negroism, then their destiny is *not* absorption by the white Americans" (Du Bois, *Conservation* 79). He made this demand for self-determination among Africans often in the years to come.

Du Bois attended Sylvester Williams' Pan-African Conference in London in 1900. The call for this conference was issued by the African Association and Williams, a lawyer from Trinidad. Du Bois was chosen to chair the "Address to the Nations of the World" Committee. In this capacity, he drafted the "Address" in which he made his now-famous statement: "The problem of the twentieth century is the problem of the color line" (Du Bois, *Souls*, 125).

Du Bois' involvement in the Pan-Africanist movement was not seen again until 1918, when he began to plan for the 1919 Pan-African Congress. The purpose for calling this and subsequent Congresses was to assess the collective grievances, desires, and aspirations of African people around the world (Du Bois, *Souls* 274), to initially help modernize Africa, to persuade European powers to treat their African "subjects" humanely, and to speak about the way forward for Africans and their interactions with other populations, especially Europeans.

From 1919 forward, Du Bois' name became synonymous with Pan-Africanism. Blaise Diagne, the Senegalese deputy to France, helped Du Bois gain permission to hold the Congress in Paris. No other country had been willing to grant Du Bois permission to conduct an international conference, and the United States tried to keep it from happening in France. Although granted permission to hold the meeting in France, Du Bois was told not to advertise it, in part because France was still under martial law. Even with this restriction, fifty-seven delegates representing fifteen different countries attended the Congress.

The delegates did not undertake proactive initiatives that would put the fate of African people in the hands of Africans. The resolutions of the 1919 Congress were not of any immediate threat to Europeans. They asked the colonial authorities to take a paternalistic position toward Africa and her people. These types of requests were in line with European colonial ambitions. For example, the Congress recommended that the League of Nations take control of the German colonies as protectorates and "demanded" that the land and natural resources be held in trust for Africans until they were ready for self-government. These types of demands were quite amenable to some Europeans. South African Prime Minister Jan Smuts, a key figure in the formation of the United Nations, wanted the former German Southwest Africa as mandate territory not for the benefit of the African inhabitants but for the source of cheap unskilled labor for South African mines, farms, and industrial businesses (Esedebe 129). Although the type of protection Africans requested from the mandate system was granted, the outcome was not desirable. In the end, the resolution empowered the League of Nations for Africans, instead of directly putting the power in the hands of the African masses.

The Second Pan-African Congress organized by Du Bois and colleagues was held in London, Brussels, and Paris in August and September of 1921. Du Bois states that the 1919 Congress provided the foundation for this meeting. Using that base, the planning for the Second Congress was much more thought out and systematic. Letters of announcement and invitation were sent to Africans in many parts of the world and to European governments that had colonies in Africa. The planning and announcements were important steps in strengthening the foundation of the Pan-African movement. This type of outreach was not possible for the 1919 Congress because of the political climate toward Africans by Europeans in Africa, the Americas, and Europe.

The Second Congress was Du Bois' attempt to assemble what he deemed to be a more authentic Pan-African Congress and movement. Although the meeting attracted 113 delegates, there were two problems as perceived by Du Bois. The first was the colonial governments' escalation of their exploitative initiatives in the colonies to compensate for their losses during World War I. The other problem encountered by Du Bois at this time was the rapid development of another Pan-African movement, which was spearheaded by Marcus Garvey. Du Bois often gave backhanded compliments to Garvey (*The Crisis*, January 1921), although it is clear that Du Bois had respect for Garvey's objectives and drive. The colonial powers were suspicious of a gathering of Africans, for they feared turmoil in the colonies where they were raising most of their capital. The colonial authorities were particularly worried about the Garvey movement and could not distinguish between the two Pan-African movements, which was Du Bois' fear.

There were two more Congresses in 1923 and 1927—the Third and Fourth, respectively—and an attempt at another in 1929, but it did not occur. After the 1927 Congress, a Fifth Congress did not occur until 1945. The 1923 conference was held in London and Lisbon, and the 1927 meeting was in New York. The resolutions from these two Congresses were slightly different from those from the previous Congresses. Whereas the First (1919) and the Second (1921) Congresses had primarily solicited League of Nations intervention on behalf of Africans on the continent, the later two Congresses tried to make a broader appeal for Africans all over the globe. So instead of demanding or asking for a form of self-government, as had been done earlier, a demand was made for a voice in the government for Africans. Although broader in its appeal, this demand was not as enabling as had been the call for self-government in the previous Congresses. Another resolution concerned the education of all children, and the development of Africa for Africans.

Du Bois says that the movement died between the Fourth and Fifth Congresses. However, several organizations kept the Pan-African movement alive: West African Students Union, League of Coloured Peoples, International African Friends of Abyssinia, and later the International African Service Bureau and the Pan African Federation (PAF). The PAF was key in the formation of the Fifth Pan-African Congress.

The Fifth Pan-African Congress was held in Manchester, England, in October 1945. The International Trade Union Conference had been held in London in February and was the main inspiration for the October meeting. Du Bois was elected as the international president of this Congress. There was a denunciation of various oppressive and paternalistic initiatives of the League of Nations and colonial governments in the Congress' resolutions. Unlike the previous Pan-African meetings, which were composed of scholars, middle-class Africans, and representatives from European governments, the Fifth Congress was attended by a diverse group of Africans. Some individuals at the previous meetings were present, but there also were union organizers, farmers, students, and labor groups. Many of those attending were from Africa. The most important contribution to the Pan-African movement from this Congress was the action-oriented stance that the delegates took in their resolutions, which set an important tone and increased awareness in the various African movements struggling for independence.

Du Bois' final contribution to the Pan-African movement was to start the process of coordinating and compiling the *Encyclopedia Africana*. "The encyclopedia hopes to eliminate the artificial boundaries created on this continent by colonial masters" (Du Bois, *World and Africa* 323). *See also*: Africa; Blyden, Edward Wilmot; Colonialism; France; Garvey, Marcus; Nkrumah, Kwame.

FURTHER READING

"The Conservation of Races." American Negro Academy Occasional Papers no. 2 (1897).

DeMarco, Joseph P. *The Social Thought of W.E.B. Du Bois*. London: University Press of America, 1983.

Du Bois, W.E.B. "Marcus Garvey." *The Crisis* 21 (1921): 112–115.

——. *The Souls of Black Folk*. Chicago: A. C. McClurg, 1903.

——. *The World and Africa: An Inquiry into the Part Which Africa Has Played in World History*. 1974. New York: International Publishers, 1985.

Esedebe, P. Olisanwuche. *Pan-Africanism: The Idea and Movement, 1917–1963*. Washington, DC: Howard University Press, 1970.

Foner, Phillip, ed. *W.E.B. Du Bois Speaks: Speeches and Addresses, 1890–1919*. New York: Pathfinder Press, 1970.

Hargreaves, John D. *Decolonization in Africa*. 2nd ed. London and New York: Longman, 1996.

Mathurin, Owen Charles. *Henry Sylvester Williams and the Origins of the Pan-African Movement, 1869–1911.* Westport, CT: Greenwood, 1976.

Nkrumah, Kwame. *Africa Must Unite.* London: Panaf Books, 1963.

Pobi-Asamani, Kwadwo O. *W.E.B. Du Bois: His Contribution to Pan Africanism.* San Bernadino, CA: Borgo Press, 1994.

Akil K. Khalfani

PEACE MOVEMENT

As early as his college days in the 1880s, when he vowed never to take up arms or serve in a military conflict, W.E.B. Du Bois expressed a consuming interest in the questions and problems of peace. Du Bois' literary stance on the subject begins to take shape in 1913 in articles written for *The Crisis.* These pieces, influenced by the encroaching and unprecedented dangers of war on a global scale, allude to the hypocrisy of so-called Christian nations that seek martial domination over other, less powerful countries. For Du Bois, such colonialism—and the racism that inevitably accompanies it—presents the most critical threat to peace and democracy in the twentieth century. As the dominant countries of Europe arm themselves to do battle with each other over their colonial holdings, it is the colonized people of Africa, Asia, and the South Seas, usually people of color, who suffer most.

As Du Bois devoted more attention during the 1920s and early 1930s to problems of race and labor both at home and abroad, he urged readers of *The Crisis* to look to the Soviet Union for alternatives to the racist policies of colonial imperialism. Du Bois also criticized the nature of the peace movement in the United States at the time. He saw it as an enclave for aristocracy rather than an active agent for democracy. And his editorials exhort U.S. foreign policy makers to aid in the process of decolonization rather than facilitate the interests of industrial capitalism.

Du Bois' work for peace became more pronounced in the aftermath of World War II. In 1945, he published *Color and Democracy: Colonies and Peace,* a work inspired by the hope that the war's end would bring a halt to racism and colonial exploitation. Under the book's guiding problematic—the present need to establish a permanent and inclusive peace—Du Bois combines a discussion of racial inequality with analyses of issues ranging from the influence of capitalist investments in former colonies to the role of the Soviet Union in international relations to the practicality of the government at the global level. Du Bois' goal in bringing these issues together is to add the voices of the colonized to a postwar peace planning process that was dominated by former colonizers.

Du Bois continued to press the importance of decolonization and peace in *The World and Africa* (1947). As it traces changing perceptions of Africa throughout history, the text employs a Marxist philosophical framework to show how colonizers have traditionally treated the continent and to emphasize that African peoples must be recognized as important agents in global development.

The publication of *The World and Africa* initiated a period of frenetic peace activism for Du Bois. In March 1949, he spoke at the Cultural and Scientific Conference for World Peace in New York. The meeting, which brought together an international collection of cultural leaders, including several from the Soviet Union, sparked criticism and protests; sessions were picketed, and some controversial figures, including Picasso, were denied visas to attend. One month later, Du Bois traveled to Paris to attend the World Peace Congress and aid in the founding of the World Council of Peace. His speech warned that a failure to eliminate colonialism could allow a return to human slavery and a third world war. In August of the same year, Du Bois was one of the twenty-five Americans invited to a Soviet Peace Conference in Moscow. Du Bois continued to make appearances and speeches at numerous conferences and meetings from 1949 through 1951—when his international activism and Communist sympathies brought him into direct conflict with Cold War intolerance and McCarthyite persecution at home.

Du Bois' *In Battle for Peace* (1952) provides an overview of his activities in the late 1940s and early 1950s: his struggle against colonialism; his association with the Peace Information Center (PIC); his campaign for a U.S. Senate seat from New York as a candidate for the American Labor Party (a local affiliate of the Progressive Party); and his indictment and trial for alleged violations of the Foreign Registration Act.

The conflict over the Peace Information Center, which existed from April 3 to October 12 of 1950, exemplifies many of the critical cultural tensions that influenced the struggle for peace after World War II. Conceived and constructed during a period of intense Red-baiting and anti-Communist sentiment, the PIC was designed to provide U.S. citizens with information on the peace and war activities of other countries. The PIC also campaigned in support of the Stockholm Appeal, an international petition to ban atomic weapons. As the situation in Korea moved closer to all-out war, the issues addressed by the Stockholm Appeal took on greater urgency, and the Center quickly became a target for conservatives who viewed its pro-peace agenda as pro-communist.

Many opponents suspected the Center of acting as an agent for the Soviet Union. Secretary of State Dean Acheson sharply criticized its activities, and the Department of Justice ordered PIC officers to register as agents of a foreign principle or risk indictment. Although the Center was dissolved in October of 1950, Du Bois and the other officers were indicted on February 9, 1951. The outcry from the international community as well as various African American groups (especially labor) was swift and harshly critical. Although significant pressure was brought to bear on the government, the Justice Department refused to drop the charges. Du Bois continued to meet with religious, political, and labor leaders across the country, and when the prosecution failed to prove its case, his acquittal became a rallying point for peace activists—one of few such victories during the Cold War.

Du Bois remained active in the peace movement throughout his life. He was named honorary chair of the American Peace Crusade in 1951, and the World Council of Peace honored his contributions by presenting him with the International Peace Prize in 1952. *See also*: Cold War; Colonialism; Color and Democracy; Cultural and Scientific Conference for World Peace; McCarthyism; Stockholm Peace Appeal.

FURTHER READING

In Battle for Peace: The Story of My 83rd Birthday. New York: Masses and Mainstream, 1952.

Paul Ryan Schneider

THE PHILADELPHIA NEGRO

In the summer of 1896, Du Bois was offered a one-year appointment as an "assistant instructor" of sociology to conduct a comprehensive study of the African American community of the Seventh Ward in Philadelphia. Politically motivated, the study of the local "social problem" was to be used as ammunition against the corrupt Republican city administrators who had formed an alliance with the African American community. Despite obvious snubs by the university—a rank inconsistent with his credentials, a minuscule salary of $900, no listing in the university catalog, no office space, and no teaching duties other than touring "a pack of idiots through the Negro slums" (Marable 251)— Du Bois enthusiastically accepted the assignment that would define his life's work.

Soon after Du Bois and his wife Nina settled in the Seventh Ward, he became submerged in his research. He conducted an extensive review of historical sources on the city covering two centuries to place the African American community within the proper economic, political, social, and cultural context. Alone, Du Bois formulated several questionnaires and spent approximately three months and 835 hours interviewing 5,000 people. As a result, he collected data on the entire ward except for a dozen families who refused to participate (Lewis 190). His exhaustive research covered topics such as family histories, community institutions, education, crime, politics, interracial sex and marriage, employment experience (particularly the consequences of the color bar), and intraracial class distinctions. His investigation often referred to the various ramifications of institutional racism and the legacy of slavery. Finally, Du Bois suggested social reforms that called upon both blacks and whites to take responsibility for eliminating the social ills revealed in the study. Advancing the philosophy of self-help and cooperative economics, Du Bois viewed the African American elite as responsible to the masses; they should provide leadership, social services, and employment. Conversely, European Americans needed to change their racist behavior and truly uphold the doctrine of equal opportunity.

In a sense, Du Bois indirectly addressed his treatment by the university. Sixty years later, he was still seething.

It would have been a fine thing if after this difficult, successful piece of work the University of Pennsylvania had at least offered me a temporary instructorship in the college or the Wharton School. The thing that galled was that such an idea never even occurred to this institution. . . . But I did not mention this rebuff. I did not let myself think of it. But then, as now, I know an insult when I see it. (Du Bois 199)

Recognized for its thoroughness yet largely ignored for its social commentary at the time of its publication, *The Philadelphia Negro* stands as a classic in both (urban) sociology and African American studies because it was the first scientific study of the Negro and the first scientific sociological study in the United States (Wilson x).

FURTHER READING

Du Bois, W.E.B. *The Autobiography of W.E.B. Du Bois*. New York: International Publishers, 1968.

Lewis, David Levering. *W.E.B. Du Bois. Biography of a Race, 1868–1919*. New York: Henry Holt, 1993.

Marable, Manning. *W.E.B. Du Bois: Black Radical Democrat*. Boston: Twayne Publishers, 1986.

Rudwick, Elliott. *W.E.B. Du Bois: Propagandist of the Negro Protest*. 2nd ed. Philadelphia: University of Pennsylvania Press, 1968.

Wilson, Walter, ed. *The Selected Writings of W.E.B. Du Bois*. New York: New American Library, 1970.

Shawn R. Donaldson

PHYLON

As chair of the Sociology Department of Atlanta University, Du Bois approached university president John Hope with the idea of publishing a social science journal that would include "literary and scientific articles of permanent value" in 1935. Hope's death left the leadership of Atlanta University to Rufus E. Clement, who was not enthusiastic about Du Bois' proposal. In May 1937, Du Bois gained support from Charles Johnson at Fisk University (Tennessee) to start a quarterly journal that would rival Carter Woodson's *Journal of Negro History* and Charles Thompson's *Journal of Negro Education*. With a thousand dollars and the understanding that each university would solicit outside funds, *Phylon, A Quarterly Review of Race and Culture* became a reality. Johnson eventually withdrew from the project, and the inaugural issue was published in 1940 under Du Bois' leadership. In his first editorial, Du Bois argued that the journal would "proceed from the point of view and the experience of black folk where we live and work to the wider world." Throughout his tenure as *Phylon*'s editor, Du Bois remained committed to publishing original scholarship on a wide range of issues concerning the treatment, life, and culture of African Americans. But it was his continued criticism of Atlanta University's leadership in the pages of *Phylon* that led to the termination of his teaching contract and his return to the National Association for the Advancement of Colored People

(NAACP). *Phylon* is still published by Atlanta University and remains dedicated to Du Bois' original purpose. *See also*: Atlanta University; Hope, John; *Journal of Negro Education.*

FURTHER READING

Du Bois, W.E.B. *The Autobiography of W.E.B. Du Bois: A Soliloquy on Viewing My Life from the Last Decade of Its First Century.* New York: International Publishers, 1968.
Marable, Manning. *W.E.B. Du Bois: Black Radical Democrat.* Boston: Twayne Publishers, 1986.

Catherine M. Lewis

POETRY

Because of his historical, sociological, and political writings, the imaginative writings of Du Bois are often neglected. He published novels (*Dark Princess*, 1928; *Mansart Builds a School*, 1959; *The Quest of the Silver Fleece*, 1911), plays, short stories, and poetry. Arnold Rampersad ("Literature") appraises Du Bois' literary output as consisting of a series of firsts.

The theme of Africa as a proper and necessary subject of black celebration was introduced into black verse . . . in his "Day in Africa." He was the first to celebrate the beauty of human blackness in his "Song of the Smoke." "The Burden of Black Women" is the first published poem to dwell on hatred as the consequence of the white destruction of crucial institutions. . . . John Jones in 1903 and Matthew Towns in 1928 had struck blows against white Americans long before Bigger rebelled. . . . *The Quest of the Silver Fleece* ended the poisonous reign of near-white heroines. . . . *Dark Princess* is the first work of art . . . to identify and promulgate the doctrine of the third world. (53)

Du Bois set down his conception for his imaginative writing in "Criteria of Negro Art."

In "Criteria of Negro Art" (*The Crisis*, October 1926) Du Bois explained that for him art is beauty, goodness, truth, and propaganda. "I stand in utter shamelessness and say that whatever art I have for writing has been used always for propaganda. . . . I do not care a damn for any art that is not used for propaganda." He resolutely asserted, "We want everything that is said about us to tell the best and highest and noblest in us. We insist that our Art and Propaganda be one." Therefore, his approach to literature was, according to Herbert Aptheker, "partisan and effective" (Aptheker x). With this rationale, art must not only embrace beauty, truth, and goodness but must also be a message against any form of oppression. However, Eric Sundquist insists that this expression "all art is propaganda" reveals Du Bois' "deeply held belief in the ethical and moral responsibility of art and literature" (304).

Du Bois believed that poetry has an added dimension: Poetry is "wisdom clothed in beauty: beauty in form, sound, and sheer fitness" (*Pittsburgh Courier*, October 23, 1937). Aptheker adds, "Du Bois's poetry welled up from his sense of outrage at oppression and injustice, or from some particular event that evoked special horror or elation" (Aptheker xi). A distinctive poetic theme was his love and admiration for blacks. Aptheker contends that "the ideas of 'Black is Beautiful' and 'Black power' " came from "The Song of the Smoke" (Aptheker xi), which celebrates the positive attributes and images of blackness. In the poem Du Bois rages against white racist crimes and casts himself as a black mythic hero crisscrossing the country, righting wrongs.

Beginning with "On the Death of the First Born" (*The Souls of Black Folk*), an essay commemorating the death of his son Burghardt, the subject of death seemed to hold a special attraction for him. The interest continued with poetic eulogies of friends and others. "Joseph Pulitzer" is a tribute to "the blind editor of the *New York World* ... who died October 29, 1911. ... His paper always treated black folk fairly in marked contrast to most New York dailies" (*The Crisis*, 1911).

Sometimes his poetry parodied aspects of American culture or history. In the introduction to "My country 'Tis of Thee," Du Bois gives alternatives to singing or rising when the song is played. His option was to write lyrics that reflected African American realities. He spoofed many traditions in other poems, all with the same sardonic bite.

Frequently Du Bois confirmed his political leanings and expressed his outrage at injustice, as in "The Rosenbergs." Julius and Ethel Rosenberg were the only American couple executed for espionage. Du Bois saw their electrocution as another in a long line of racial atrocities. He also published poems that expressed an international political philosophy: "A Day in Africa," "The United Nations," "I Sing to China," and "Ghana Calls."

Reacting strongly to gender oppression, Du Bois contributed much toward the liberation of black women. He favored giving women the vote, supported their reproductive freedom, and criticized men for encouraging women's economic dependence. Further, because he respected black women and abhorred their negative images, he denounced their sexual abuse and identified with their fight to end discrimination in the predominantly white women's suffrage movement. Thus, in "The Burden of Black Women," he attacks the white-created stereotypes that black women endure. Du Bois continued writing in support of black women in the essay "The Damnation of Women," in *Darkwater: Voices from Within the Veil* (1920).

Possibly his most intense poetic themes come from African American history, and the most powerful example is "A Litany of Atlanta." The poem was the result of the September 22, 1906, Atlanta riot that occurred after an election in which black disfranchisement was the dominant issue. Fallacious newspaper reporting of four assaults on white women by black men instigated the riot. Whites rampaged for five hours, committing acts of inexpressible barbarity—using a black child for target practice, crucifying several blacks on telephone poles. Informed of the pogrom, Du Bois, who was out of town at the time, rushed home to his wife and daughter. During the trip, he began composing "A Litany of Atlanta." Rampersad points out in *The Art and Imagination of*

W.E.B. Du Bois that "the most telling characteristic of Du Bois' poetry is that even his greatest ragings repeatedly resolve themselves into the language and form of religion. God, Christ, Heaven and Hell are omnipresent in his verse . . . repeatedly translated into questions of divine judgment and intervention" (105). In "A Litany of Atlanta" Du Bois uses biblical oratory to express African American hopelessness and rage. He beseeches God to rescue his suffering disciples. He casts aside one of Christianity's basic doctrines—turn the other cheek—and encourages blacks to retaliate against white inhumanity. Also in "Litany," the poet strikes out at Booker T. Washington and his associates, who advocated subservience, compromise, and the postponement of constitutional rights and protection.

Du Bois matched African American spiritual practices with historical events or personal beliefs as a basis for much of his poetry. He used religious tradition in other poems: "A Hymn to the People," "The Prayers of the Bantu," "The Christ of the Andes," and "The Prayers of God."

Du Bois' poetry reflected his myriad interests in conditions that affected African Americans. Using themes of history, religion, and blackness, he created a body of poetry that should not be allowed to languish in obscurity or be a footnote to his other writings. *See also*: Art and Literature.

FURTHER READING

Aptheker, Herbert, ed. *Creative Writings by W.E.B. Du Bois*. White Plains, NY: Kraus-Thomson Organization, Ltd., 1985.

Capeci, Dominic J. "Reckoning with Violence: W.E.B. Du Bois and the 1906 Atlanta Race Riot." *Journal of Southern History* 62 (1996): 727–766.

"Criteria of Negro Art" *The Crisis* (October 1926).

Rampersad, Arnold. *The Art and Imagination of W.E.B. Du Bois*. Cambridge: Harvard University Press, 1976.

——. "W.E.B. Du Bois as a Man of Literature." *American Literature* 51 (1979): 50–68.

Sundquist, Eric J. *The Oxford W.E.B. Du Bois Reader*. New York: Oxford University Press, 1996.

Mary Young

PROGRESSIVE PARTY

This third party, not to be confused with the party of the same name that challenged Harry Truman in 1948, was formed in 1912 by progressive Republicans dissatisfied with President William Taft. Shortly after Taft succeeded Theodore Roosevelt in the White House in 1909, western Republicans, led by Wisconsin's Senator Robert La Follette, joined with southern Democrats in denouncing the protective tariff and other business-friendly measures of eastern Republicans. With control of the party apparatus still safely in hand, however, Taft secured renomination in 1912, despite a disastrous showing in the primaries. Insurgent Republicans, meeting in a rump convention in Chicago, nominated Roosevelt, who championed a platform calling for powerful governmental action to regulate business and enact a wide range of social reforms. His campaign at the head of the "Bull Moose" party, as it became known, attracted a wide array of middle- and upper-class reformers but split the Republican Party, as Roosevelt ran second to the Democrat Woodrow Wilson, while Taft ran a distant third, carrying only Utah and Vermont.

The Progressive Party ran "lily-white" tickets in the southern states, as Republicans continued their search for a successful southern strategy. For Du Bois and other black intellectuals such as William Monroe Trotter, then, the time seemed ripe for African Americans to turn away from the party of Lincoln, which appeared increasingly unsympathetic to their interests. Du Bois threw his support to the seemingly benign Wilson, a decision not rewarded when Wilson showed little sympathy for black political aspirations. The Progressive Party fared indifferently in the 1914 elections and in 1916 endorsed Republican Charles Evans Hughes after Roosevelt refused the Progressive nomination. Fading after its 1916 convention, the Progressive Party was never successful in winning votes for candidates other than the charismatic Roosevelt but did manage to see many of its 1912 platform planks become law. See also: La Follette, Robert; Roosevelt, Theodore; Trotter, William Monroe.

FURTHER READING

Cooper, John Milton. *Pivotal Decades: The United States, 1900–1920.* New York: Norton, 1990.

Gable, John Allen. *The Bull Moose Years: Theodore Roosevelt and the Republican Party.* Port Washington, NY: Kennikat Press, 1978.

Harbaugh, William Henry. *Power and Responsibility: The Life and Times of Theodore Roosevelt.* New York: Farrar, Straus and Cudahy, 1961.

Mowry, George E. *Theodore and the Progressive Movement.* Madison: University of Wisconsin Press, 1947.

Trent Watts

PROTAGONISTIC AND ANTAGONISTIC VIEWS

One of Du Bois' greatest strengths as an African American spokesperson was to articulate the "double consciousness" or dual cultural identity that African Americans experienced. Du Bois recognized the twoness of African American identity as both an American and a black experience. While he believed in integration, he also advocated racial solidarity and self-help and felt a strong sense of community with black people all over the world. Du Bois also challenged the beliefs of many black activists and organizations, including those with which he had an affiliation. He was both revered and hated by many of his black contemporaries.

One of Du Bois' first publicly controversial stances was against Booker T. Washington's agenda. Washington's plan encouraged black people to remain in the South and receive a useful education and job, to attain enough money to buy a piece of property, and subsequently to "earn" their full American citizenship. Washington believed that when African Americans proved themselves to whites, black civil rights would naturally follow. Washington's platform of accommodation advocated that African Americans adapt to a white-dominated country by focusing on their own self-discipline and economic advancement while accepting their own disenfranchisement. They were to defer to the white South on political matters and focus their own energies on a practical education and a useful occupation. Of course, Washington received much support from white southerners.

While Washington's viewpoint reflected the sentiments of many white and black Americans at the turn of the century, Du Bois articulated an emerging African American viewpoint that directly challenged notions of accommodation. Du Bois had been on good terms with Washington until their ideas began to conflict over the role of education in African American emancipation. Washington advocated an industrial education offered at Tuskegee Institute, whereas Du Bois envisioned leadership training for black intellectuals. Washington sought progress through the establishment of a black economic base of farmers, artisans, and businessmen. Du Bois, on the other hand, sought the leadership of highly educated African Americans to lead the race out of oppression.

Both Washington and Du Bois agreed on the importance of self-help and racial solidarity. Du Bois' vision of the "Talented Tenth" was a more elitist vision of racial uplift than Washington's whereas Du Bois and his disciples charged that the Tuskegee students were most useful in agricultural settings. Du Bois and his followers represented the emerging viewpoints of African Americans as the twentieth century progressed.

As Du Bois emerged as a prominent leader of black civil rights at the turn of the century, he attempted to locate black protest within the framework of socialism. He incorporated socialism into his philosophy and began to see the parallels between the oppression of both black and white workers. Du Bois' form of socialism, shared by much of the National Association for the Advancement of Colored People (NAACP), was not rigidly Marxist in content but acknowledged the similarities in the class oppression of both blacks and whites. His affiliation with the NAACP and their elitist tactics for black civil rights did not fit the Socialist Party's definition of socialism. In fact, A. Philip Randolph offered a socialist critique of Du Bois in an editorial written for *The Messenger* in 1919.

In this editorial, Randolph criticized Du Bois for abandoning a more radical stance against racial and class oppression of African Americans. He argued that Du Bois' platform fell short of socialist revolution in that he never advocated unionizing black workers for higher wages and better working conditions. On the contrary, Randolph recounted that Du Bois took a stance against the Industrial Workers of the World, which was the only union that had extended itself toward black workers. Randolph also criticized the NAACP for ignoring the black working class in its agenda. Randolph argued that no social group has ever been liberated without a social revolution and cited the

Civil War as a historical example. He accused Du Bois of complicity with maintaining the status quo with his less-than-radical solutions for eradicating black oppression.

Du Bois' relationship with the NAACP was both antagonistic and protagonistic. The NAACP grew out of Du Bois' own vision of racial progress through the enforcement of African American civil rights. He was, however, moving beyond the scope of the organization's agenda when he officially joined it in 1910. Evidence for the tensions between Du Bois and the NAACP can be seen in his role as editor of *The Crisis*. He was aware of the fact that *The Crisis* belonged to the NAACP and was supposed to function essentially as propaganda for the organization. These tensions arose repeatedly and usually involved Du Bois' attempt to expand the scope of the magazine to include things other than American legal issues concerning African American civil rights. For example, Du Bois' interest in Pan-Africanism around 1920 went beyond what the NAACP thought appropriate for its publication. Du Bois felt progressively confined by the limitations placed on the expression of his own broadening agenda.

By the early 1930s, the depression had created desperate economic circumstances for black Americans. Du Bois became increasingly frustrated with the NAACP's unwillingness to reorganize its agenda to meet these new economic circumstances. By now he had abandoned his vision for a black elite and instead advocated an economic separatist strategy for African Americans. With his distrust of white labor, his vision included acknowledging the segregation of African Americans from European Americans both in community living and all-black franchises. Du Bois ostensibly had diminished faith in socialism but still adapted socialist theory to envision a twentieth-century black cooperative economy. He challenged and even rejected the policies of the NAACP in its own publication, *The Crisis*. The NAACP was opposed to his conception and particularly to his apparent endorsement of segregation. Du Bois' argument was that segregation did not necessarily mean discrimination, and historically it was the latter that the NAACP had opposed, not the former. The NAACP's response was a forceful restatement of the old platform and specifically a denunciation of segregation and racial separatism of any kind. Soon after, Du Bois resigned from the NAACP. It had become clear that these arguments were not leading to any kind of mutual resolution.

Throughout his life, Du Bois maintained an often adversarial stance against many of the African American activists around him. From Booker T. Washington to the socialist movement and the NAACP, Du Bois challenged those around him to expand the scope of their agenda. As a result, he had many enemies. Du Bois also had many supporters but was notorious for being not easy to work with and demanding of those around him. Many of Du Bois' biggest critics were also his greatest advocates. Du Bois remained, however, one of the most prominent African American spokespersons of the twentieth century. *See also*: *The Crisis*; Integration versus Segregation; National Association for the Advancement of Colored People (NAACP); Pan-Africanism; Socialism/Communism; Talented Tenth; Tuskegee Institute; Washington, Booker T.

FURTHER READING

Aptheker, Herbert. *Annotated Bibliography of the Published Writings of W.E.B. Du Bois.* Millwood, NY: Kraus-Thomson Organization, 1973.

Du Bois, W.E.B. *The Autobiography of W.E.B. Du Bois: A Soliloquy on Viewing My Life from the Last Decade of Its First Century.* New York: International Publishers, 1968.

Lewis, David. *W.E.B. Du Bois: Biography of a Race.* New York: A John Macrae Book, Henry Holt Company, 1993.

Meier, August, ed. *Black Protest Thought in the Twentieth Century.* New York: Macmillan Publishing Company, 1971.

Amy Bowles

THE QUEST OF THE SILVER FLEECE, RURAL
UTOPIANISM IN

> There is no God but Love and Work is his prophet—help us to realize this truth O Father which thou so often in word and deed has taught us. Let the knowledge temper our ambitions and our judgements. We would not be great but busy—not pious but sympathetic—not merely reverent, but filled with the glory of our Life-Work. God is Love & Work is His Revelation.
>
> Rampersad 121

Du Bois is often credited with focusing his efforts on examining and aiding the plight of urban African Americans. As he squared off in philosophical positioning with Booker T. Washington, of the Tuskegee Institute, Du Bois seemed clearly to urge blacks to reject agrarian labor favored by Washington; instead, he urged blacks to explore their creativity and professional abilities. After 1910, he wrote from Harlem, and his actions and utopianism seemed to compel southern blacks to flee the rural United States for urban centers to explore their own economic and creative horizons. Specifically, Du Bois, the sociologist, vehemently criticized the "color line" that Washington and others chose to accept as an opportunity for gradual change. The interaction with southerners of other classes and races, writes Du Bois, provided the means that "[t]he American Negro and all backward peoples must have for effectual progress" (*The Souls of Black Folk* 74). Du Bois, the novelist, however, did not limit his hopes to the "Talented Tenth" but instead looked to the land. In *The Quest of the Silver Fleece* (1911), Du Bois creates a novel clear in its image of rural utopianism and seemingly incongruous with much of his own logic.

Quest is an epic of cotton, similar in its naturalist texture with Frank Norris' story of wheat, *The Octopus*. Du Bois follows cotton from its planting by black hands in the South on lands owned by whites to its manufacture and distribution by white business and industrial interests, mainly in the North. At the center of the epic is a black couple, Blessed Alwyn and Zora Cresswell, who rise from virtual serfdom in Alabama to attain a sense of independence through their love and the field of cotton (silver fleece) that they tend in the secrecy of a surrounding swamp. The other black agriculturalists in *Quest*, as either tenants or sharecroppers, have been drawn into a scheme inspired by a New York businessman to corner the cotton market nationally. This scheme combines with the repression of the Alabama color line to rid southern blacks of nearly all autonomy during the nineteenth century. Their carefully tended field allows Bles and Zora to figuratively and literally exist outside this difficulty.

The importance of "marginal" areas during slavery and throughout the Jim Crow era has been well documented. Zora lives with her mystic mother, Elspeth, deep in the swamp. The "veil" of racism and inequality that Du Bois sees everywhere in Alabama culture rarely penetrates the swamp. The magical aura of the swamp links it with dreams of progress and opportunity. "And over yonder behind the swamps," Zora tells Bles, "is great fields full of dreams, piled high and burning" (14). The swamp, in other words, acts as a buffer between southern white control and African American opportunity. This marginal zone becomes the sheltered site in which Zora and Bles find opportunity by planting and tending a wondrous crop of cotton in their quest for the "silver fleece." Du Bois suggests that landownership is not necessary for success; however, the status quo of growing crops for white southerners did not possess the necessary autonomy. Education, in the form of Susan Smith's northern-supported school for ex-slaves, also failed to bring automatic success. While Smith personifies moral excellence and compassion and leads Bles and Zora to personal enrichment, these accomplishments come through Smith's friendship and not necessarily through the institution of education. Du Bois' imagery is clear: While education is not an automatic route to equality, autonomy in land use and ownership can be. In the summary image, Zora uses proceeds from cotton sales to purchase the swamp lands to establish an all-black community with social and economic self-sufficiency. Mr. Cresswell and other white landowners, of course, belittle her for thinking such a positive outcome can derive from wasteland.

The route to success involves more than land. Specifically, the purveyor of personal autonomy here is a familiar character to southern blacks: cotton. As Bles talks with Miss Smith, the white educator, he introduces the northerner to the meaning of the crop more with his tone than his actual descriptions. Du Bois writes, Bles' "eyes lighted, for cotton was to him a very real and beautiful thing and a lifelong companion, yet not one whose friendship had been coarsened and killed by heavy toil. He leaned against his hoe and talk half dreamily . . . [of cotton]" (31). As Bles and Zora consider their future capabilities, he suggests that "yonder lies the Silver Fleece spread across the brown back of the world; let's get a bit of it, and hide it." Zora responds that she knows just the place "down in the heart of the swamp—where dreams and devils live" (52). The care and accomplishment of their crop bring very personal rewards to Bles and Zora. Du Bois intentionally accentuates the paternal role of the toilers when he writes:

In the field of the Silver Fleece all her possibilities were beginning to find expression. These newborn green things hidden far down in the swamp, begotten in want and mystery, were to her a living wonderful fairy tale come true. All the latent mother in her brooded over them; all her brilliant fancy wove itself about them. They were her dream-children, and she tended them jealously; they were her Hope, and she worshipped them. (125)

However, similar to the plight of black southerners overall, the exercise of control over one's own life and "family" causes Du Bois' characters considerable strain. Zora's strength of will, and her seizing the opportunity to exhibit it, ultimately ensures their personal success.

Clearly, Du Bois is not arguing that the southern blacks' progress relies on learning a viable trade; instead, he argues for a personal or spiritual autonomy that derives from economic and cultural control over one's life. Historian Mart Stewart finds the main thrust of Du Bois' *Quest* as the formation of cultural identity, particularly through the formation of meanings of place. The controlling yoke of slavery, peonage, and Jim Crow took such cultural autonomy from southern blacks. In *Quest*, the swamp offers the opportunity for redemption. What Cresswell sees as a wasteland, Zora sees as a sanctuary. Her success, of course, is unlike that to be found for African Americans in urban areas; grounded in the meaning of a specific crop and location, this path to success fuses some of Washington's belief in remaining in the South with a dash of Du Bois separatism.

To explore Du Bois' intention, literary scholar Arnold Rampersad focuses on the composition of Zora's personal "university," located within her utopian community. The limited library contains the works of the world's great writers and, with carefully placed, specific mention, an encyclopedia of agriculture. Rampersad writes, "The fields of the country, not the streets of the city, provide the most auspicious landscape for social regeneration" (Rampersad 129). However, there must be the requisite autonomy; the tilling must be neither slavery nor serfdom. *Quest* clearly reveals that the rural utopia worked for Du Bois as a literary form. He likely even hoped it would work in reality. However, when Du Bois became a national leader entrusted with divining the African American future, he rarely repeated the romanticism of his *Quest. See also*: Art and Literature.

FURTHER READING

Du Bois, W.E.B. *The Quest of the Silver Fleece.* Chicago: A. C. McClurg & Co., 1911. Boston: Northeastern University Press, 1989.

——. *The Souls of Black Folk.* Chicago: A. C. McClurg & Co., 1903. New York: Random House, 1994.

Rampersad, Arnold. *The Art and Imagination of W.E.B. Du Bois.* Cambridge: Harvard University Press, 1976.

Stewart, Mart A. *"What Nature Suffers to Groe": Life, Labor, and Landscape on the Georgia Coast, 1680–1920.* Athens: University of Georgia Press, 1996.

Brian C. Black

R

RACE RIOTS

Intermittent periods of active racial unrest mark a tragic pattern in U.S. history. Riots appeared not only in response to numerous antebellum slave conspiracies and insurrections but also in contemporary mob violence against free blacks living in northern cities. Isolated riots persisted during the Reconstruction era, but racially motivated violence upon the individual through lynching became the primary instrument used to perpetuate the mythology of cultural dominance and superiority. During the 1898–1920 era, the incidence of racially motivated mob violence escalated to a level unsurpassed until the civil rights conflagration of the 1960s.

The Great Migration created demographic and economic pressures that fostered racial discontent in the early twentieth century. Pressures of depopulation upon a sharecropping-based South and rapidly expanding migration upon a job-poor North burdened both regions, thus producing economic distress coupled with overt racism. Riots in Wilmington, North Carolina (1898), Statesboro, Georgia (1904), and Atlanta, Georgia (1906) motivated similar occurrences in Springfield, Ohio (1904), Greensburg, Indiana (1906), and Springfield, Illinois (1908). Subsequent race riots occurred in twenty-three northern cities between 1910 and 1920.

The Atlanta Riot of September 22, 1906, influenced the intellectual temper of W.E.B. Du Bois, then professor of history and economics at Atlanta University. While conducting research in Lowndes County, Alabama, Du Bois learned that a mob of 10,000 white youths ruled Atlanta's streets, beating and killing blacks at will. Returning by train to protect his home and family, Du Bois became a participant–activist as he sat on his porch with a shotgun and buckshot, defending his wife and daughter. Officials reported that two dozen African Americans died in the rioting, but Du Bois wrote that "the Atlanta

Riot was if anything worse than reports." In writing "A Litany of Atlanta" for *The Independent* (October 11, 1906), Du Bois seemed exasperated and almost blasphemous as he searched for meaning in the chaos of "a city . . . in travail," even questioning, "Is not the God of the Fathers dead?" Disheartened by the carnage wrought from bigotry, Du Bois viewed the Atlanta Riot as a consequence of Booker T. Washington's "Atlanta Compromise," which had stymied racial advancement in the name of social harmony. Yet Du Bois' recently created Niagara Movement appeared ineffective at preventing the Atlanta Riot.

Two years later a northern riot inspired creation of an integral component of Du Bois' crusade for social justice. On August 14, 1908, a white mob rampaged through Springfield, Illinois, attacking black residents and shouting, "Lincoln freed you, we'll show you where you belong!" Causing eight deaths and an estimated $200,000 in property damage, this event showed Du Bois and other Niagara Movement leaders that the racial problem was a national disgrace as the former abolitionist heartland now condoned methods previously employed in the South. Accordingly, Du Bois and others worked tirelessly to establish a powerful national organization in 1909, the National Association for the Advancement of Colored People (NAACP), to advance the cause of racial justice in the United States. Though sporadic race riots persisted, the NAACP, an organization forged from violent racial discord, worked unceasingly to transform narrow-minded rage into progressive social reform. *See also*: National Association for the Advancement of Colored People (NAACP); Niagara Movement; Poetry; Racism; Slave Uprisings; Washington, Booker T.

FURTHER READING

"The Arkansas Riot." *New York World* (November 28, 1919).
Urban Race Riots. New York: Garland Pub., 1991.

Junius Rodriguez

RACISM

Du Bois was a critical figure in debates and intellectual discussions about racism and oppression from the late nineteenth century until his death. To say that Du Bois was outspoken in his concern about racism is an understatement of the greatest proportion. Throughout his life, Du Bois was an advocate of antiracist policies and practice. Du Bois often found himself misunderstood by both blacks and whites.

In 1897, Du Bois studied inner-city life in Philadelphia and published the results in 1899, *The Philadelphia Negro.* In that study, Du Bois observed that the city was a "social environment of excuse, listless despair, careless indulgence, and lack of inspiration to work." Du Bois noted that the inner city functioned as a social entity for economic and social subordination. He also noted that blacks were receiving lower wages than usual for less desirable work and, because of that work and wages, were forced to live in less pleasant quarters than others and pay higher rents for the privilege.

By some, Du Bois was viewed as a black leader who was justifying the white system of racism by placing the blame for black failures on the shoulders of those blacks who were in oppressive situations. However, this was not the case. Du Bois presented a powerful argument against institutional racism. Du Bois said that by discouraging blacks from entering certain trades and labor unions, and through segregation and political and social oppression, white society condemned all African Americans "behind a wall of social injustice."

Du Bois joined the faculty of Atlanta University in 1897 as a history and economics professor. He went there, to an institution he called an "Ivory tower of race," "to explain the difficulties of race and the ways in which these difficulties caused political and economic troubles."

While en route to Atlanta University in July and August of 1897, Du Bois collected data in Farmville, Virginia, a town he selected because many blacks in his Philadelphia study were from this area. Again, much like the Philadelphia study, Du Bois noted irregular employment opportunities as problematic.

In a powerful statement that served, in some ways, to summarize Du Bois' view of race relations, Du Bois presented a paper at the American Negro Academy entitled "The Conservation of Races." In this paper he asserted that each of the world's great racial groups has distinct cultural and "spiritual" characteristics and that African Americans have only begun to give to civilization the full spiritual message they can give. This work was one example of how Du Bois conveyed his view of the races, not as a segregationist but as an advocate of cultural pluralism.

Du Bois has written that, "One ever feels his twoness—an American, a Negro; two souls, two thoughts, two unreconciled strivings; two warring ideas in one dark body, whose dogged strength alone keeps it from being torn asunder." Du Bois asserts that blacks in the United States are unable to simply be Americans; they are daily bombarded with information that reminds them of their status in society. While European Americans are rarely reminded that they are white, black Americans were unable to function in society without having to address issues of racism and prejudice. Segregation, lynchings, and general injustice were constant reminders that to be black was not to be an American in the sense that blacks could not participate in the benefits of society at the same level as whites.

Du Bois' work *The Souls of Black Folk* (1903) contained more of his powerful statements concerning the state of race relations in the United States and his perspectives on the effects of racism. In *The Souls of Black Folk*, Du Bois again addresses the problems of institutionalized racism. By referring to institutionalized racism as a veil that made blacks virtually invisible to whites, and kept blacks from attaining a clear view of their own circumstances, Du Bois provided the reader with imagery that represented the situation in which blacks found themselves in the United States.

Further, Du Bois suggested that racism grows from the exploitation of people and that exploitation affects all parties involved, both the exploiter and the exploited. Because of his knowledge of history, Du Bois could point out the fact that race as a means of categorizing people only gained wide acceptance after the onset of slavery in the New World. Races were then assigned certain psychological and physical characteristics that had little to do with the individual members of the racial group. The need to make a distinction between people of different races grows from two sources: the first, when a group of people is increasingly identified solely through the marks of their oppression; the second, the evolving set of beliefs used to justify the treatment of those individuals as infrahuman.

When contrasted with Booker T. Washington, Du Bois appeared radical. As Washington gained popularity, he spoke of blacks taking up their own financial systems and working within the segregated society in which they lived to achieve their financial goals. Du Bois was willing, at first, to be an advocate for Washington; however, as time progressed, Du Bois became less satisfied with Washington's perspective. While Washington urged the creation of black society, independent of white society and not making demands on white society, Du Bois pushed for "perfect equality before the law" for blacks.

Early in his fight against racism, Du Bois envisioned democracy within the system of American capitalism as a way to end oppression of blacks and racism. He said that the "power of the ballot" was an important tool, and striving to preserve the democratic rights of African Americans was crucial. Later in life, Du Bois believed socialism would be a better tool for achieving equality, and ending racism, than democracy.

At the 1947 National Association for the Advancement of Colored People (NAACP) convention, Du Bois stated, "Every leading land on earth is moving toward some form of socialism, so as to restrict the power of wealth, introduce democratic methods in industry, and stop the persistence of poverty, ignorance, disease, and crime." His perspective on the value of socialism grew in part from a distaste for class distinctions. Du Bois had believed that in the black community the most intelligent and most learned would provide leadership to the working classes. He referred to these "most intelligent members" of black society as "the Talented Tenth." As time passed, he became aware that the Talented Tenth were separating themselves from the working classes, and instead of providing leadership, they were taking part in a capitalistic society, sometimes to the point of exploiting other blacks. Du Bois saw these class divisions in the black community as a threat to unity, and as such, it would also be a threat to social reform.

Du Bois was one of America's most outspoken intellectual leaders from the late nineteenth to the midtwentieth century. His belief in cultural pluralism and his dedication to ending racism and oppression transcended color and country. Through his many writings, Du Bois managed to generate discussion at the highest levels of government. Du Bois left behind a legacy of critical inquiry into the problems of race and racism that continues to provide clarification of the situation of blacks and whites in the United States. *See also*:

Atlanta University; National Association for the Advancement of Colored People (NAACP); *The Philadelphia Negro*; *The Souls of Black Folk*; Talented Tenth; Washington, Booker T.

FURTHER READING

Aptheker, Herbert, ed. *Against Racism: Unpublished Essays, Papers, Addresses, 1887–1961.* Amherst: The University of Massachusetts Press, 1985.
"Strivings of the Negro People." *Atlantic Monthly* (August 1897).
Wintz, Cary D., ed. *African American Political Thought, 1890–1930. Washington, Du Bois, Garvey, and Randolph.* Armonk, NY: M. E. Sharpe, 1996.

Ladonna Rush

RELIGION

Critical of religion as practiced by European Americans, Du Bois frequently pointed out that the church was the most racist and segregated institution in the United States. "Of course, it is the Churches which are the most discriminatory of all institutions!" (*Phylon*, 1941).

In 1913 (*The Crisis*, December) he devoted several paragraphs to the Episcopal Church, attacking it for its racism, concluding that it is "the church of John Pierpont Morgan and not the church of Jesus Christ." Later (*The Crisis*, May 1917), Du Bois excoriated the European American church for its racism, asking: "Is there not a spirit of moral leadership in this powerful aggregation of men that can touch with mighty hands our real problems of modern life and lead us?"

As he had earlier reproached the Episcopal Church, Du Bois also had harsh words for the Catholic Church. In "The Catholic Church and Negroes: A Correspondence" (*The Crisis*, July 1925), Du Bois writes: "Because Catholicism has so much that is splendid in its past and fine in its present, it is the greater shame that 'nigger' haters clothed in its episcopal robes should do to black Americans in exclusion, segregation and exclusion from opportunity all that the Ku Klux Klan ever asked." With the election of Pope Pius XI, Du Bois succinctly noted: "The question that concerns us is whether or not he is going to continue catering to the wealth of American Catholics; will continue to allow the American hierarchy, despite some of its nobler souls, to refuse to train and ordain Negro priests?" (*The Crisis*, April 1922).

By 1949 Du Bois was still attacking the European American church, insisting that the church had consistently stood on the side of wealth and power, and he expected it would remain so in the future. However, he wryly noted, if equality were ever achieved, the church would take the credit.

Neither did Du Bois spare the black church. In "The Negro Church" (*The Crisis*, May 1912), he denounced black ministers, calling them "pretentious, ill-trained men and in far too many cases . . . dishonest . . . immoral . . . hustling businessmen, eloquent talkers, suave companions and hale fellows." In 1928, in Washington, D.C., black ministers closed their churches to a proposed lecture by Clarence Darrow because of his agnosticism. Du Bois wrote in "Postscript" (*The Crisis*, 1928) that the ministers had committed a disgraceful act. "Such witch hunting would have barred Lincoln and Garrison and Douglass ... [and] the greatest of religious rebels was Christ."

On the other hand, Du Bois believed that "the religion of Black folk has served as a basic rock to which they have clung—the triumph of Good in the end. Its method has influenced all religious practice in the United States and the Salvation Army copied wholesale from our style" (*The Amsterdam News*, November 2, 1940). *See also*: African Methodist Church; Jesus Christ.

FURTHER READING

"The Catholic Church and Negroes: A Correspondence," *The Crisis* (July 1925).

Malaika Horne

REPUBLICAN PARTY

Originally a coalition of forces that opposed the extension of slavery, the Republican Party united after the disintegration of the Whig Party. The founding of the Republican Party can be traced to a nonpartisan meeting at Ripon, Wisconsin, in February 1854. It was at this meeting that the name "Republican" was suggested. As the party of Lincoln, it enjoyed black support for many years following the Civil War. However, in 1877 Republican Rutherford B. Hayes was elected president by one electoral vote in a much disputed election. Under Hayes, efforts to reconstruct the South and secure black rights were abandoned, and the southern states returned to the control of white Democrats.

As early as 1883 Du Bois was questioning the Republican commitment to blacks, and throughout his life, he was consistent in his criticism of the Republican Party's racial policies. By 1906 (*Voice of the Negro*, December 1906), he was denouncing Theodore Roosevelt for the low number of blacks with the party. He claimed that undue pressure and a lack of commitment to black needs caused a substantial decrease in black membership.

In 1908 (*The Horizon*), Du Bois emphatically stated that the Republican Party had forfeited any claim to the black vote and that the Democratic Party deserved a trial because between the two parties he must choose Democratic (*The Crisis*, August 1915). He also observed that the Republican Party had completely disenfranchised blacks with no public protest.

Du Bois predicted that Herbert Hoover's efforts to create a blackless Republican Party would have unseen consequences. Eventually, Du Bois opined, the absence of blacks might lead to a breakdown of white supremacy in the South. In a May 1930 *Crisis* article, Du Bois revealed the accuracy of his prophecy, noting that Hoover "now finds scandal after scandal emanating from the greed of his lily white Southern Republicans."

Later in his life, Du Bois was still critical of the Republican Party, writing that "the choice between Democrats and Republicans is not a real choice at all. Both agree on capitalism—on greed" (*The Chicago Defender*, October 5, 1946). Displaying his sense of humor yet maintaining his critical stance, Du Bois noted "the habit of insulting animals in English—such as snaky, dumb as sheep, the jackass and the Democratic Party, the elephant and the Republican Party, etc.—all of which is insulting to the beasts." *See also*: Roosevelt, Theodore.

FURTHER READING

Coolidge, Calvin. *The Republican Case*. Chicago: Republican National Committee, 1932.
National Guardian (December 18, 1952).
New York Globe (October 20, 1883).

Mary Young

ROBESON, PAUL (1898–1976)

I agree with Paul Robeson absolutely that Negroes should never willingly fight in an unjust war. I do not share his honest hope that all will not. A certain sheep-like disposition, inevitably born of slavery, will, I am afraid, lead many of them to join America in any enterprise, provided the whites will grant them equal rights to do wrong.

W.E.B. Du Bois, *Daily Worker*, May 2, 1949

Robeson, son of an ex-slave turned preacher, was first famous as an All-American athlete and Phi Beta Kappa valedictorian at Rutgers (New Jersey), then as a singer/interpreter of Negro spirituals during the Harlem Renaissance, particularly his title role in *Othello*, and eventually, with Du Bois, as a fervent advocate for racial equality. Yet for his political convictions—mainly, speaking for all oppressed peoples, from every nation, creed, or color—he was not recognized for the Renaissance man he was until a Robeson revival began some two decades ago.

Friendship between Robeson and Du Bois began in Harlem, particularly around their memberships in the National Association for the Advancement of Colored People (NAACP) in the postwar period. Du Bois had written about Robeson's football exploits in *Crisis* columns. On September 23, 1946, the anniversary of Lincoln's Emancipation Proclamation, the two collaborated to launch a federal antilynching law. In 1948, when they were elected to serve on the new World Peace Council, Robeson and Du Bois were increasingly linked both personally and professionally. As part of a response to McCarthyism, in 1950 Robeson helped establish a Harlem newspaper, *Freedom*, which frequently included writings by Du Bois. A good example is the January 1953 issue on *One Hundred Years in the Struggle for Negro Freedom*, which rejected the notion of blacks forming their own nation and instead favored the idea of cultural unity—the solutions: ending all Jim Crow regulations and customs, increasing black-white labor unity, both universal suffrage and free education, and a more equitable distribution of wealth.

Robeson and Du Bois cooperated on the newly formed journal, *Freedom*, co-chaired the Council on African Affairs, were implicated in the anti-Communist fervor of the 1950s because of their pro-Russian attitudes, supported Pan-Africanism, worked fervently for civil rights, and with their wives, remained firm friends throughout their lives, despite the wide age differences. Shirley Graham Du Bois writes about a photo she snapped of Robeson and her husband at Stratford-on-Avon after his operatic performance there: "He towers like a giant over my husband, but both of them stand so straight and gratified that their pride and joy in each other are caught by the camera" (Graham Du Bois, *Du Bois*, 134).

On the occasion of Du Bois' ninetieth birthday, he railed in his autobiography over government persecution of Robeson's affinities for a Soviet Union that had welcomed and accepted him: "Robeson has done nothing to hurt or defame this nation. He is, as all know, one of the most charming, charitable and loving of men . . . Robeson, who more than any living man has spread the pure Negro folk song over the civilized world" (*Autobiography*). Reciprocally, it seems worthy to reprint, despite its faulty translation, Robeson's cable to Shirley Graham Du Bois in Accra, on the occasion of the esteemed leader's death.

Thankful doctor lived to see practical achievements resulting from his magnificent contributions to African independence and unity Negro militant of this wonderful. He enjoyed universal recognition appreciation respect and love in last years. Always think of him proudly as our distinguished scholar and elder statesman as we reach toward our rightful place in the world. Our warmest sympathy and thanks to you.

Affectionately, Paul and Eslanda Robeson
(Graham Du Bois, *His Day* 368)

As many scholars have pointed out, while W.E.B. Du Bois may have been the intellectual leader for most blacks, Paul Robeson was their "soulful" leader. Du Bois summed it up best in a March 1950 issue of *Negro Digest*, "The only thing wrong with Robeson is in having too great faith in human beings." *See also*: Art and Artists; Du Bois, Shirley Graham; Dyer Anti-Lynching Bill; McCarthyism.

FURTHER READING

Duberman, Martin Bauml. *Paul Robeson*. New York: Alfred A. Knopf, 1988.

Du Bois, Shirley Graham. *His Day Is Marching On*. New York: Lippincott, 1971.

——. *Du Bois: A Pictoral Biography*. Chicago: Johnson, 1978.

Du Bois, W.E.B. *The Autobiography of W.E.B. Du Bois*. New York: International Publishers, 1968.

Freedomways, eds. *Paul Robeson: The Great Forerunner*. New York: Dodd, Mead and Co., 1965.

Hamilton, Virginia. *Paul Robeson: The Life and Times of a Free Black Man*. New York: Harper and Row, 1974.

"Paul Robeson. Right or Wrong? Right, Says W.E.B. Du Bois." *Negro Digest* 7 (1950): 8, 10–14.

Robeson, Paul. *Here I Stand*. New York: Othello Associates, 1958.

Salk, Erwin A. *Du Bois–Robeson: Two Giants of the 20th Century: The Story of an Exhibit and a Bibliography.* Chicago: Columbia, 1977.

Linda K. Fuller

ROOSEVELT, THEODORE (1858–1919)

The presidency of Theodore Roosevelt, 1901–1909, coincided with an increase in violence toward blacks, including the highest rate of lynchings. Moreover, what political support blacks had previously built up in the South was by this time severely eroded. There was also a decrease in the number of black federal appointees. While in some cases Roosevelt defended black equality, he nevertheless was calculatingly cautious. After two terms in office, he concluded that the Republican Party had "been ruined" by its "rotten borough [Black] Republican delegates from the Southern states" (Harbaugh 445).

Writing in the January 1907 issue of *The Horizon,* Du Bois expressed to his readership that "if the truth must be told, Theodore Roosevelt does not like black folk." However, such was not Du Bois' earlier viewpoint, as he later recalled in *The Seventh Son.* "I was attracted to Roosevelt by his attitude toward my folk in the appointing of [Dr. William] Crum to the port of collectorship in [Charleston] South Carolina and his defense of the little black postmistress [Minnie Cox] at Indianola, Mississippi. Also, I knew he was right in his fight against trusts. His luncheon with Booker T. Washington raised such a row in the South that it made me a strong Roosevelt partisan" (*The Seventh Son* 589).

From Du Bois' perspective, Roosevelt lost political credibility in his response to the Brownsville incident of 1906. In August of that year, black troops of the 25th Infantry Regiment allegedly attacked Brownsville, Texas, killing one white and injuring two others. In November after determining that there was a conspiracy of silence, Roosevelt summarily dismissed the entire army unit. Except for a handful, all of its members were given dishonorable discharges. Du Bois regarded Roosevelt's action as the most flagrant hypocrisy of the times:

Because a few blacks were suspected of treating Southerners as Southerners treated them, without trial or hearing, Theodore Roosevelt dismissed them from the United States Army in disgrace not only those suspected but scores of others never accused, denied them the ordinary rights of American citizens and even tried to contravene the constitution—and all this to tarnish the hitherto unblemished record of a soldiery who saved the Union and saved Roosevelt himself on San Juan Hill. (*The Seventh Son* 57)

Shortly after becoming president, Roosevelt invited Booker T. Washington to dine at the White House, a gesture that was significant in terms of honoring the black leader. Yet it was at the same time an endorsement of Washington's accommodationist policy. Four years later, Du Bois and other black "radicals" formed the Niagara Movement for the cause of gaining full political and economic rights for blacks, which was a direct rejection of Washington's conciliatory approach. This action was felt eight years later, during the formation of the Progressive Party. As part of the new party's platform, Du Bois offered an antidiscrimination plank; Joel Spingarn, representing the National Association for the Advancement of Colored People (NAACP), presented a watered-down version at the Chicago convention. The plank was forthrightly rejected by Roosevelt, who took the time to label Du Bois a "dangerous person." *See also*: Brownsville Raid; Niagara Movement; Republican Party.

FURTHER READING

Cashman, Sean Dennis. *African-Americans and the Quest for Civil Rights, 1900–1990.* New York: New York University Press, 1991.

Du Bois, W.E.B. "From McKinley to Wallace." In *The Seventh Son*, ed. Julius Lester. Vol. II. New York: Random House, 1971.

——. *Writings in Periodicals Edited by W.E.B. Du Bois: Selections from* The Horizon. Ed. Herbert Aptheker. White Plains, NY: Kraus-Thomson Organization Limited, 1985.

Dyer, Thomas G. *Theodore Roosevelt and the Idea of Race.* Baton Rouge: Louisiana State University Press, 1980.

Gable, John Allen. *The Bull Moose Party: Theodore Roosevelt and the Progressive Party.* Port Washington, NY: Kennikat Press, 1970.

Harbaugh, William Henry. *The Life and Times of Theodore Roosevelt.* New York: Collier Books, 1963.

Hart, Albert Bushnell, and Herbert Ronald Ferleger, eds. *Theodore Roosevelt Cyclopedia.* New York: Roosevelt Memorial Association, 1941.

Lane, Ann J. *The Brownsville Affair: National Crisis and Black Reaction.* Port Washington, NY: Kennikat Press, 1971.

Rudwick, Elliott M. *W.E.B. Du Bois: Propagandist of the Negro Protest.* 2nd ed. Philadelphia: University of Pennsylvania Press, 1968.

Roger Chapman

ROSENBERGS

Ethel Greenglass Rosenberg (1915–1953) and Julius Rosenberg (1918–1953), born in New York, are the only Americans ever executed for espionage by the judgment of a civilian court. The charge against them was giving vital information on the atomic bomb to the USSR. The primary evidence against them was the testimony of Ethel's brother, David Greenglass. Greenglass testified that while working at a secret base in Los Alamos, New Mexico, Julius encouraged him to give information to a Russian agent. Because of Greenglass' testimony, the fear of communism, and McCarthyism, not necessarily because they were guilty, the judge sentenced the Rosenbergs to death.

Judge Irving S. Kaufman assessed the death sentence because their treason had "altered the course of history to the disadvantage of our country" (Goldstein 42). The Rosenbergs maintained their innocence, but after many appeals, they were executed at Sing Sing Prison in 1953.

The trial and execution stirred worldwide controversy, and at the forefront of this public debate was Du Bois. Du Bois considered the arrest, trial, conviction, and execution of the couple insidious, equal to that of Sacco and Vanzetti. At a "Save the Rosenbergs" rally in New York, Du Bois presented a cogently reasoned, comprehensive analysis of the case. Besides his public appearances in support of the Rosenbergs, Du Bois published many articles against their executions including: "A Negro Leader's Plea to Save the Rosenbergs" (*Worker*, 1952) and "The Rosenbergs" (*Masses & Mainstream*, 1953). *See also*: McCarthyism; Socialism/Communism.

FURTHER READING

"A Negro Leader's Plea to Save the Rosenbergs." *Worker* (November 16, 1952).

Goldstein, Alvin H. *The Unquiet Death of Julius and Ethel Rosenberg*. New York: Lawrence Hill & Co., 1975.

Neville, John F. *The Press, The Rosenbergs, and the Cold War*. Westport, CT: Praeger, 1995.

Mary Young

RUSSIAN REVOLUTION AND THE SOVIET UNION

The world's largest country, by territory, Russia, had suffered under an extremely oppressive form of government for centuries before the 1917 revolution. Eventually there were several revolutions, not one. The first rebellion, known as the Decembrist uprising, occurred in December 1825. Members of the propertied class, including many military officers, rebelled after the death of Alexander I. The revolt failed but inspired generations of dissidents.

There was another abortive revolution in 1905 following Russia's defeat in the Russo-Japanese War. For a short time, it seemed that public discontent would force Czar Nicholas II to establish a constitutional monarchy. However, such a change would have satisfied neither the czar nor his opponents. Radical revolutionaries continued to fight for a democratic republic, and the czar wanted to retain control.

The next two revolutions were successful, taking place during World War I, when Russian military forces were hard-pressed by the Germans. The March Revolution of 1917 led to the abdication of Nicholas and the establishment of a provisional government. Alexander Kerensky was the leader of this government, who when forced from power immigrated to the United States.

The last revolution took place in November 1917. Because the date was in October on the old Russian calendar, it is usually called the October Revolution. This successful uprising brought to power the Bolshevik wing of the Communist Party, led by Lenin. The Bolsheviks established the Union of Soviet Socialist Republics under the Communist Party.

It was the Revolution of 1917 that concerned Du Bois, although during the 1920s and 1930s he seemed ambivalent. Poet and novelist Claude McKay accused Du Bois of not paying sufficient attention to the Russian Revolution and deriding its program of socialism. Du Bois replied: "[I am not] prepared to dogmatize with Marx and Lenin. . . . At the same time it would be just as foolish for us to sneer or even seem to sneer at the blood-entwined writhing of hundreds of millions of our whiter human brothers" (*The Crisis*, July 1921).

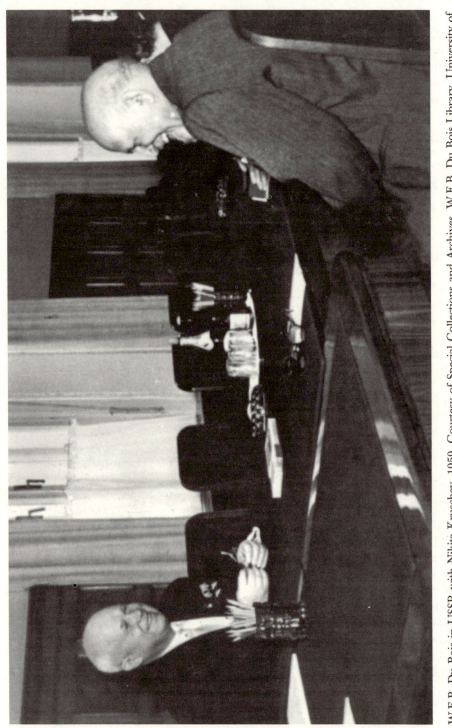

W.E.B. Du Bois in USSR with Nikita Kruschev, 1959. Courtesy of Special Collections and Archives, W.E.B. Du Bois Library, University of Massachusetts Amherst.

While Du Bois chose not to grapple with the revolution then, he astutely recognized the anti-Russian campaign carried on by the West. He wrote in 1927 that "Russia is trying to make the workingman the main object of industry," although organized capital in the United States and western Europe "has used every modern weapon to crush Russia" (*The Crisis*, 1927). Later, continuing his apologia, Du Bois referred to Russia as a "victim of a determined propaganda of lies" (*Labor Defender*, 1928).

Western criticism of Russia continued and so did Du Bois' critique of the propaganda techniques used by the West: "At first we were told the Russian Revolution was bound to fail and the Russians would starve to death. Now we are told the Russians are dumping products on the rest of the world and threatening it with starvation. Somehow the Russians are not able to suit us" (*The Crisis*, December 1930). Finding the inherent discrepancies in the West's arguments, Du Bois' reactions to Russia and its revolution became more definitive.

In the 1940s Du Bois began to defend the revolution and the USSR against determined Western antagonism.

I never considered the Russians even after the revolution as supermen. I expected them to stagger on in blood and tears toward their magnificent goal with many a stumble and retreat. I love the victim Radek more than the tyrant Stalin—but the accomplishments of that revolution and of the peoples of the U.S.S.R. have been enormous and therefore, I still believe in Russia. (*The Amsterdam News*, February 24, 1940)

Maintaining his support, a year later Du Bois declared that the Russian Revolution had more depth than the French Revolution.

By 1947 Du Bois seemed more firmly committed to the revolution, pronouncing the USSR the most "hopeful state in the world today." "Not" he added, "because its efforts have been perfection or without mistakes, but because it has attacked the fundamental problems of our day" (*Soviet Russia Today*, 1947).

For Du Bois the greatest events of the twentieth century were India's struggles with Britain and the Russian Revolution. Consequently, American blacks should look to the two events with "reverence, hope and applause" (*The Crisis*, July 1930). *See also*: Integration versus Segregation; McKay, Claude; Socialism/ Communism; Washington, Booker T.

FURTHER READING

Du Bois, W.E.B. "The Most Hopeful State in the World Today." *Soviet Russia Today* (November 1947).

——. "The World Peace Movement." *New World Review* (May 1955).

Mary Young

S

SILENT PROTEST AGAINST LYNCHING

The Silent Protest against Lynching was an attempt to secure President Woodrow Wilson's attention, a man who before being elected had promised to treat African Americans fairly. After his election, Wilson repudiated his promise by further segregating the federal government. The march, a response to the bloody East St. Louis, Illinois, riot (1917) in which nine whites and forty blacks were killed by rampaging mobs, occurred on July 28, 1917, in New York City. First proposed by Oswald Garrison Villard, one of the founders of the National Association for the Advancement of Colored People (NAACP), and involving between 8,000 and 10,000 black people, the march was silent except for "the steady roll of muffled drums carried by several men at the head," down Fifth Avenue. Male participants were dressed in dark suits, while women and children were dressed in white. In a widely reprinted photograph of the march, Du Bois can be seen in the second row behind the drummers. Several protesters carried signs and banners. On one, carried by a child, was the question, "Mother, Do Lynchers Go to Heaven?" On another was the charge, "Your Hands Are Full of Blood." Taken with the 1915 national campaign against D. W. Griffith's film *The Birth of a Nation*, there could no longer be any doubt that there was now an active, "aggressive national civil rights organization representing black people" in its quest for social-democratic rights, the outcome of which would be a test of what the nation had put on paper at its inception. *See also*: *The Birth of a Nation*; Dyer Anti-Lynching Bill; Racism; Villard, Oswald Garrison.

FURTHER READING

The Crisis (September 1917).

William M. King

SLATER FUND

In 1882, the businessman John F. Slater pledged $1 million for the education of former slaves and their descendants. Eight years later, Rutherford B. Hayes, then the Fund's chair, told an audience at Johns Hopkins University that the Slater Fund would be willing to finance a European education for any young black men who showed intellectual promise. Du Bois, then at Harvard, read this speech when it was published in the *Boston Herald*.

Du Bois quickly applied to the Slater Fund. Though Du Bois' letters of support from Harvard's top faculty members all attested to his intellectual aptitude, Hayes declined the application. Du Bois responded to the former president of the United States with a damning letter, implicitly accusing him, and all white philanthropists, of hypocrisy. Hayes must have been taken aback by the letter because he encouraged Du Bois to reapply for the following year. Du Bois reapplied and in 1891 was awarded enough aid—one half as a grant, the other half as a loan—to finance a year's study abroad. Du Bois spent the year at the University of Berlin and was later granted a year's renewal under the same terms. He was only one semester shy of receiving his Ph.D. from Berlin when the Fund refused his request for a special one-semester renewal. With the rise of Booker T. Washington's philosophy of industrial education for blacks, the Slater Fund decided to award no more funds to advanced students. Du Bois returned to the United States without his German Ph.D., without a job prospect, and without a way to repay his $700 debt to the Fund's trustees. *See also*: Harvard; University of Berlin.

FURTHER READING

"As the Crow Flies." *Amsterdam News* (October 19, 1940).
"As the Crow Flies." *Amsterdam News* (March 7, 1942).

Todd Gibson

SLAVERY

As Du Bois grew older his views on the causes and implications of slavery increasingly reflected the influences of Marx and Freud. Du Bois' first work, *The Suppression of the African Slave Trade to the United States of America, 1638–1870*, couches slavery in terms of Northern morals subjugated to Southern economics in return for the high revenues generated by the slave trade. Later, his correspondence and articles such as "Marxism and the Negro Problem" show his growing association of slavery with class struggle. Indeed, in 1954 he wrote what may be considered the best critique of *Suppression*, and *Apologia*, which outlines how his views changed in the sixty years after the former was written.

Suppression traces the evolution of slavery from the rise of the English slave trade, through the American Revolution and Emancipation Proclamation, and finally to the "freedom" long sought after by blacks. It places much of the blame for slavery on the Founding Fathers at the Constitutional Convention. And he believed that a firm stance against slavery at the time would have prevented the Civil War. Du Bois states that the Northern shipping interests entered into an immoral pact with Southern planters because of the highly profitable slave trade. He cites a letter from Luther Martin, a delegate to the convention, to his constituents, stating, "I found the Eastern States, notwithstanding their aversion to slavery, were very willing to indulge the Southern States with at least a temporary liberty to prosecute the slave trade, provided the Southern States, in their turn, gratify them by laying no restrictions on navigation acts" (*Suppression* 64). Although noting that farming colonies checked the slave trade primarily because it was not profitable, Du Bois did not make the connection until his later years between this complete subjugation of morals and the role of economics and chose instead to play North against South and emphasize the issue of morality.

In *The Souls of Black Folks* (1903), Du Bois described the yearning of slaves to be free but decries that they are "bound by law and custom to an economic slavery, from which the only escape is death or the penitentiary." Here Du Bois makes reference to the de facto economic slavery à la Marx, as opposed to the legal slavery supposedly removed by the Emancipation Proclamation. In *Marxism and the Negro Problem* (1933), he wrote, "They [the white proletariat] have similar complaints against capitalists, save that the grievances of the Negro workers are more fundamental and indefensible, ranging as they do since the day of Karl Marx from chattel slavery, to the worst paid, sweated, mobbed, and cheated labor in any civilized land" (*The Crisis*, May 1933). And he later went as far as to declare, "I still dabble in Marx, I think he is one of the greatest philosophers of the day. I believe in Marxism" (*The Crisis*, May 1933).

Finally, in his *Apologia*, Du Bois suggests that his work could be completely written in Freudian and Marxist terms. More Freud would have meant less of his own New England moral code in the text, and more Marx would have clearly indicated "that the real difficulty rested in the willingness of a privileged class of Americans to get power and comfort at the expense of degrading a class of black slaves, by not paying them what their labor produced" (103ff). *See also*: Slave Uprisings; *The Souls of Black Folks*.

FURTHER READING

Aptheker, Herbert, ed. *The Correspondence of W.E.B. Du Bois*. Vol. I, *Selections, 1877–1934*. Amherst: University of Massachusetts Press, 1973.

——. *The Correspondence of W.E.B. Du Bois*. Vol II, *Selections, 1934–1944*. Amherst: University of Massachusetts Press, 1976.

——. *The Correspondence of W.E.B. Du Bois*. Vol. III, *Selections, 1944–1963*. Amherst: University of Massachusetts Press, 1978.

Du Bois, W.E.B. "Marxism and the Negro Problem." *The Crisis* 40 (May 1933): 103–104, 118.

——. *The Souls of Black Folks*. In *Three Negro Classics*. New York: Doubleday & Co., 1973.

——. *The Suppression of the African Slave Trade to the United States of America, 1638–1870*. New York: Longmans, Green and Co., 1896. New York: Russell & Russell Inc., 1965.

Lewis, David Levering. *W.E.B. Du Bois: Biography of a Race, 1868–1919.* New York: Henry Holt, 1993.

Marable, Manning. *W.E.B. Du Bois. Black Radical Democrat.* Boston: Twayne Publishers, 1986.

Alphine Jefferson

SLAVE UPRISINGS

In 1839, forty-nine men, one boy, and three young women were taken from their homes, family, and friends in West Africa and sold as slaves. These people from Mendeland, an area on the west coast of Africa, crossed the Atlantic Ocean to Cuba on the slave ship *Tecora.* In Cuba two Spaniards, José Ruiz and Pedro Montes, bought the group and transferred them to the *Amistad* that sailed for the western end of the island.

While the Africans did not all come from the same village or family, they understood each other. And before the *Amistad* reached its destination, the Africans, led by (Joseph) Cinque (Sengbeh Pieh), revolted, attacking the crew. The enraged Africans killed the captain and the cook; other crew members escaped. The Africans took the slave owners, Ruiz and Montes, prisoner. Ordered to sail the *Amistad* back to West Africa, the Spanish slavers followed a confusing course, hoping a British or American ship would stop them. The U.S. Navy captured the *Amistad* off the coast of Long Island, New York, and again the Africans found themselves in a strange land. Cinque and thirty-eight survivors were charged with murder and piracy. Women and children were also held.

However, Cinque and the other African were no longer in slave territory. Many in New England considered slavery a barbaric practice, inappropriate for a democracy. At the center of the event stood the slavers, Ruiz and Montes, who illegally transported the Africans to Cuba (Spain had technically abolished the slave trade in 1820). In Cuba, Cinque's and the other Africans' documents were altered, stating they had been born in Cuba, where slavery was legal.

There followed a series of trials, the issues of salvage, murder, the legalities of the Spanish slave trade, forgery—and whether the Africans should be regarded as human or cargo. The case moved from a circuit court in Hartford (Connecticut) to the U.S. District Court in New Haven (Connecticut). The judge, Andrew Judson, found in the Africans' favor, but President Martin Van Buren pressed the government to appeal. However, the abolitionists on the defense committee convinced the seventy-three-year-old John Quincy Adams to argue the case before the U.S. Supreme Court. After Adams had argued eloquently for eight hours, the justices upheld the lower court ruling. Months after the Supreme Court decision, the surviving Africans—some had died during their confinement—sailed for Africa.

Seemingly, slave insurrections fascinated Du Bois because they contradicted the myth of slave docility. Because of his interest in history, Du Bois frequently wrote about slavery and slave uprisings. In 1906, he published *The Negro*

Church: Report of a Social Study Made under the Direction of Atlanta University: together with the Proceedings of the Eighth Conference for the Study of Negro Problems, held at Atlanta University, May 26, 1903, in which he included a full discussion of Toussaint L'Ouverture (Haiti, 1743?–1803) and slave rebel leaders in the United States, such as Gabriel Prosser, Denmark Vessey, and Nat Turner. Subsequently, in his *Amsterdam News* column (February 10, 1940), "He recalled the history of the American Missionary Association, and the connection therewith of the *Amistad* Case and of John Quincy Adams."

Later (*Amsterdam News*, December 8, 1940) Du Bois celebrated the one hundredth anniversary of the *Creole* mutiny. The ship was en route from Hampton, Virginia, to New Orleans, Louisiana. Overpowering the crew, the slaves took control of the vessel and sailed to the Bahamas, where they were granted asylum and freedom.

Earlier (1931) Du Bois had traveled to Charleston, South Carolina (*The Crisis*, August 1931), where he visited the tree from which Denmark Vessey was hung. Continuing to write of slave rebellions, Du Bois "wrote a stirring historical introduction to the reproduction of three panels on the theme of the *Amistad* mutiny done by Hale Woodruff (1900–1980) for the library at Talladega College" (*Phylon*, 1941). *See also*: Brown, John; Douglass, Frederick; Slavery.

FURTHER READING

"African Testimony." *New York Journal of Commerce,* January 10, 1840:2.

Aptheker, Herbert. *American Negro Slave Revolts.* New York: International Publishers, 1969.

"The Captured African of the Amistad." *New York Morning Herald,* October 4, 1839:2.

Du Bois, W.E.B. *The Negro Church: Report of a Social Study Made under the Direction of Atlanta University: together with the Proceedings of the Eighth Conference for the Study of Negro Problems, held at Atlanta University, May 26, 1903.* Atlanta: Atlanta University Press, 1903.

"An Incident." *New York Commercial Advertiser,* September 26, 1839.

Jones, Howard. *Mutiny of the Amistad: The Saga of a Slave Revolt and Its Impact on American Abolition, Law, and Diplomacy.* New York: Oxford University Press, 1987.

Kramer, Helen. *Amistad Revolt, 1839.* Cleveland, OH: Pilgrim Press, 1997.

"Testimony of James Covey in the United States District Court." National Archives, November 20, 1839.

Courtney Young

SOCIALISM/COMMUNISM

Socialism and communism, both grounded in the work of Karl Marx and Friedrich Engels, posit an economic class–based oppression that crosses national boundaries around the world. Socialist ideals have informed W.E.B. Du Bois' work since his college days at Fisk University and were cemented, most argue, by a journey abroad in 1893; this journey permitted him to see a class oppression in a racially homogeneous context (Berlin) that was no less insidious than the racial oppression of his home country. Du Bois' political thought evolved throughout the course of his public life and work to include both socialism and communism in the struggle for black liberation.

In 1909, joined by several other radical black liberationists as well as three white Socialist compatriots, Du Bois formed the National Association for the Advancement of Colored People (NAACP). With these same three people, Charles Edward Russell, William English Walling, and Mary White Ovington, Du Bois became a member of the American Socialist Party in 1910. Resigning his membership in 1912 to support Woodrow Wilson in a misguided attempt to garner pragmatic political gain for American blacks, Du Bois nonetheless continued to push both his friends and fellow Socialists to address the issue of race oppression now, rather than wait for it to disappear with the onset of the socialist utopia. While many have focused upon Du Bois as a writer of race issues (e.g., Brotz), Du Bois, from the start of his intellectual development, believed, in the words of Drake, that "race was an evolutionary product of a materialist reality" that created a uniquely invidious form of exploitation that required immediate corrective attention.

Despite his ongoing acknowledgment of economic gain as the primary method of black liberation, Du Bois struggled to incorporate an interlocking analysis of race and class in his landmark study *The Philadelphia Negro* (1899). While Du Bois sought to focus upon a racial analysis of the situation of blacks, he was forced to recognize that "[t]here is no doubt that in Philadelphia the centre and kernel of the Negro problem so far as the white people are concerned is the narrow opportunities afforded Negroes for earning a decent living. . . . Industrial freedom of opportunity has by long experience been proven to be generally best for all" (394). The principles of the Niagara Movement (1905) more explicitly blended race and class equality by addressing labor issues in addition to political rights. Both works reflect Du Bois at the start of the process of incorporating the class-based analysis offered by socialism into his antiracist work.

Black Reconstruction (1935) represents Du Bois' initial work in the Marxist method. His first extensive visit to the Soviet Union in 1926 reinforced Du Bois' dissatisfaction with American Socialists' focus on economic determinism and partially inspired his shift to a critical race analysis (which necessarily included class) in the manner of Karl Marx himself. The international aspect of European socialism blended with his own travel around the world (1936) and lifetime commitment to black liberation to form a groundwork for his own political and theoretical creation, Pan-Africanism.

A key distinction between socialism and communism lies in the strategy each ideology proposes to ensure the triumph of the working class. Despite Du Bois' previous trips, in 1940 Du Bois remained a staunch socialist. In his autobiography *Dusk of Dawn*, he stated:

I was not and am not a communist. I do not believe in the dogma of inevitable revolution in order to right economic wrong. I think war is worse than hell, and that it seldom or never forwards the advance of the world. On the other hand, I believed and still believe that Karl Marx was one of the greatest men of modern times and that he put his finger squarely upon our difficulties when he said that economic foundations . . . are the determining factions in the development of civilization.(303)

The distress caused by his 1950–1951 trial and acquittal of federal charges of failing to register as a foreign agent heightened Du Bois' sensitivity to intraracial class stratification:

I thought this inner Negro cultural ideal would be built on ancient African communism, supported and developed by the memory of slavery and the experience of caste, which would drive the Negro group into a spiritual unity precluding economic class development and inner class struggle. This was once possible, but now improbable. (*Autobiography* 392).

Du Bois critiqued American blacks for failing to realize that southern whites had seized upon the charge of "Communist" to thwart his race work. The very organization he had formed with blacks and Socialists alike, the NAACP, led such efforts in the black community with its willful blindness to the strategy used by the white elite. This blindness was most painfully demonstrated by the NAACP Legal Defense Fund's snub of the Du Bois case.

Toward the end of his life, Du Bois, discouraged by his rebuffed attempts to "racialize" white American socialists and to radicalize the black bourgeoisie, embraced the solution offered by communism. While Du Bois had in the past winked at the excesses of Stalin's purges in recognition of the destabilizing international intrigue committed by the United States, his personal experiences with the horrors of McCarthyism and the silence of his race leadership moved Du Bois toward revolutionary belief. At this point, encouraged by the anticolonial movements in Africa, Du Bois turned a realistic eye on the legacy of Stalin and recognized the nature of his rule. Nevertheless, Du Bois maintained his Marxist methodology, praising the Soviet state for its positive influences upon the national liberation movements in Africa, Asia, and the Americans as being conducive to this theory of Pan-Africanism and the ultimate goal of black liberation. In an interlude in *The Autobiography of W.E.B. Du Bois* (1968), he stated:

I now state my conclusion frankly and clearly. I believe in communism. I mean by communism a planned way of life in the production of wealth and work designed for building a state whose object is the highest welfare of its people and not merely the profit of a part.

He joined the Communist Party, USA in 1961 before moving to Ghana. *See also: Dusk of Dawn*; National Association for the Advancement of Colored People (NAACP): Ovington, Mary White; Pan-Africanism; University of Berlin; Walling, William English.

FURTHER READING

Brotz, Howard. *African American Social and Political Thought. 1850–1920*. New Brunswick, NJ: Transaction Publishers, 1992.

Drake, Willie Avon. *From Reform to Communism:The Intellectual Development of W.E.B. Du Bois*. Ann Arbor, MI: University Microfilms International, 1985.

Du Bois, W.E.B. *The Autobiography of W.E.B. Du Bois: A Soliloquy on Viewing My Life from the Last Decade of Its First Century*. New York: International Publishers, 1968.

——. *Dusk of Dawn: An Essay toward an Autobiography of a Race Concept*. New York: Harcourt Brace, 1940.

——. *The Philadelphia Negro*. Philadelphia: Published for the University, 1899.

Fried, Richard M. *Nightmare in Red: The McCarthy Era in Perspective*. New York: Oxford University Press, 1990.

Horne, Gerald C. *Black and Red: W.E.B. Du Bois and the Afro-American Response to the Cold War, 1944–1963*. Albany: State University of New York Press, 1986.

Marable, Manning. "Why Black Americans Are Not Socialist." In *Speaking Truth to Power: Essays on Race, Resistance and Radicalism*. Boulder: Westview Press, 1996.

Ange-Marie Hancock

THE SOULS OF BLACK FOLK

Published by the Chicago firm of A. C. McClurg and Company in 1903, *The Souls of Black Folk* contains fourteen chapters. For the book Du Bois revised nine previously published essays and incorporated five new ones. He gave each chapter two epigraphs—one, words from a "white" poetic source, the other, a few bars from a "black" spiritual. The book, then, addresses audiences on both sides of the color line.

"The Negro," Du Bois writes in the introductory chapter of *Souls*, "sees his life through the eyes of a white world." This practice forces on him a double consciousness and leads him to develop two separate souls and two competing sets of ideals. The history of blacks in the United States, Du Bois states, is the history of this struggle within the individual self. Du Bois claims that blacks at the opening of the twentieth century desire to merge these two selves into a hybrid that retains the positive aspects of each. To do this, African Americans must continue to struggle for freedom and liberty and must begin to strive for knowledge. Although such knowledge enables double consciousness to be overcome, it heightens black outrage at the injustices of racial inequality and makes him a target for new forms of prejudice. The remainder of *Souls*, then illustrates these ideas through chapters written in literary genres that range from memoir and history to fiction and the literary essay. Today *The Souls of Black Folk* stands as one of Du Bois' most important pieces of writing and one of the most influential books of its era.

FURTHER READING

Andrews, William L. *Critical Essays on W.E.B. Du Bois*. Boston: G. K. Hall, 1985.

Todd Gibson

SOUTH AFRICA

As a Pan-Africanist, W.E.B. Du Bois kept his readers apprised of the situation in South Africa. Although he never wrote an extensive publication on South Africa, Du Bois' regular updates in the editorials of *The Crisis*, surveys of global race relations in *Phylon*, and weekly column "Pan Africa" in *People's Voice* and other newspaper columns were in keeping with his insistence of "Africa for Africans." Moreover, Du Bois never failed to mention South Africa within the context of the ongoing worldwide struggle of African people. In essence, his commentary, spanning several decades, provides a rare glimpse of South Africa as apartheid rule evolved.

In 1911, for example, Du Bois relayed that a man of mixed ancestry—or a "colored"—had been appointed as the Treasurer General of South Africa. The Constitution predicated such a position on European ancestry; however, the law was interpreted to include this candidate as well. Likewise, *The Crisis* editorial also reported that this was an occasion for great optimism on the part of a Dr. Boon who predicted that "we are already on the road toward a Native Parliament which is only 100 years off" (*The Crisis*, January 1911). Furthermore, Du Bois' section "A Chronicle of Race Relations" in *Phylon* (1940–1944) provided information on various topics such as medical facilities/training for Africans, housing segregation, strikes, manipulation of the census, crime rates, racism within student unions, and particularly the plight of the African laborer under the subheadings of "Africa" and "South Africa."

This type of straightforward reporting stands in sharp contrast to the tone of other editorials. Obviously outraged, Du Bois (February 1930) used the occasion of Jan Smuts' visit to the United States to expose the unforgivable flaw of this "great, international statesman," namely, his hand in the racist policy of his country. After listing the injustices suffered by indigenous South Africans, Du Bois concluded, "Jan Smuts, as Prime Minister and leading statesman, has raised no effective voice and merely calls them patient asses." In comparison, Du Bois recognized the centennial anniversary of David Livingstone's death with a tribute to "an honest practical man" (*Phylon*, 1941). Quoting extensively from Murray, Du Bois' *Phylon* entry emphasized Livingstone's humanitarianism, rejection of racial stereotypes, and genuine friendship with Africans (*Phylon*, 1941). With his piercing sarcasm, Du Bois viewed the "war in South Africa" as a current labor strike within a global context: "In Chicago, in St. Louis, in New Orleans and Oklahoma, in Liverpool and South Africa, it has been the White laborer who has driven the black man out into the desert and then stands there stupidly wondering why black folks are 'scabs' and do not 'understand' the labor movement" (*The Crisis*, May 1922). And after describing the political chaos and contradictions in South Africa, Du Bois called white rule a "medieval slave-driven oligarchy . . . a situation too tragic to be ridiculous" (*People's Voice*, October 1947).

Du Bois reported on South Africa according to his objective scientific training and as a passionate advocate for the social, economic, and political equality of Africans worldwide. *See also*: Africa; Racism.

FURTHER READING

The Crisis. (February 1930).
People's Voice (October 4, 1947).
Phylon (1941).

Shawn R. Donaldson

SOUTHERN EDUCATION BOARD

Founded in 1901 and funded in part by the General Education Board, the announced purpose of this group was that of directing a regional public school crusade in the states of the Old Confederacy. Composed of eleven northern moderates and fifteen southern progressives during its thirteen-year existence, this intersectional partnership embraced the belief that carefully formed and selectively encouraged and supported educational activity was the key to liberation of the locals from the shibboleths of the past. However, what the members had not anticipated in their planning was the impact of the white supremacy movement in the South that had been building since the collapse of Radical Reconstruction and the kinds of compromises they would have to make to ensure their own modest survival and few meager achievements. Writing in the June 1914 issue of *The Crisis*, in a review of W.T.B. Williams' *Duplications of Schools for Negro Youth*, a John F. Slater Fund occasional paper, Du Bois observes that while the Board had been established to work for and coordinate the cause of black education, something that had not been done before, it gradually evolved into a group supportive of all education before its final evolution into an agency " 'for white people only' with the cheerful assent of its Northern promoters." Consequently, black folk were slowly disabused "of any assumption they have had that the board had the slightest interest in them or intended to help except in the most casual and niggardly way (*The Crisis*, June, 1914). *See also*: Educational Philosophy; *Journal of Negro Education*; Slater Fund.

FURTHER READING

Autobiography of W.E.B. Du Bois. New York: International Publishers, 1968.

William M. King

SPINGARN MEDAL

The Spingarn Medal is an annual award instituted by the National Association for the Advancement of Colored People (NAACP) and named in honor of Joel Elias Spingarn (1875–1939). Spingarn, one of the founders of the NAACP, created the prize in 1914. The medal is awarded annually to the African American who reached the highest achievement in the previous year or during a lifetime. Du Bois was honored in 1920 for his efforts to foster racial solidarity. *See also*: National Association for the Advancement of Colored People (NAACP).

FURTHER READING

Douglas, Melvin I. *Black Winners: A History of Spingarn Medalists, 1915–1983*. Brooklyn, NY: T. Gaus. Distributed by D. A. Reid Enterprises, 1984.

Mary Young

STOCKHOLM PEACE APPEAL

In the book *In Battle for Peace* (1952), Du Bois describes the Stockholm Peace Appeal as "the greatest piece of literature which came out of the World Wars." On March 15, 1950, at a conference in Sweden, representatives from eighteen nations—including both the USSR and the United States—adopted these statements.

"We demand the absolute banning of the atomic weapon, an arm of terror and of mass extermination of populations."

"We demand the establishment of strict international control to ensure the implementation of this ban."

"We consider that the first government henceforth to use the atomic weapon against any country whatsoever will be committing a crime against humanity and should be treated as a war criminal."

"We call on all people of goodwill throughout the world to sign this appeal."

Du Bois had been active in the international peace movement, from 1949 to 1951 attending conferences in Paris, New York, Moscow, and Prague. To help spread information in the United States about the movement, he participated in the founding of the Peace Information Center in New York City and was elected chair of the Center. This group distributed "peacegrams" to raise American consciousness about worldwide antinuclear peace activities.

Central to the mission of the Peace Information Center was the circulation of the Stockholm Peace Appeal. The Center was in official existence from April 3 to October 12, 1951, and in that time it printed and distributed 485,000 copies of the Appeal, garnering over 1 million signatures in the United States.

This activity in the name of peace against atomic destruction was interpreted by anti-communist forces as Soviet machinations against U.S. foreign policy, particularly in light of the Korean War. Secretary of State Dean Acheson called the Appeal a Soviet "propaganda trick"; the House Un-American Activities Committee also attacked it as "Communist chicanery" (Broderick 210).

Du Bois responded by reiterating the international commitments to peace "regardless of beliefs and affiliations" and by naming some of the international luminaries who had signed the document, including politicians, scientists, clerics, and a Nobel Peace Prize winner.

Nevertheless, the circulation of the Appeal became the basis for a federal indictment of Du Bois and four other officials of the Center, issued on February 9, 1951. The Center was accused of failing to register as an "agent of a foreign principal."

The trial of Du Bois lasted five days, from November 8 to November 13, 1951. Recall that at the time Du Bois was already eighty-three years old. Ultimately Du Bois was deemed innocent of the charges levied against him. Du Bois never had to take the stand, as the government failed to provide any credible evidence to prove its assertions that Du Bois and the others were pawns of Soviet-directed international communism.

It seems evident, however, that during this entire process, as McCarthyism was taking its toll in U.S. politics, Du Bois himself was shifting the emphasis of his concern more directly to the issue of world socialism, and from 1952 on—if not before—he believed the Soviet Union presented the best option for the future. *See also*: McCarthyism; Peace Movement.

FURTHER READING

Du Bois, W.E.B. *In Battle for Peace: The Story of My 83rd Birthday.* New York: Masses and Mainstream, 1952.
Broderick, Francis L. *W.E.B. Du Bois, Negro Leader in a Time of Crisis.* Stanford, CA: Standford University Press, 1959.

Scot Guenter

T

TALENTED TENTH

Du Bois' theory of the "Talented Tenth" was the second chapter in *The Negro Problem, a Collection of African American Essays* (1903). In the essay, Du Bois explained his theory, maintaining that in the nineteenth century there was a talented group that existed even before he formulated the concept. He contended that there was a distinguished group of persons of exceptional abilities who were among the best of their time. For Du Bois early examples of these "talented tenthers" were abolitionists Henry Highland Gannet, Sojourner Truth, Alexander Crummel, and Frederick Douglass. "They stood as living examples of the possibilities of the Negro race. . . . They were the men [sic] who made American slavery impossible."

Now, he suggests that this group should come from the class of educated blacks, not only those with a liberal arts education but also those with vocational training: "I believe that next to the founding of the Negro colleges the most valuable addition to Negro education since the war, has been industrial training for black boys. Nevertheless, I insist that the object of all true education is not to make men carpenters, it is to make carpenters men."

He wished to limit the group to 10 percent because at the time he speculated that only 10 percent of African Americans had the education or training that he envisioned was necessary for the advancement of the race.

Education was not the only factor to determine "Talented Tenth" membership but also hard work, a sense of personal worth, and commitment to racial uplift. Although superficially the theory seems elitist, Du Bois was facing the realities of the time. Many groups, including the National Association for the Advancement of Colored People, the Urban League, the Association for Negro History, the Brotherhood of Sleeping Car Porters, and other organizations, formed around Du Bois's Talented Tenth theory.

FURTHER READING

The Negro Problem. New York: James Pott and Company, 1903.
Worlds of Color. New York: Mainstream Pub., 1961.

Malaika Horne

TROTTER, WILLIAM MONROE (1872–1934)

A businessman, editor, and civil rights leader, Trotter was born into a financially comfortable family on his grandparents' farm near Chillicothe, Ohio. In 1891 he entered Harvard, where he became the first African American admitted to Phi Beta Kappa. He worked at various jobs until 1902, when he founded the *Boston Guardian*.

Trotter established the *Guardian* specifically to oppose the Tuskegee Machine. He was a militant of whom Du Bois observed that he had an "intense hatred of all racial discrimination and segregation. He was particularly incensed at the compromising philosophy of Booker T. Washington" (*The Crisis*, May 1934).

Washington was not the sole focus of Trotter's animosity. In November 1914 he went to the Wilson White House to protest Wilson's racial policies. After a forty-five-minute argument between the two, Wilson ordered Trotter from the White House because of "insulting language."

Trotter's personal philosophy was as uncompromising with African Americans as it was with European Americans. A member of the Niagara Movement, he refused to attend a conference called by Oswald Garrison Villard because he distrusted the motives of whites.

An apparent suicide, Trotter died on his sixty-second birthday. At his death, Du Bois wrote in *The Crisis* (May 1934):

> I can understand his death. I can see a man of sixty, tired and disappointed, facing poverty and defeat. Standing amid indifferent friends and triumphant enemies. So he went to the window of his Dark Tower, and beckoned to Death; up from where She lay among the lilies. And Death, like a whirlwind, swept up to him. I shall think of him as lying silent, cold and still; at last at peace, dreamless and serene. Let no trumpet of doom disturb him from his perfect and eternal rest.

See also: *Boston Guardian*; Niagara Movement; Villard, Oswald Garrison; Washington, Booker T.

FURTHER READING

Fox, Stephen. *The Guardian of Boston: William Monroe Trotter*. New York: Atheneum, 1970.

Mary Young

TUSKEGEE INSTITUTE

In 1881 Booker T. Washington—then on the staff of the Hampton Institute—was sent to Tuskegee, Alabama, to start a similar program of industrial education for blacks. Through Washington's indefatigable personal effort,

Tuskegee grew steadily in size and influence. Washington clearly expressed his belief in the necessity of combining physical with intellectual labor and his conciliatory stance toward southern segregation in his famous "Atlanta Compromise" address of 1895. The near universal approval of his message further increased the flow of northern money into Tuskegee. In less than twenty years Tuskegee became the most powerful black educational institution in the United States.

In 1894, Washington responded to Du Bois' request for employment by offering him a position teaching mathematics; however, Washington's telegram arrived after Du Bois had already accepted a position at Wilberforce University (Ohio). Washington offered Du Bois a position as head of a proposed sociological institute in 1899. They discussed the position through the remainder of the year and into early 1900 before Du Bois refused the offer—this time because he was uncomfortable with Washington's philosophy of education and his conciliatory views on segregation. After 1901 Du Bois began to voice criticism of Washington's educational philosophy and of Tuskegee. Du Bois' third chapter of *The Souls of Black Folk*, "Of Mr. Booker T. Washington and Others," opened the breach between them that later solidified with Du Bois' organization of the Niagara Movement. Du Bois continued his attacks on Washington and his "Tuskegee Machine" by charging that Washington was bribing the black press to print material supportive of Tuskegee and to withhold criticism. *See also*: *The Souls of Black Folk*; Washington, Booker T.; Wilberforce University.

FURTHER READING

Du Bois, W.E.B. *The Souls of Black Folk*. Chicago: A. C. McClurg, 1903.
"The Overlook." *Horizon* (January 1907).

Todd Gibson

U

UNIONS AND STRIKES

After the Emancipation Proclamation, some labor unions welcomed blacks as a way of ending poverty and other social ills. In 1876, the Knights of Labor held its first national convention and proclaimed no distinctions of "race, creed or color." Union campaigns proceeded in the South, resulting in fourteen unions of black carpenters and marking the beginning of unionized black workers. Unfortunately, dissension within the ranks of the Knights of Labor led to its decline. On its heels emerged the American Federation of Labor (AFL) as a larger and more successful movement. The AFL, however, seemed less inclined to include black workers, and the AFL allowed its unions to amend its laws to exclude blacks.

Between 1881 and 1900, there were fifty strikes by U.S. workers protesting black employment and their nonunion status. Paradoxically, these same union protesters opposed blacks joining unions. Thus, African Americans began a protracted struggle for their democratic rights as workers and citizens.

W.E.B. Du Bois' interest in unions was piqued by his growing realization that it was not just the poor white laboring classes responsible for the suppression of blacks in unions. His studies revealed a universal problem of the exploitation of labor by management and big business. Upon examining labor problems in the United States, Africa, Asia, and the Caribbean, Du Bois realized that imperialism drove the world economy and that its primary aim was to obtain cheap materials and labor to compensate for private profits and higher wages paid to white workers in Europe and the United States. Du Bois also took a great interest in apartheid in South Africa and sharply criticized its political, economic, and legal discrimination against blacks and other people of color.

Because African Americans were not allowed to join labor unions, some worked as scabs to break strikes. European American workers charged that the low pay of blacks also kept white wages down. Black workers were thus pitted against white workers, further increasing racial tension.

Du Bois strongly favored a less-market-driven economy. He supported a socialist government that controlled and planned industry and eschewed the idle rich or privileged classes. For example, the objective of unions in Russia was not to strike since management and labor were not antagonistic. They had a common interest he felt, that is, to increase production and improve the quality of life for its workers.

According to Du Bois, trade unions, under capitalism, kept blacks out of unions, supported world wars, and condemned socialism. Moreover, he continued, work under capitalism was for private profits, which put workers at a distinct disadvantage. Nonetheless, these unions did have some merit. The Congress of Industrial Organizations (CIO) was lauded for its unionizing of both skilled and unskilled workers. It also brought blacks and whites together, resulting in greater racial tolerance and understanding.

From 1900 to 1930, black membership in trade unions increased from 30,000 to 100,000. During World War II, there were an estimated 1 million black union workers.

Du Bois believed that a true democracy is intricately connected to labor and gives workers a voice in the government. Thus, to sustain a true democracy, the government must protect the rights of all workers despite race, creed, or color. *See also*: Socialism/Communism; South Africa.

FURTHER READING

"A Chronicle of Race Relations." *Phylon* (1941).
The Crisis (November 1916).
"Postscript." *The Crisis* (March 1932).

Malaika Horne

UNITED NATIONS

The United Nations Conference on International Organization (UNCIO) convened at San Francisco on April 25, 1945. Washington officials understood that the United States would be a global leader in the postwar world. They wanted to defeat the isolationism characteristic of the interwar period and avert possible Senate rejection of UN membership. Policymakers wanted to "sell" the public on the peace process, if only at a symbolic level. The State Department accordingly asked certain influential organizations, including the National Association for the Advancement of Colored People (NAACP), to send consultants to the proceedings. Representatives from these groups observed the plenary sessions and met occasionally with official U.S. delegates to share their organizations' views. This government initiative created opportunities for activists to raise civil rights and human rights concerns and to have these addressed in charter documents and in the structure of the organization.

The NAACP chose secretary Walter White, vice president Mary McLeod Bethune, and Du Bois, the Association's director of special research, as consultants. The NAACP polled other civil rights and black organizations so that the consultants could carry their various views to the U.S. delegation.

While in San Francisco, Du Bois and Walter White pressed the United States and other delegates to adopt an international bill of rights, undertake colonial reform, and prohibit racial discrimination. They also disclosed what they learned to black organizations that lacked official status. Pressure from nongovernmental organizations helped secure token recognition of human rights from the official conferees and reference to human rights in the charter documents. *See also*: National Association for the Advancement of Colored People (NAACP).

FURTHER READING

Autobiography of W.E.B. Du Bois. New York: International Publishers, 1968.

Brenda Gayle Plummer

UNIVERSITY OF BERLIN

W.E.B. Du Bois studied social science at the University of Berlin for two years without receiving his Ph.D. Although he rapidly completed the requirements for the doctorate, a combination of bureaucratic and political factors prevented him from securing the degree. In 1892 Du Bois won a fellowship from the Slater Fund to support his German education. At the University he joined a generation of early American social scientists in receiving instruction from German historical economists who argued that economies developed from their social and political contexts; they were not the products of laissez-faire's abstract laws. From this premise, they argued for a strong state role in economic policymaking and the improvement of social conditions. Du Bois returned from Germany with a deep belief in the power of social science to engender social reforms. Du Bois traveled throughout Europe while a student at Berlin. To his delight he often traveled without systematic discrimination and enjoyed the company of Europeans. Yet he was often mistaken for a Jew and came to compare Europe's deep anti-Semitism with the U.S. system of race relations.

Du Bois returned to the United States in 1894 after the Slater Fund refused to extend his funding and the University denied his application for an early examination for the doctorate. The Slater Fund hastily backed away from the idea that they might support graduate education for African Americans. When they turned their support toward education in the manual arts, Du Bois' cause was lost. In 1894 he returned to Great Barrington, Massachusetts, and quickly accepted a teaching position at Wilberforce University in Ohio. *See also*: Germany; Great Barrington, Massachusetts; Slater Fund; Wilberforce University.

FURTHER READING

Autobiography of W.E.B. Du Bois. New York: International Publishers, 1968.

Drew VandeCreek

UNIVERSITY OF PENNSYLVANIA

In 1895 Du Bois was not happy in his position as professor of ancient languages at Wilberforce University (Ohio). When the opportunity arose for a one-year appointment as an "assistant instructor in sociology" at the University of Pennsylvania in Philadelphia, Du Bois took it without hesitation. Later he attributed the unusual title—and the fact that he was given neither teaching responsibilities nor office space at the university—to the administration's reluctance to hire a black.

Du Bois' appointment came in a roundabout manner. In 1895, Susan P. Wharton, philanthropist and member of the College Settlement Association's executive committee, contacted the university's administration to ask if the university would join her organization in conducting a sociological survey of the city's black population. She suggested the study be headed by Samuel McCune Lindsay, an assistant professor of sociology at the university, but Lindsay demurred, thinking the study would be better conducted by an African American. Du Bois was awarded the post and was charged with completing a survey of blacks living in the city's Seventh Ward, the area where most of Philadelphia's black population resided. Once established there, Du Bois began surveying its residents about all aspects of their lives. It has been estimated that he spent 835 hours in the field interviewing twenty-five households. His study was published by the university in 1899 as *The Philadelphia Negro*. By this point he had accepted a position at Atlanta University. Years later, Du Bois would write about his bitterness at not having been offered a full-time position by the University of Pennsylvania after the successful completion of the project. *See also*: *The Philadelphia Negro*.

FURTHER READING

Logan, Rayford, W., ed. "My Evolving Program for Negro Freedom." *What the Negro Wants*. Chapel Hill: University of North Carolina Press, 1944.

Todd Gibson

V

VERSAILLES

Following World War I, European nations and the United States met at Versailles near Paris to arrange "terms of peace" for all countries. During the time of the Peace Conference at Versailles, Du Bois was organizing the Pan-African Congress of 1919 in Paris. Its purpose was to bring together leaders of black people throughout the world to plan political, economic, and educational reforms for all people of color. Du Bois' proposal was not a call for racial separatism but a call for the centralization of race effort and the recognition of racial harmony.

At the conclusion of the Pan-African meeting, Du Bois focused on three main ideas. First, European and American powers would be asked to turn over German colonies to an international organization. Next, they would be asked to establish a code of law for the protection of black Africans. Finally, the Allies would be asked to administer equal and fair treatment in the governing of African people.

Du Bois attended the Peace Conference at Versailles as a delegate of the NAACP. Du Bois lobbied for his ambitious ideas of colonization and the issues of the people of color as set forth at the Pan-African Congress. Unfortunately, the diplomats at the conference were not sympathetic to his ideas.

Even though the Pan-African Congress of 1919 did not influence the deliberations at the Peace Conference at Versailles, Du Bois believed it was successful because it brought to the forefront the concerns of Black people worldwide. *See also*: Colonialism; France; Pan-Africanism.

FURTHER READING

The Chicago Defender (May 26, 1945).
"Opinion." *The Crisis* (May 1919).

Faye P. Snorton

VILLARD, OSWALD GARRISON (1872–1949)

Villard, a New York philanthropist and publisher, was born in Germany on March 13, 1872. He was the son of Helen Garrison Villard (1835–1928), a reformer and suffragist, and Henry Villard (1835–1900), a railroad magnate who owned *The Nation* and the *New York Evening Post*. Villard graduated from Harvard in 1893, and in 1897, he joined his father's staff at the *New York Evening Post*. In 1900, he became owner and president. Like his maternal grandfather, William Lloyd Garrison, Villard was one of the United States' foremost liberal editors and authors, espousing pacifism, anti-imperialism, women's suffrage, and civil rights for blacks.

In 1909 Villard and his mother were among the founders of the National Association for the Advancement of Colored People (NAACP). Villard's reputation, energy, and organizational skill made him the dominant figure for the first five years, but his support of Booker T. Washington, and promise that the NAACP would not oppose him, led to tensions. His conservative views on race and expectations that black members should be humble and grateful for his patronage offended Du Bois and others.

Du Bois recalled that Villard's wife, Julia Breckenridge Sandford, was a southerner who refused to attend integrated events with blacks or Jews. In 1915 Villard resigned as NAACP treasurer and chairman because he could not share authority with Du Bois, the editor of the NAACP magazine, *The Crisis*. Villard was a pioneer in racial justice who is remembered as an indefatigable reformer and publisher limited by his ties to the conservative social elite. He died in New York City on October 1, 1949. *See also*: Harvard; National Association for the Advancement of Colored People (NAACP); Washington, Booker T.

FURTHER READING

Humes, Dollera Joy. *Oswald Garrison Villard, Liberal of the 1920's*. Syracuse: Syracuse University Press, 1960.
Wreszin, Michael. *Oswald Garrison Villard, Pacifist at War*. Bloomington: Indiana University Press, 1965.

Peter C. Holloran

W

WALLING, WILLIAM ENGLISH (1877–1936)

William Walling English, best known for his role in founding the National Association for the Advancement of Colored People (NAACP), was born in Louisville, Kentucky, in 1877 to a wealthy and well-connected family. His great-grandfather was a Democratic candidate for vice president. While attending Harvard Law School, after graduating from the University of Chicago, he retained his southern-bred distaste for being thrown into the company of blacks. After dropping out of law school he spent several years becoming a radical journalist and social reformer. Although he was never able to completely free himself from the racial culture in which he had been reared, he recognized it, isolated it, and acted in spite of it. When in 1908 the European American citizens of Abraham Lincoln's former home of Springfield, Illinois, went on a rampage against their African American neighbors, Walling and his socially conscious wife, Anna Strunsky Walling, were soon on the scene to investigate.

Walling's celebrated article on the riot in *The Independent* (September 3, 1908), "Race War in the North," touched off a series of events leading to the founding of the NAACP by Walling, Mary White Ovington, Henry Moskowitz, Charles Edward Russell, and Oswald Garrison Villard, all prominent European American socialists or liberals. It was, of course, the existence of Du Bois' predominantly black Niagara Movement that helped pave the way for the new civil rights organization. After the group's founding in 1910, Walling was largely responsible for arranging for Du Bois to move to New York and become publicity director and editor of *The Crisis*. Without Du Bois and the bulk of the Niagara Movement, the NAACP might have been condemned to remain primarily an organization of white social reformers, instead of gradually being able to achieve a depth of support within the black community. Walling continued to support Du Bois against his critics in the organization, chief of whom was Oswald Garrison Villard, the publisher of the *New York Evening Post*. Villard was a major financial and political backer of the group in its early years but frequently engaged in power struggles with Du Bois. Walling's frequent support helped make it possible for Du Bois to continue working in the NAACP until 1934, when Du Bois resigned. Walling himself remained a member of the board until his death in 1936. Having worked for much of his adult life on behalf of labor and also blacks, Walling died in Europe attempting to aid victims of the Nazis.

Du Bois reassured Walling some twenty years after the founding that he was surely "the real founder of the NAACP." Ironically, the two men were not merely thrown together for a common historical task, however. They were quite certainly both descended from Chretian Du Bois, a farmer near Lille, France, two of whose sons emigrated to the New World in the mid-seventeenth century. Du Bois seems never to have been aware of this relationship—possibly as tenth cousins—but Walling may have been later in his life. *See also*: Harvard; National Association for the Advancement of Colored People (NAACP); Niagara Movement; Ovington, Mary White; Race Riots; Villard, Oswald Garrison.

FURTHER READING

Boylan, James. *Revolutionary Lives: Anna Strunsky and William English Walling*. Amherst: University of Massachussets Press, 1998.

Jack Stuart

WAR AND PEACE

The source of World War I, according to Du Bois, lay in colonialism and imperialist exploitation. To end this abuse of power, European colonial patterns would have to be reversed. But, if there must be war, then "its basic purpose . . . must be an end to poverty" (*The Amsterdam News*, March 31, 1942).

During the Great War there were organizations dedicated to peace that included on their program limited eradication of colonial expansion. Du Bois, however, noted the presence of racism in these national and international organizations and that racism trivialized their announced intentions.

The basic sources of peace, on the other hand, for Du Bois required not only organizations but a structured program that would include an agreement to outlaw war, an agreement on modes of arbitration, and an agreement on disarmament. However, Du Bois asserted that "until the realities of racism, colonialism and imperialism are faced and overcome . . . these are basic sources of war" (*The Crisis*, March 1925)

Along with the elimination of the sources of war, Du Bois argued that the "emancipation of the black masses of the world is one guarantee of a firm foundation for world peace" (*The Chicago Defender*, November 11, 1947). Nevertheless, there is an overriding necessity for peace, Du Bois suggested. However, the forces for peace are usually those driven from power by social revolution and those enriching themselves in the West who want war.

Advancing a similar argument during the Korean War, Du Bois chided those who maintained that the action in Korea was patriotic. He wrote that it was "our bounded duty to stop the fighting . . . and to help see to it that Koreans make their own decisions without United States help" (*The Chicago Defender*, September 23, 1950).

At the height of the Cold War, Du Bois earnestly maintained in "I Take My Stand for Peace" (1950) that the United States wanted war because war was necessary for the economy. "We must have war. . . . [I]n no other way can we keep our workers employed and maintain huge profits save by spending seventy thousand million dollars a year for war preparation and adding to the vast debt of over 200 thousand millions" (*Masses and Mainstream*, April 1951). With the war in Korea, the United States was prepared for war with the Soviet Union. Instead the Russians "did not fight and issued a call for world peace, for union against the atomic bomb." The United States did not heed the Soviet call; instead, the U.S. government jailed peace advocates. For Du Bois, to escape the insidious eschewing of civil liberties, an individual must publicly and repeatedly proclaim:

- that he hates Russia.
- that he opposes Socialism and Communism.
- that he supports wholeheartedly the war in Korea.
- that he is ready to spend any amount for further war, anywhere, anytime.
- that he is ready to fight the Soviet Union, China and any other country, or all countries together.
- that he believes in the use of the atom bomb or any other weapon of mass destruction, and regards anyone opposed as a traitor.
- that he not only believes in and consents to all these things but is willing to spy on his neighbors and denounce them if they do not believe as he does ("*I Take My Stand for Peace*").

These public pronouncements are necessary because, Du Bois argued, the leaders of the United States are afraid of an idea—socialism. After World War I the United States envisioned itself as the successor "of the empire on which the sun already sets." Unsuccessful in its imperialist designs, the United States promoted war with the Soviet Union.

Consequently, Du Bois was unwavering in his stance. "I take my stand beside the millions in every nation and continent and cry *Peace—No More War!*" ("*I Take My Stand for Peace*"). *See also*: Cold War; Colonialism; Peace Movement; Racism; Stockholm Peace Appeal; World War I.

FURTHER READING

Du Bois, W.E.B. "The African Roots of the War." *Atlantic Monthly* (May 1915).
——. "The World Problem of the Color Line." *Manchester (NH) Leader* (November 16, 1914.
——. "I Take My Stand for Peace." *Masses and Mainstream* (April 1951).

Mary Young

WASHINGTON, BOOKER T. (1856–1915)

Washington has been viewed as the ideological antipode of Du Bois. However, their early encounters were far from antagonistic. At one point, the "Wizard of Tuskegee" actually offered Du Bois a teaching post, just as Du Bois was quite uncritical–initially–of Washington's infamous "Atlantic Compromise speech" of 1895, which fundamentally endorsed racial segregation. Du Bois, in fact, congratulated Washington on this address and suggested that his words might form the basis for an equitable racial settlement.

At the turn of the century, Washington offered to hire Du Bois as director of research, but Du Bois did not accept, perhaps because of apprehension that he would be dominated like other faculty of Tuskegee. But shortly after that, Du Bois, in reviewing Washington's memoir *Up from Slavery*, deplored what he saw as the crassness of Washington's educational and social programs, which he saw as overly influenced by millionaire elites. Then in 1903, Du Bois' book *The Souls of Black Folk* was published. Included was an essay, "Of Mr. Washington and Others," that sharply assailed Washington's philosophy–particularly industrial education and racial accommodation. Du Bois felt that Washington's crass materialism and his compromises with powerful forces denied African Americans all manner of rights. He felt that Washington's philosophy meant the abandonment of political power, civil rights, and higher education–losses that Du Bois felt were irreparable. Du Bois conceded that Washington's fostering of self-help and his opposition to some forms of racial injustice were noteworthy. But this concession only made the thrust of his critique seem more reasonable.

When Du Bois played a role in the founding of the National Association for the Advancement of Colored People (NAACP), opposition to the reigning philosophy of Washington was a significant animating factor. Du Bois found ludicrous Washington's deriding of the study of French and Latin. Washington's jokes about educated blacks were anathema to Du Bois.

Unsurprisingly, Washington began to view Du Bois as a leading antagonist and sought to use against him tactics he had deployed against other presumed foes in the past, for example, using his vast influence among African American newspapers to guarantee negative coverage of Du Bois and his various initiatives.

However, the deprivation of black voting rights, the proliferation of lynching, the continued exploitation of Africa, the persistence of employment dis-

Booker T. Washington. Courtesy of Historical Collections of Berea College.

crimination, and residential segregation meant that many African Americans were willing to entertain an alternate voice. By the time of Washington's death, the NAACP was well on its way to becoming the premier voice of protest against racism in the United States. *See also*: *The Souls of Black Folk*; National Association for the Advancement of Colored People (NAACP); Tuskegee Institute.

FURTHER READING

Harlan, Louis R. *Booker T. Washington: The Wizard of Tuskegee, 1901–1915.* New York: Oxford University Press, 1983.

Gerald Horne

WILBERFORCE UNIVERSITY

In 1894, Wilberforce University (Ohio) offered Du Bois a professorship in the classics with his primary responsibilities the teaching of Greek and Latin. Du Bois immediately accepted the position and prepared to leave for Ohio, to teach at this small African Methodist Episcopal (AME) university. This was the first professional university teaching position held by Du Bois. Ironically, one week after accepting the Wilberforce position, two additional offers came from Tuskegee Institute in Alabama and Lincoln University in Missouri. Nevertheless, his tenure at Wilberforce lasted from 1894 to 1896.

Initially, Du Bois was stimulated about having the opportunity to teach at Wilberforce. Consequently, the stimulus would change to discontent. His professorship at Wilberforce was perplexing. From the beginning, university officials had problems with Du Bois' dress: example, top hat, white gloves, Van Dyck beard, and ideology. On the other hand, Du Bois was extremely critical of the general education curriculum, the acquisition of books, and the university's mission to promote higher education of black students. Manning Marable, a Du Boisian scholar, writes that Du Bois was "tactless and thoughtlessly blunt" in communicating with university and AME officials. Wilberforce's administration saw his manner and behavior as insubordination. Du Bois once described the religious requirements imposed by Wilberforce's administration as "increasingly irksome." In addition, Marable notes that the religious dogmatism of Wilberforce University severed the relationship between the ideological thought of Du Bois and the mission of the university. Nevertheless, there were positive factors of Du Bois' tenure at Wilberforce, such as meeting Paul Laurence Dunbar and Charles Young. Du Bois' association with these men in later years would prove extremely productive to his continued learning. Besides Du Bois' teaching-administrative duties, he spent much of his time revising his doctoral dissertation, *The Suppression of the African Slave Trade.*

Despite the opposition Du Bois encountered at Wilberforce, he remained a vigilant scholar–activist. In 1895, Du Bois received his doctorate in history from Harvard University. After receiving his degree, his dissertation was published by Longmans, Green and Co. in 1896. At this point in Du Bois' intellectual career, his research interests were becoming more interdisciplinary with a curricular emphasis in sociology and history. In 1896, Du Bois left Wilberforce University to accept a position as assistant instructor of sociology at the University of Pennsylvania. The purpose of this appointment was for Du Bois to conduct a survey research project of the black community in Philadelphia. Eventually, the study was published in 1899 as *The Philadelphia Negro*. Equally important, his study was considered one of the first major sociological studies conducted in the United States.

Years later, after leaving Wilberforce University, Du Bois remained consistent and critical of the method, procedure, and mission of the institution. In 1940, Du Bois gave the commencement address at Wilberforce "where he spoke the truth as he saw it." In a letter dated October 16, 1940, John M. Gandy thanked Du Bois for his commentary on and analysis of Wilberforce. In Du Bois' commentary, "The Future of Wilberforce University," he questioned the inability and unwillingness of institutional leadership and urged that Wilberforce become a productive force in black higher education. He also noted that Charles Harris Wesley was wise in rejecting Wilberforce University's offer to become president in 1932. Eventually, Wesley accepted the position in 1942, and Du Bois said, "I admire the courage of Charles H. Wesley who has undertaken the rebuilding of Wilberforce" (*The Amsterdam News*, July 11, 1942).

The experience Du Bois acquired from his brief tenure at Wilberforce University provided a context that prepared him to confront dilemmas encountered by black scholars. *See also*: African Methodist Church; Harvard; *The Philadelphia Negro; The Souls of Black Folk*.

FURTHER READING

"The Future of Wilberforce." *Journal of Negro Education* (October 1940).
"Wilberforce." *The Crisis* (August 1920).

James L. Conyers Jr.

WOMEN'S RIGHTS

W.E.B. Du Bois, like Frederick Douglass, was a nineteenth-century feminist before support of women's rights was in vogue. As early as 1887, he proclaimed his advocacy for the political and economic equality of women. In the *Fisk Herald* (December 1887), Du Bois recognized "that 'The Age of Women' is surely drawing." Du Bois' position on women's issues was best demonstrated in his many *Crisis* editorials, particularly entries written as the nation and, more important, black men debated the proposed constitutional amendment to enfranchise women. Also, *The Crisis* column "Man of the Month" featured the achievements of men and women in keeping with Du Bois' view that every reference to "man/men" was not gender specific. As each state considered the

Nineteenth Amendment for ratification, Du Bois kept his readers informed of upcoming elections and the potential impact of a black voting bloc. Moreover, he urged them to vote affirmatively in spite of racism within the suffrage movement and more generally among white women.

Du Bois exposed the leadership of the national American Woman Suffrage Association by printing their own accounts of the Louisville Convention (*The Crisis*, June 1912). On the one hand, the president, Anna Shaw, denied discrimination in the organization. Yet a resolution to denounce the disenfranchisement of blacks in the South was conveniently and forever stalled by bureaucratic procedures and supposed time constraints. Furthermore, Shaw stated:

I am in favor of colored people voting but white women have no enemy in who does more to defeat our amendment, when submitted, than colored men, and until women are recognized and permitted to vote, I am opposed to introducing into our women suffrage convention a resolution on behalf of men who, if our resolution were carried, would go straight to the polls and defeat us every time.

Initially, Du Bois refuted Shaw's accusation that the black male was the enemy of white suffragists, but later he admitted, "American negro [*sic*] voters have, in the majority of cases, not been favorable to women suffrage" (*The Crisis*, November 1917). He fully understood why this group of voters may use their experiences of victimization and the threat of a united, intensified white front as justification for voting against a woman's right to vote. It was preposterous to believe that white women would be "any more intelligent, liberal or humane toward the black, the poor and the unfortunate than white men" (*The Crisis*, August 1914). Still, Du Bois believed that white women could eventually grow empathetic to black issues through education and drawing parallels between their plight and similar oppressive circumstances. Even if hopes of an alliance with white women were inconceivable, every woman still deserved the right to vote, to become full participants in the political system of the country.

It follows that Du Bois found the moral arguments for black and female disenfranchisement inseparable: "Let every black man and woman fight for a new democracy which knows no race or sex" (*The Crisis*, May 1913). According to Du Bois, the perception of women as the weaker sex was "sheer rot" (*The Crisis*, April 1915). Their capabilities, despite sex discrimination, as contributors to the economy and civilization were quite evident throughout the society and the world. In addition, it was erroneous to assume that women's interests were protected by male voters. As the unmarried, never married, deserted, and separated, millions of women were denied even a plausible secondary voice. Furthermore, marriage held no guarantees for women.

It is conceivable, of course, for a country to decide that its unit of representation should be the family and that one person in the family should express its will. But by what possible process of rational thought can it be decided that the person to express that will should always be the male, whether he be genius or drunkard, imbecile or captain of industry? (*The Crisis*, April 1915)

Finally, his writings on women's issues often recognized and revered the unique circumstances of black womanhood. The poem "The Burden of Black Women" (*Horizon*, November 1907) and the essay "The Damnation of Women" (1920) celebrated African American women while demonstrating the extent of their denigration and exploitation within a historical context. In the fable "The Woman" (*The Crisis*, May 1911), Du Bois elevated black women to near sainthood as a lone black woman humbly went to war for the king. When the creation of a black mammy statue was under advisement, Du Bois penned his retort in "The Black Mother" (*The Crisis*, December 1912). Rather than an immortalized dedication to the "perversion of motherhood," he suggested a more fitting tribute: "Let the colored mother of today build her own statue, and let it be the four walls of her own unsullied home" (*The Crisis*, December 1912). Even in the short-lived children's periodical *The Brownies' Book*, he educated his youthful readers on the life and contributions of Sojourner Truth, a righteous defender of human and civil rights for blacks and women (*The Crisis*, April 1920). Accordingly, Du Bois had steadfast faith in the integrity of the approximately 3.3 million prospective black women voters. He insisted that they could not be physically deterred from voting or bribed like their male counterparts and therefore would bring strength to the black political voice (*The Crisis*, September 1912). *See also: The Brownies' Book*; Manliness.

FURTHER READING

"Abraham Lincoln." *Voice of the Negro* (June 1907).
"The Burden of Black Women." *Horizon* (November 1907).
Du Bois, W.E.B. "The Damnation of Women." *Darkwater: Voices from within the Veil.* New York: Harcourt, Brace, and Howe, 1920.

Shawn R. Donaldson

WOODSON, CARTER G. (1875–1950)

This pioneering black historian was born in New Canton, Virginia, one of nine children of James Henry and Anna Eliza Woodson. As a young man Woodson worked on the family's farm and later in West Virginia's coal mines. Inspired by his mother, Woodson became determined to obtain a formal education. After the family moved to Huntington, West Virginia, Woodson entered Frederick Douglass High School at the age of twenty and completed the four years in less that two. Woodson then enrolled at Kentucky's Berea College, an institution committed to interracial education, and completed his degree in 1903, one year before Kentucky's Day Act prohibited biracial education in the state.

After traveling overseas, including a teaching stint in the Philippines, in 1907

Carter G. Woodson. Courtesy of Historical Collections of Berea College.

Woodson entered the University of Chicago, where he earned a B.A. and an M.A. in history. His thesis was on eighteenth-century French diplomatic history. Woodson furthered his education at Harvard University, where he completed his Ph.D. in 1912 with a study of the secession movement in western Virginia. He became the only African American born to formerly enslaved parents to earn a doctorate in history. Woodson spent much of the next decade teaching in the high schools of Washington, D.C. In 1919 he became dean of Howard University's School of Liberal Arts, and the following year he accepted an appointment as a dean at West Virginia State College.

Scholar, editor, publisher, and teacher, Woodson was devoted to the proposition that black Americans had a significant history worthy of respect and study, a proposition that ran counter to the era's popular and academic views of African Americans. One of Woodson's greatest legacies was his founding in 1915 of the American Association of the Study of Negro Life and History. The Association began publishing the *Journal of Negro History* in 1916, with Woodson serving as editor, a position he held until 1950. The *Journal* served as the chief vehicle for scholarship on the black experience in the United States. The annual *Negro History Week*, begun in 1926, was another of Woodson's attempts to carry scholarship to the public. In 1937 Woodson began the *Negro History Bulletin* to provide black teachers and students with material for classroom use.

Woodson was a well-respected scholar, and his book *The Negro in Our History* went through nine editions and was for years the standard college-level text in the field. Woodson's scholarship was chronologically and geographically wide-ranging, moving from the colonial era to the twentieth century and taking in people of African descent throughout the Western Hemisphere. He also founded Associated Publishers in 1921 to undertake projects in black history that mainstream presses largely dismissed. Woodson retired from teaching in 1922 to devote more time to his publishing and other duties with the Association.

Du Bois consistently reviewed Woodson's publications positively; in 1916 Du Bois congratulated Woodson and the *Journal of Negro History* on completing the first year of publication (*The Crisis*, December 1916). Later, Du Bois chided Woodson for declining to join him in initiating a unified effort for the proposed three-volume *History of Black People (The Crisis*, May 1919).

Active in the National Urban League and the National Association for the Advancement of Colored People (NAACP), Woodson believed that education and black economic advancement went hand in hand. A purposeful man of vision, Woodson is now widely regarded as "the Father of Black History."

Upon Woodson's death Du Bois bemoaned that scholars like Woodson received little or no financial support for their research projects. "No white university ever recognized his work; no white scientific society ever honored him. Perhaps this was his reward" (*Chicago Globe*, April 19, 1950). *See also:*

Harvard; National Association for the Advancement of Colored People (NAACP).

FURTHER READING

Woodson, Carter G. *The Negro in Our History*. Washington, DC: Associated Pub., 1941.

Trent Watts

WORLD WAR I

Du Bois widened the scope of his cultural and intellectual agenda because of World War I in Europe. Du Bois' commentary and editorials during wartime reveal large issues at hand in the United States: the identity crisis of African American leadership; the discussion surrounding the resistance or acquiescence to cultural and intellectual mobilization; the potential fragmentation of the African American intelligentsia; and the reconstruction of leadership in the wake of problems and setbacks caused by World War I. His commentary transcended the debates surrounding the war aims and objectives, thereby relocating the discussion to issues of colonialism, European imperialism, the sovereignty of African states, and Pan-Africanism. As a result Du Bois did not quite adhere to the conventional spectrum of wartime commentary that ranged from condemnation and dissent to enthusiasm and approbation. On the contrary, Du Bois examined World War I as an enumeration of its ramifications for people of color worldwide. His foremost priority centered around two questions: What have the Allies and Central Powers done for people of color in the past? What can the Allies and Central Powers do for people of color in the present? Du Bois took the debate out of a European context and placed it in Africa, Asia, and the United States.

In 1915, "The African Roots of the War" appeared in the May issue of the *Atlantic Monthly*; it was one of Du Bois' most provocative and compelling commentaries. Du Bois concluded that imperialism in Africa was an important motivation of World War I. Suggesting that western Europe's intentions in Africa were not honorable, Du Bois queried, "What shall the end be? The world-old fearful things, War, Murder and Luxury? Or shall it be a new thing—a new peace and new democracy of all races; a great humanity of equal men? '*Semper novi ex quid Africa!*' " During the first year of the war in 1914, Du Bois abstained from formally approving U.S. intervention. Assuming the United States would enter on the side of the Allies, he urged American citizens, both African American and European American, to ponder the implications and consequences of entanglements in Europe and Africa.

A few years later Du Bois' brief editorial "Close Ranks" appeared in the July 1918 issue of *The Crisis*. The United States officially joined the Allied effort almost sixteen months earlier in April 1917 when Du Bois wrote, "We of the colored race have no ordinary interest in the outcome. . . . Let us, while this war lasts, forget our special grievances and close our ranks. . . . With our fellow citizens and the allied nations that are facing for democracy" (*The Crisis*). African Americans answered the call to arms immediately after the United States declared war on Germany in 1917, and though his article appeared after the fact, his message was for African Americans to take an active and enthusiastic part in the war for the sake of the Allies and for democracy.

Soon after the war's end, Du Bois returned to the social agenda he had constructed as a part of the Niagara Movement. He traveled to Paris in December 1918 to collect documents and personal narratives concerning African American soldiers for a book about "their reaction to their treatment and the effect of all this on modern culture" ("Documents of the War," *The Crisis*, May 1919). Du Bois was also in Paris to confirm rumors that European American soldiers had actually treated their German enemies better than they had African American troops. After almost four months of research, Du Bois had collected enough data to put together more than 750 pages. Unfortunately, he was unable to complete the book because he lacked funds, time, and assistance. In 1919 Du Bois organized and attended a Pan-African Congress in Paris; fifty-seven delegates were present, including sixteen African Americans, twenty West Indians, twelve citizens from various African states, and representatives from France, Belgium, and Portugal. Although the conference garnered few substantial results, Du Bois continued to work through the setbacks caused by World War I.

As a member of the African American intelligentsia during wartime, Du Bois also responded to the destructive racial atmosphere in the immediate postwar years. During this period of the late 1910s and early 1920s, African Americans, like European American women, were expected to return to pre-war roles of servitude and separation. Du Bois was unable to counter the conservative backlash, as the aftermath of World War I caused a schism and fragmentation in African American leadership. The building momentum from the success of his prewar works, like *The Souls of Black Folk* (1903), gradually waned to a standstill by November 1918, and it took almost six years before he could get his Pan-African agenda back on track. As for his social programs, after the war Du Bois concentrated his efforts on editing *The Crisis*, combating the widespread problem of lynching (especially during the Red Scare of the early 1920s), and counteracting the worsening race relations in the United States.

In the 1920s, Du Bois watched eagerly as a younger generation of African American intellectuals and leaders were emerging in the spotlight. A. Philip Randolph, Claude McKay, Cyril Briggs, and Marcus Garvey all captured the attention of the African American audience and emphasized self-sufficiency, self-empowerment, uplift, and community. In the five or six years after the war, this reassembly of African American cognoscenti began in earnest. By the end of the 1920s, the Harlem Renaissance provided even newer voices and newer visions that were direct beneficiaries of the factionalization ten years earlier. *See also*: Colonialism; Garvey, Marcus; Germany; Harlem Renaissance; McKay, Claude; *The Souls of Black Folk.*

FURTHER READING

Countee, Clarence. "W.E.B. Du Bois and African Nationalism." Diss., American University, 1970.

Du Bois, W.E.B. "The African Roots of the War." *Atlantic Monthly* (May 1915): 707–714.

——. "Close Ranks." *The Crisis* (July 1918): 111.

——. "World War and the Color Line." *The Crisis* (November 1914): 28.

Franklin, Robert. *Liberating Visions: Human Fulfillment and Social Justice in African American Thought.* Minneapolis, MN: Fortress Press, 1990.

Logan, Rayford. *The Betrayal of the American Negro: From Rutherford B. Hayes to Woodrow Wilson.* New York: Collier Books, 1954.

Quarles, Benjamin. *The Negro in the Making of America.* New York: Collier Books, 1964.

Nikki Brown

Selected Bibliography

SELECTED WRITINGS OF W.E.B. DU BOIS

The Suppression of the African Slave Trade to the United States of America, 1638–1870. New York: Longmans, Green and Co., 1896.

The Philadelphia Negro, A Social Study. Philadelphia: Published for the University, 1899.

The Souls of Black Folk. Chicago: A. C. McClurg & Co., 1903.

John Brown. Philadelphia: G. W. Jacobs & Company, 1909.

The Quest of the Silver Fleece: A Novel. Chicago: A. C. McClurg & Co., 1911.

The Negro. New York: H. Holt, 1915.

Darkwater: Voices from Within the Veil. New York: Harcourt, Brace and Howe, 1920.

The Gift of Black Folks: Negroes in the Making of America. Boston: Stratford Co., 1924.

Dark Princess: A Romance. New York: Harcourt, Brace and Co., 1928.

Africa, Its Geography, People and Products. Girard, KS: Haldeman-Julius Publications, 1930.

Africa—Its Place in Modern History. Girard, KS: Haldeman-Julius Publications, 1930.

Black Reconstruction in America, 1860–1880: An Essay toward a History of the Part which Black Folk Played in the Attempt to Reconstruct Democracy in America. New York: Harcourt, Brace and Co., 1935.

Black Folk Then and Now: An Essay in the History and Sociology of the Negro Race. New York: H. Holt and Co., 1939.

Dusk of Dawn: An Essay toward an Autobiography of a Race Concept. New York: Harcourt Brace, 1940.

Color and Democracy: Colonies and Peace. New York: Harcourt, Brace and Co., 1945.

The World and Africa: An Inquiry into the Part Which Africa Has Played in World History. New York: Viking Press, 1947.

Peace is Dangerous. New York: National Guardian, 1951.

In Battle for Peace: The Story of My 83rd Birthday, with Comment by Shirley Graham. New York: Masses & Mainstream, 1952.

The Black Flame: A Trilogy
    The Ordeal of Mansart. New York: Mainstream Publishers, 1957.
    Mansart Builds a School. New York: Mainstream Publishers, 1959.
    Worlds of Color. New York: Mainstream Publishers. 1961.

The Autobiography of W.E.B. Du Bois: A Soliloquy on Viewing My Life from the Last Decade of Its First Century. New York: International Publishers, 1968.

An ABC of Color: Selections from Over a Half Century of the Writings of W.E.B. Du Bois. New York: International Publishers, 1969.

Africa: It's Place in Modern History. Millwood, NY: Kraus-Thomson, 1977.

SOURCES OF SELECTED DU BOIS POETRY

"A Litany of Atlanta." *The Independent* (October 11, 1906).

"The Song of the Smoke." *The Horizon* (February 1907): 4–6.

"A Day in Africa." *The Horizon* (January 1908): 5.

"The Song of America." *The Horizon* (February 1908): 20.

"In God's Garden." *The Crisis* (April 1912): 235.

"Easter Emancipation." *The Crisis* (April 1913): 285–288.

"The Burden of Black Women." *The Crisis* (November 1914): 31.

"The Christmas Prayers of God." *The Crisis* (December 1914): 83–84.

"Unrest." *The Crisis* (March 1920): 195.

"The Rosenbergs." *Masses & Mainstream* (July 1953): 10–12.

"Suez." *Masses & Mainstream* (December 1956): 42–43.

"I Sing to China." *Peking: China Welfare Institute* (June 1959): 6, 7.

"To Kwame Nkrumah." *Freedomways* (Winter 1962): 98–101.

"Ghana Calls." *Freedomways* (Winter 1965): 98–101.

AFRICA

Ascherson, Neal. *The King Incorporated. Leopold II in the Age of Trusts.* Garden City, NY: Doubleday and Co., 1964.

Clarke, John H. *Marcus Garvey and the Vision of Africa.* New York: Vintage Books, 1974.

Countee, Clarence. "W.E.B. Du Bois and African Nationalism." Diss., American University, 1970.

Du Bois, W.E.B. "The African Roots of the War." *Atlantic Monthly* (May 1915): 707–714.

——. "Not Separatism." *The Crisis* (February 1919): 166.

——. "Reconstruction and Africa." *The Crisis* (February 1919): 165–166.

——. "What Is Africa to Me?" In *Dusk of Dawn: An Essay toward an Autobiography of a Race Concept.* New York: Harcourt Brace, 1940.

——. *The World and Africa: An Inquiry into the Part which Africa Has Played in World History.* 1947. New York: International Publishers, 1985.

Emerson, Barbara. *Leopold II of the Belgians. King of Colonialism.* New York: St. Martin's Press, 1979.

Hargreaves, John D. *Decolonization in Africa.* 2nd ed. London and New York: Longman, 1996.

Lynch, Hollis. *Black American Radicals and the Liberation of Africa: The Council on African Affairs 1937–1955.* Ithaca, NY: Africana Studies and Research Center, Cornell University, 1978.

Nkrumah, Kwame. *Africa Must Unite.* London: Panaf Books, 1963.

BIOGRAPHY

Broderick, Francis L. *W.E.B. Du Bois: Negro Leader in a Time of Crisis.* Stanford, CA: Stanford University Press, 1959.

Clarke, John Henrik, et al., eds. *Black Titan: W.E.B. Du Bois: An Anthology by the Editors of Freedomways.* Boston: Beacon Press, 1970.

Du Bois, Shirley Graham. *His Day Is Marching On. A Memoir of W.E.B. Du Bois.* New York: Lippincott, 1971.

Du Bois, W.E.B. "I Bury My Wife." *Negro Digest* (1950).

Horne, Gerald C. *Black and Red: W.E.B. Du Bois and the Afro-American Response to the Cold War, 1944–1963.* Albany: State University of New York Press, 1986.

Lacy, Leslie Alexander. *The Life of W.E.B. Du Bois: Cheer the Lonesome Traveler.* New York: Dial Press, 1970.

Lewis, David Levering. *W.E.B. Du Bois: Biography of a Race, 1868–1919.* New York: Henry Holt, 1993.

Marable, Manning. *W.E.B. Du Bois: Black Radical Democrat.* Boston: Twayne Publishers, 1986.

Moore, Jack B. *W.E.B. Du Bois.* Boston: Twayne Publishers, 1981.

Salk, Erwin A. *Du Bois–Robeson: Two Giants of the 20th Century: The Story of an Exhibit and a Bibliography.* Chicago: Colombia, 1977.

BIRTH CONTROL

Du Bois, W.E.B. "Black Folk and Birth Control." *Birth Control Review* 16 (June 1932).

Hart, Jamie. "Who Should Have the Children? Discussions of Birth Control among African American Intellectuals, 1920–1939." *Journal of Negro History* (Winter 1994).

BUSINESS

Du Bois, W.E.B. *The Negro in Business: Report of a Social Study Made under the Direction of Atlanta University; together with the Proceedings of the Fourth Conference for the Study of the Negro Problems, Held at Atlanta University, May 30–31, 1899.* Atlanta, GA: Atlanta University, 1899.

Johnson, Charles S. *The Economic Status of Negroes.* Nashville, TN: Fisk University Press, 1933.

Kinzer, Robert H., and Edward Sagarin. *The Negro in American Business.* New York: Greenberg, 1950.

COLONIALISM

Hargreaves, John D. *Decolonization in Africa.* 2nd ed. London and New York: Longman, 1996.

Lynch, Hollis. *Black American Radicals and the Liberation of Africa: The Council on African Affairs 1937–1955.* Ithaca, NY: Africana Studies and Research Center, Cornell University, 1978.

COMMUNISM, SOCIALISM

Du Bois, W.E.B. "Marxism and the Negro Problem." *The Crisis* 40 (1933): 103–104, 118.

——. "Revolution." In *Dusk of Dawn: An Essay toward an Autobiography of a Race Concept.* New York: Harcourt Brace, 1940.

Horne, Gerald C. *Black Liberation/Red Scare: Ben Davis and the Communist Party.* Newark: University of Delaware Press, 1994.

Lenin, V. I. *Imperialism: The Highest Stage of Capitalism. A Popular Outline.* 1917. New York: International Publishers, 1939.

Marable, Manning. "Why Black Americans Are Not Socialist." In *Speaking Truth to Power: Essays on Race, Resistance and Radicalism.* Boulder, CO: Westview Press, 1996.

Naison, Mark. *Communists in Harlem during the Depression.* Urbana: University of Illinois Press, 1983.

Shannon, David A. *The Socialist Party of America: A History.* New York: Macmillan, 1955.

Wiatrowski, Lily Phillips. "W.E.B. Du Bois and Soviet Communism: *The Black Flame* as Socialist Realism." *South Atlantic Quarterly* 94 (1995): 837.

CONFERENCES

Du Bois, W.E.B. "The Bandung Conference." In *Writings in Periodicals Edited by Others* 4:237–247. Millwood, NY: Kraus-Thomson Organization, 1982.

——. "Pan-Colored." In *Writings in Periodicals Edited by Others* 4:225–236. Millwood, NY: Kraus-Thomson Organization, 1982.

Wright, Richard. *The Color Curtain.* Jackson: University of Mississippi Press, 1995.

DRAMA

Daniel, Walter C. "W.E.B. Du Bois' First Efforts as a Playwright." *CLA Journal* (June 1990): 415–427.

Du Bois, W.E.B. "Can the Negro Serve the Drama?" *Theatre* 38 (July 1923): 12+.

——. "Krigwa Players Little Negro Theater." *The Crisis* 32 (July 1926): 134–136.

——. "The National Emancipation Exposition." *The Crisis* 6 (November 1913): 339–341.

——. "The Negro and the American Stage." *The Crisis* 28 (June 1924): 56–57.

——. "A Pageant." *The Crisis* 10 (September 1915): 230–231.

——. "Paying for Plays." *The Crisis* 23 (November 1926): 7–8.

——. "The Star of Ethiopia." *The Crisis* 11 (December 1915): 90–93.

Fisher-Stitt, Norma Sue. "W.E.B. Du Bois and 'The Star of Ethiopia' Pageant: Education through Participation." In *Society of Dance History Scholars.* St. Paul: University of Minnesota Press, 1996.

EDUCATION

Aptheker, Herbert, ed. *The Education of Black People: Ten Critiques, 1906–1960.* New York: Monthly Review Press, 1973.

Bacote, Clarence. *The Story of Atlanta University: A Century of Service, 1865–1965.* Princeton, NJ: Princeton University Press, 1969.

Davis–Du Bois, Rachel. *Get Together Americans: Friendly Approaches to Racial and Cultural Conflicts through the Neighborhood-Home Festival.* New York: Harper and Brothers, 1943.

Davis-Du Bois, Rachel, and Corann Okarodudu. *All This and Something More: Pioneering in Intercultural Education.* Bryn Mawr, PA: Dorrance, 1984.

Dennis, Rutledge M. "Du Bois and the Role of the Educated Elite." *Journal of Negro Education* (1977): 388–402.

Du Bois, W.E.B. "Does the Negro Need Separate Schools?" *Journal of Negro Education* 4 (July 1935): 328–335.

——. *Report of the First Conference of Negro Land Grant Colleges for Coordinating a Program of Cooperative Social Studies.* Atlanta, GA: Atlanta University Press, 1943.

Franklin, V. P. "W.E.B. Du Bois and the Education of Black Folk." *History of Education Quarterly* (Spring 1976): 111–118.

——. "Whatever Happened to the College Bred Negro?" *History of Education Quarterly* (Fall 1984): 411–418.

Leavell, Ullin Whitney. *Philanthropy in Negro Education.* Nashville, TN: George Peabody College for Teachers, 1930.

Rubin, Louis D., Jr., ed. *Teaching the Freeman: The Correspondence of R. B. Hayes and the Slater Fund for Negro Education.* Vol. 2. Baton Rouge: Louisiana State University Press, 1959.

Sears, Jesse Brundage. *Philanthropy in the History of American Higher Education.* Washington, DC: Government Printing Office, 1922.

Sollars, Werner, et al. *Blacks at Harvard: A Documentary History of the African-American Experience at Harvard and Radcliff.* New York: New York University Press, 1993.

Wolters, Raymond. *The New Negro on Campus.* Princeton, NJ: Princeton University Press, 1975.

EUROPE

Ascherson, Neal. *The King Incorporated. Leopold II in the Age of Trusts.* Garden City, NY: Doubleday and Co., 1964.

Barkin, Kenneth. "W.E.B. Du Bois and the *Kaiserreich*–Articles–An Introduction to Du Bois's Manuscripts on Germany." *Central European History* (1998): 155.

Emerson, Barbara. *Leopold II of the Belgians. King of Colonialism.* New York: St. Martin's Press, 1979.

Morel, E. D. *Great Britain and the Congo: The Pillage of the Congo Basin.* 1909. New York: H. Fertig, 1969.

HISTORY

Aptheker, Herbert, ed. *A Documentary History of the Negro People in the United States.* Vol. 2. New York: Citadel Press, 1951.

Cooper, John Milton. *Pivotal Decades: The United States, 1900–1920.* New York: Norton, 1990.

Cronon, Edmund D. *Black Moses: The Story of Marcus Garvey and the Universal Negro Improvement Association.* Madison: University of Wisconsin Press, 1955.

Dorfman, Joseph. "The Role of the German Historical School in American Economic Thought." *American Economic Review,* Supp. (May 1955): 17–28.

Franklin, V. P. *Black Self-Determination: A Cultural History of African American Resistance.* Brooklyn, NY: Lawrence Hill Books, 1992.

——. *Living Our Stories, Telling Our Truths: Autobiography and the Making of the African-American Intellectual Tradition.* New York: Charles Scribner's, 1995.

Ginger, Ray. *The Bending Cross.* New Brunswick, NJ: Rutgers University Press, 1949.

Herbst, Jurgen. *The German Historical School in American Scholarship.* Ithaca, NY: Cornell University Press, 1965.

Lane, Ann J. *The Brownsville Affair: National Crisis and Black Reaction.* Port Washington, NY: Kennikat Press, 1991.

Logan, Rayford. *The Betrayal of the American Negro: From Rutherford B. Hayes to Woodrow Wilson.* New York: Collier Books, 1954.

Oates, Stephen B. *To Purge This Land with Blood: A Biography of John Brown.* New York: Harper and Row, 1970.

Quarles, Benjamin. *The Negro in the Making of America.* New York: Collier Books, 1964.

Renehan, Edward. *The Secret Six: The True Story of the Men Who Conspired with John Brown.* New York: Crown Publishers, 1995.

Roediger, David R. *The Wages of Whiteness: Race and the Making of the American Working Class.* New York: Verso, 1991.

Shannon, David A. *The Socialist Party of America: A History.* New York: Macmillan, 1955.

Warren, Robert Penn. *John Brown: The Making of a Martyr.* New York: Payson and Clarke, 1929.

Weaver, John D. *The Brownsville Raid.* College Station: Texas A & M University Press, 1992.

INTELLECTUAL HISTORY

Brotz, Howard. *African American Social and Political Thought. 1850–1920.* New Brunswick, NJ: Transaction Publishers, 1992.

DeMarco, Joseph P. *The Social Thought of W.E.B. Du Bois.* London: University Press of America, 1983.

Drake, Willie Avon. *From Reform to Communism: The Intellectual Development of W.E.B. Du Bois.* Ann Arbor, MI: University Microfilms International, 1985.

Franklin, Robert. *Liberating Visions: Human Fulfillment and Social Justice in African American Thought.* Minneapolis, MN: Fortress Press, 1990.

Meier, August, ed. *Black Protest Thought in the Twentieth Century.* New York: Macmillan, 1971.

Moon, Henry Lee, ed. *The Emerging Thought of W.E.B. Du Bois: Essays and Editorials from The Crisis.* New York: Simon and Schuster, 1972.

Zamir, Shamoon. *Dark Voices: W.E.B. Du Bois and American Thought, 1888–1903.* Chicago: University of Chicago Press, 1995.

JEWS, ANTI-SEMITISM

Diner, Hasia R. *In the Almost Promised Land: American Jews and Blacks. 1915–1935.* Westport, CT: Greenwood, 1977.

West, Cornel. "On Black-Jewish Relations." In *Race Matters.* Boston: Beacon, 1993.

LITERATURE

Aptheker, Herbert. *The Literary Legacy of W.E.B. Du Bois.* White Plains, NY: Kraus International, 1989.

——, ed. *Creative Writings by W.E.B. Du Bois.* White Plains, NY: Kraus-Thomson Organization, Ltd., 1985.

Bruce, Dickson D., Jr. "W.E.B. Du Bois and the Idea of Double Consciousness." *American Literature* (1992): 299–309.

Byerman, Keith E. *Seizing the Word: History, Art, and Self in the Work of W.E.B. Du Bois.* Athens: University of Georgia Press, 1994.

Du Bois, W.E.B. "Criteria of Negro Art." *The Crisis* 32 (October 1926): 290–297.

Elder, Arlene A. "Swamp versus Plantation: Symbolic Structure in W.E.B. Du Bois' *The Quest of the Silver Fleece.*" *Phylon* (December 1973): 358–367.

Finkelstein, Sidney. "W.E.B. Du Bois' Trilogy: A Literary Triumph." *Mainstream* (October 1961): 6–17.

Gibson, Lovie N. "W.E.B. Du Bois as a Propaganda Novelist." *Negro American Literature Forum* (Autumn 1976): 75–77, 79–83.

Gooding-Williams, Robert. "Philosophy of History and Social Critique in *The Souls of Black Folk.*" *Social Science Information* (1987): 99–114.

Kostelanetz, Richard. *Politics in the African-American Novel: James Weldon Johnson, W.E.B. Du Bois, Richard Wright and Ralph Ellison.* New York: Greenwood, 1991.

Lewis, David Levering. *When Harlem Was in Vogue.* New York: Knopf, 1981.

Moses, Wilson J. "The Lost World of the Negro, 1895–1919: Black Literary and Intellectual Life before the 'Renaissance.'" *Black American Literature Forum* (Summer 1987): 61–84.

Rampersad, Arnold. *The Art and Imagination of W.E.B. Du Bois.* 1976. Reprint, New York: Schocken Books, 1990.

——. "W.E.B. Du Bois as a Man of Literature." *American Literature* (1979): 50–68.

Stewart, James B. "Psychic Duality of Afro-Americans in the Novels of W.E.B. Du Bois." *Phylon* (June 1983): 93–107.

Wiatrowski, Lily Phillips. "W.E.B. Du Bois and Soviet Communism: *The Black Flame* as Socialist Realism." *South Atlantic Quarterly* 94 (1995): 837.

MCCARTHY, MCCARTHYISM

Fried, Richard M. *Nightmare in Red: The McCarthy Era in Perspective.* New York: Oxford University Press, 1990.

NEWSPAPERS, MAGAZINES

Arndt, Murray Dennis. "The *Crisis* Years of W.E.B. Du Bois, 1910–1934." Diss., Duke University, 1970.

Fraser, Gerald C. "*The Crisis*, 1910–1980: 'A Record of the Darker Races.'" *The Crisis* (1980): 468–472.

Vaughn-Roberson, Courtney, and Brenda Hill. "*The Brownies' Book* and *Ebony Jr.*: Literature as a Mirror of the Afro-American Experience." *Journal of Negro Education* (1989): 494–510.

ORGANIZATIONS

Weiss, Nancy J. *The National Urban League, 1910–1940*. New York: Oxford University Press, 1974.

PAN-AFRICANISM

Esedebe, P. Olisanwuche. *Pan-Africanism: The Idea and Movement (1917–1963)*. Washington, DC: Howard University Press, 1970.

Heiting, Thomas James. "W.E.B. Du Bois and the Development of Pan-Africanism, 1900–1930." Diss., Texas Technological College, 1969.

Mathurin, Owen Charles. *Henry Sylvester Williams and the Origins of the Pan-African Movement, 1869–1911*. Westport, CT: Greenwood, 1976.

Nkrumah, Kwame. *Africa Must Unite*. London: Panaf Books, 1963.

Pobi-Asamani, Kwadwo O. *W.E.B. Du Bois: His Contribution to Pan Africanism*. San Bernadino, CA: Borgo Press, 1994.

Romero, Patricia W. "W.E.B. Du Bois, Pan-Africanists and Africa, 1963–1973." *Journal of Black Studies* (1976): 321–366.

Stanford, Max. "The Pan-African Party." *Black Scholar* (1976): 26–30.

PAPERS AND WRITINGS

Aptheker, Herbert, ed. *Against Racism: Unpublished Essays, Papers, Addresses, 1887–1961*. Amherst: University of Massachusetts Press, 1985.

——. *Annotated Bibliography of the Published Writings of W.E.B. Du Bois*. Millwood, NY: Kraus-Thomson, 1973.

——. *The Correspondence of W.E.B. Du Bois*. Vol. I, *Selections, 1877–1934*. Amherst: University of Massachusetts Press, 1973.

——. *Pamphlets and Leaflets by W.E.B. Du Bois*. White Plains, NY: Kraus-Thomson, 1986.

——. *Writings in Periodicals Edited by W.E.B. Du Bois: Selections from* The Horizon. White Plains, NY: Kraus-Thomson Organization Limited, 1985.

Foner, Philip, ed. *W.E.B. Du Bois Speaks: Speeches and Addresses*. New York: Pathfinder Press, 1970.

Horne, Gerald. "The Papers of W.E.B. Du Bois, 1877–1965." *Journal of American History* (March 1992): 1538.

Lester, Julius, ed. *The Seventh Son: The Thoughts and Writings of W.E.B. Du Bois*. New York: Vintage Books, 1971.

Lewis, David Levering, ed. *W.E.B. Du Bois: A Reader*. New York: Henry Holt, 1995.

McDonnell, Robert W. *The Papers of W.E.B. Du Bois (1877–1963): A Guide*. Sanford, NC: Microfilming Corporation of America, 1981.

Walden, David, ed. *W.E.B. Du Bois:* The Crisis *Writings*. Greenwich, CT: Fawcett Publications, 1972.

Weinberg, Meyer, ed. *W.E.B. Du Bois: A Reader*. New York: Harper and Row Publishers, 1970.

Wilson, Walter, ed. *The Selected Writings of W.E.B. Du Bois*. New York: New American Library, 1970.

PERSONAGES

Benjamin, George J. *Edward W. Blyden: Messiah of the Black Revolution.* New York: Vantage Press, 1979.

Bunche, Ralph. *A World View of Race.* Washington, DC: Associates in Negro Folk Education, 1936.

Cronon, Edmund D. *Black Moses: The Story of Marcus Garvey and the Universal Negro Improvement Association.* Madison: University of Wisconsin Press, 1955.

——. *Marcus Garvey.* Englewood Cliffs, NJ: Prentice-Hall, 1973.

Cullen, Countee. *On These I Stand: An Anthology of the Best Poems of Countee Cullen.* New York: Harper and Brothers, 1947.

Davis, Benjamin J. *Communist Councilman from Harlem: Autobiographical Notes Written in a Federal Penitentiary.* New York: International Publishers, 1969.

Duberman, Martin Bauml. *Paul Robeson.* New York: Alfred A. Knopf, 1988.

Du Bois, W.E.B. "Marcus Garvey." *The Crisis* 21 (1921): 112–115.

Dyer, Thomas G. *Theodore Roosevelt and the Idea of Race.* Baton Rouge: Louisiana State University Press, 1980.

Fax, Elton C. *Garvey: The Story of a Pioneer Black Nationalist.* New York: Dodd, Mead, 1972.

Fox, Stephen R. *The Guardian of Boston: William Monroe Trotter.* New York: Atheneum, 1970.

Gable, John Allen. *The Bull Moose Years: Theodore Roosevelt and the Republican Party.* Port Washington, NY: Kennikat Press, 1978.

Hamilton, Virginia. *Paul Robeson: The Life and Times of a Free Black Man.* New York: Harper and Row, 1974.

Harbaugh, William Henry. *Power and Responsibility: The Life and Times of Theodore Roosevelt.* New York: Farrar, Straus and Cudahy, 1961.

Harlan, Louis R. *Booker T. Washington: The Wizard of Tuskegee, 1901–1915.* New York: Oxford University Press, 1983.

Hart, Albert Bushnell, and Herbert Ronald Ferleger, eds. *Theodore Roosevelt Cyclopedia.* New York: Roosevelt Memorial Association, 1941.

Helm, MacKinley. *Angel Mo' and Her Son, Roland Hayes.* Boston: Little, Brown and Co., 1942.

Henry, Charles P. *Ralph Bunche.* New York: New York University Press, 1999.

Humes, Dollera Joy. *Oswald Garrison Villard, Liberal of the 1920's.* Syracuse: Syracuse University Press, 1960.

Hunton, Dorothy. *Alphaeus Hunton: The Unsung Valiant.* N.P.: Privately printed, 1986.

Janken, Kenneth Robert. *Rayford W. Logan and the Dilemma of the African American Intellectual.* Amherst: University of Massachusetts Press, 1993.

Lynch, Hollis. *Edward Wilmot Blyden: Pan-Negro Patriot, 1832–1912.* London: Oxford University Press, 1967.

Mathurin, Owen Charles. *Henry Sylvester Williams and the Origins of the Pan-African Movement, 1869–1911.* Westport, CT: Greenwood, 1976.

"Paul Robeson. Right or Wrong? Right, Says Du Bois." *Negro Digest* 7 (1950): 8, 10–14.

Robeson, Paul. *Here I Stand.* New York: Othello Associates, 1958.

Rubin, Louis D. Jr., ed. *Teaching the Freeman: The Correspondence of R. B. Hayes and the*

Slater Fund for Negro Education. Vol. 2. Baton Rouge: Louisiana State University Press, 1959.

Salk, Erwin A. *Du Bois–Robeson: Two Giants of the 20th Century: The Story of an Exhibit and a Bibliography*. Chicago: Columbia, 1977.

Salvatore, Nick. *Eugene Debs: Citizen and Socialist*. Urbana: University of Illinois Press, 1982.

Shucard, Alan W. *Countee Cullen*. New York: Twayne, 1984.

Talbot, Edith Armstrong. *Samuel Chapman Armstrong*. New York: Doubleday, Page & Co., 1904.

Villard, Oswald Garrison. *John Brown, 1800–1859: A Biography Fifty Years After*. Boston: Houghton Mifflin Company, 1911.

Waltzer, Kenneth. "The FBI, Congressman Vito Marcantonio, and the American Labor Party." In *Beyond the Hiss Case. The FBI, Congress, and the Cold War*, ed. Athan C. Theoharis. Philadelphia: Temple University Press, 1982.

Washington, Booker T. *Up from Slavery*. New York: Doubleday, 1901.

Weinstein, Brian. *Eboue*. New York: Oxford University Press, 1972.

White, John. *Black Leadership in America from Booker T. Washington to Jesse Jackson*. London: Longman Publishers, 1990.

Wilkerson, Doxey. "William Alphaeus Hunton: A Life that Made a Difference." *Freedomways* (Winter 1970).

Wreszin, Michael. *Oswald Garrison Villard, Pacifist at War*. Bloomington: Indiana University Press, 1965.

PROTEST

Boxill, Bernard Romaric. "A Philosophical Examination of Black Protest Thought." Diss., University of California at Los Angeles, 1971.

Meier, August, ed. *Black Protest Thought in the Twentieth Century*. New York: Macmillan, 1971.

Rudwick, Elliot. *W.E.B. Du Bois: Propagandist of the Negro Protest*. 2nd ed. Philadelphia: University of Pennsylvania Press, 1968.

RACE, RACISM, RACE RELATIONS

Appiah, Anthony. "The Uncompleted Argument: Du Bois and the Illusion of Race." *Race, Writing, and Difference*, ed. Henry Louis Gates, Jr. Chicago: University of Chicago Press, 1985. 21–37.

Aptheker, Herbert. *Against Racism: Unpublished Essays, Papers, Addresses, 1887–1961*. Amherst: University of Massachusetts Press, 1985.

———. *W.E.B. Du Bois and the Struggle against Racism in the New World*. New York: United Nations, 1983.

Baber, Willie L. "Capitalism and Racism: Dicontinuities in the Life and Work of W.E.B. Du Bois." *Critique of Anthropology* (1992): 339–364.

Biddis, Michael D. *Father of Racist Ideology. The Social and Political Thought of Count Gobineau*. New York: Weybright and Talley, 1970.

Chicago Commission on Race Relations, eds. *Negro in Chicago: A Study of Race Relations and a Race Riot*. Chicago: Ayer Co. Publishers, 1978.

Stoddard, Lothrop. *The Revolt against Civilization: The Menace of the Under Man.* New York: Charles Scribner's Sons, 1922.

——. *The Rising Tide of Color against World Supremacy.* New York: Charles Scribner's Sons, 1920.

RACE RIOTS

Capeci, Dominic J. "Reckoning with Violence: W.E.B. Du Bois and the 1906 Atlanta Race Riot." *Journal of Southern History* 62 (1996): 727–766.

Ellsworth, Scott. *Death in a Promised Land: The Tulsa Race Riot of 1921.* Baton Rouge: Louisiana State University Press, 1992.

Finkelman, Paul, ed. *Lynching, Racial Violence, and Law.* Detroit: Garland Publishing, 1992.

Moses, Wilson J. "W.E.B. Du Bois's 'The Conservation of the Races' and Its Context: Idealism, Conservation and Hero Worship." *Massachusetts Review* (1993): 275–294.

Rudwick, Elliott M. *Race Riot at East St. Louis, July 2, 1917.* Jackson: University of Illinois Press, 1982.

Williams, Lee E. *Anatomy of Four Race Riots: Racial Conflict in Knoxville, Elaine, Arkansas, Tulsa and Chicago, 1919–1921.* Jacksonville: University Press of Mississippi, 1972.

RELIGION

Du Bois, W.E.B. *Prayers for Dark People.* Ed. Herbert Aptheker. Amherst: University of Massachusetts Press, 1980.

Marable, Manning. "The Black Faith of W.E.B. Du Bois: Sociocultural and Political Dimensions of Black Religion." *Southern Quarterly* (1985): 15–33.

SLAVERY

"African Testimony." *New York Journal of Commerce,* January 10, 1840: 2.

Aptheker, Herbert. *American Negro Slave Revolts.* New York: International Publishers, 1969.

——. "Some Comments of W.E.B. Du Bois on Slave Revolts." *Journal of Negro History* (Summer 1997): 353–357.

"The Captured Africans of the Amistad." *New York Morning Herald,* October 4, 1839: 2.

"An Incident." *New York Commercial Advertiser,* September 26, 1839.

Jones, Howard. *Mutiny on the Amistad: The Saga of a Slave Revolt and Its Impact on American Abolition, Law, and Diplomacy.* New York: Oxford University Press, 1987.

Kramer, Helen. *Amistad Revolt, 1839.* Cleveland, OH: Pilgrim Press, 1997.

"Testimony of James Covey in the United States District Court." National Archives, November 20, 1839.

SOCIOLOGY

Bowser, Benjamin. "The Contribution of Blacks to Sociological Knowledge: A Problem of Theory and Role to 1950." *Phylon* (1981): 180–193.

Deegan, Mary Jo. "Du Bois and the Women of Hull House." *American Sociologist* (1988): 301–311.

Du Bois, W.E.B. *The Philadelphia Negro: A Social Study.* Philadelphia: Published for the University, 1899.

Fine, Sidney. *Laissez Faire and the General Welfare State.* Ann Arbor: University of Michigan Press, 1956.

Green, Dan S., and Edwin D. Driver, eds. *W.E.B. Du Bois on Sociology and the Black Community.* Chicago: University of Illinois Press, 1980.

Green, Danforth Stuart. "The Truth Shall Make Ye Free: The Sociology of W.E.B. Du Bois." Diss., University of Massachusetts, 1973.

Lange, Werner J. "W.E.B. Du Bois and the First Scientific Study of Afro-America." *Phylon* (1983): 135–146.

Miller, Zane. "Race-ism and the City: The Young Du Bois and the Role of Place in Social Theory, 1893–1901." *American Studies* (1989): 89–102.

Ross, Dorothy. *Origins of American Social Science.* New York: Cambridge University Press, 1991.

Watts, Jerry. "Reconsidering Park, Johnson, Du Bois, Frazier and Reid: A Reply to Benjamin Bowser's 'The Contribution of Blacks to Sociological Knowledge.' " *Phylon* (1982): 273–291.

WOMEN

Aptheker, Bettina. "W.E.B. Du Bois and the Struggle for Women's Rights: 1910–1920." *San Jose Studies* (1975): 7–16.

Burrow, Rufus, Jr. "Some African American Males on the Black Woman." *Western Journal of Black Studies* (1992): 64–73.

Du Bois, W.E.B. "A Pioneer Suffragist." *The Brownies' Book* (1920): 120–121.

——. "Suffering Suffragettes." *The Crisis* (1912): 76–77.

——. "Suffrage and Women." *The Crisis* (1916): 182.

——. "Votes for Women." *The Crisis* (1917): 8.

——. "The Woman." *The Crisis* (1911): 19.

——. "Woman's Suffrage." *The Crisis* (1913): 29.

——. "Woman's Suffrage." *The Crisis* (1915): 29–30.

Morton, Patricia. *Disfigured Images: The Historical Assault on Afro-American Women.* New York: Praeger, 1971.

Yellin, Jean Fagan. "Documentation: Du Bois' *Crisis* and Women's Suffrage." *Massachusetts Review* (1973): 365–375.

PAPERS

Fisk University. This is a significant collection that includes manuscripts of Du Bois' writings, most notably drafts and research material for his study of the black soldier in World War I, as well as unpublished short stories. The collection also includes routine correspondence.

Schomburg Center for Research in Black Culture. There is a small amount of material in the Hugh Smythe Papers. The material includes drafts of several essays, articles, and speeches. The collection also contains Du Bois' student materials, such as philosophy notes from Harvard University and other miscellaneous items.

University of Massachusetts at Amherst. The W.E.B. Du Bois Papers collection is comprehensive and includes virtually every stage in his career. For example, the correspondence files include more than 100,000 items. The files, containing only a few items from his youth, are more complete for Du Bois' student days in the 1880s and 1890s and the beginning of his career as a scholar and educator in the 1890s and 1900s. They are most complete during his period with the NAACP as editor of *The Crisis* (1910–1934), and they remain nearly as abundant for the last thirty years of his life (1934–1963).

Yale Library. The collection contains manuscripts for *Dusk of Dawn, The Gift of Black Folk, Darkwater, The Negro, The World and Africa,* and several articles and poems. There are also files regarding the Amenia Conferences, the United Nations, and other areas.

WORKS BY DU BOIS ON THE WEB

"The Freedman's Bureau." From The English Server, Carnegie Mellon University. Available at: http://eng.hss.cmu.edu/

"Lynching." Editorial from *The Crisis.* Available at: http://members.tripod.com/~Du Bois/library.html

"A Negro Schoolmaster in the New South." From The English Server, Carnegie Mellon University. Available at: http://eng.hss.cmu.edu/

"Of the Sorrow Songs." Available at: http://members.tripod.com/~DuBois/library.html

"Of the Training of Black Men." From The English Server, Carnegie Mellon University. Available at: http://eng.hss.cmu.edu/

"The Rosenbergs." Available at: http://members.tripod.com/~DuBois/library.html

"The Song of Smoke." Available at: http://members.tripod.com/~DuBois/library.html

The Souls of Black Folk. From the Bartleby Project. Available at: http://www.bartleby.com/index.html

"Strivings of the Negro People." From The English Server, Carnegie Mellon University. Available at: http://eng.hss.cmu.edu/

INTERESTING WEB SITES

Pan-Africanism

A Global View of Pan-Africanism
    http://www.angelfire.com/ny/PanafricanColours/Page1.html
    "You've certainly heard about the struggle of our brothers and sisters throughout the world. Here are some of the people who summarize best the intensity of this fight for freedom and recognition. Moreover, you have the opportunity to learn about the hidden History of the World."

W.E.B. Du Bois

African American Journey: Du Bois, W.E.B.
    http://fcis.oise.utoronto.ca/~daniel_schugurensky/assignment1/dubois.html

Short biography, links. "W.E.B. Du Bois . . . a sociologist and educator, challenged the current system of education as restricting rather than socially and economically advancing African Americans. He challenged what was called the 'Tuskegee machine' of Booker T. Washington."

The History Channel
http://www.historychannel.com/cgi-bin/framed.cgi
Short biography of Du Bois with links.

How did the views of Booker T. Washington and W.E.B. Du Bois toward woman suffrage change between 1900 and 1915?
http://womhist.binghamton.edu/webdbtw/Doclist.htm
Contains a list of documents that support thesis: letters, reports, editorials, *Crisis* articles, etc.

Marcus Garvey and W.E.B. Du Bois
http://www.ritesofpassage.org/g-dubois.htm
Also contains references to Washington.

The W.E.B. Du Bois Page [San Antonio College (TX) Lit.]
http://www.accd.edu/SAC/english/bailey/dubois.htm
Selected bibiography, links.

W.E.B. Du Bois
http://ishi.lib.berkeley.edu/history/7B/W_E_B_DuBois.htm
"Comprehensive information about Du Bois' life and . . . *The Souls of Black Folk*."
Links, study questions.

The W.E.B. Du Bois Virtual University
http://members.tripod.com/~DuBois/index.html
Created and maintained by Jennifer Wager. Five pages: bibliography, biography, classroom, conferences, library, and scholars.

The Souls of Black Folk

Book #62: The Souls of Black Folk *by W.E.B. Du Bois*
http://userpage.fu-berlin.de/~tanguay/book62.htm
A review by Edward Tanguay, May 7, 1997. Online Reading Club Reviews.

A Homeric Life: A Comprehensive Biography of W.E.B. Du Bois [USIA AF History]
http://www.usia/gov/usia/blackhis/web.htm

W.E.B. Bu Dois Page [Black Excellence in World History]
http://ww2.csusm.edu/Black_Excellence/documents/pg-du-bois1.htm
Three chapters from *The Souls of Black Folk*.

W.E.B. Du Bois (1868–1963)
http://history.hanover.edu/19th/dubois.htm
Four articles from the *Atlantic Monthly, The Souls of Black Folk* (Project Bartleby).

We Shall Overcome—W.E.B. Du Bois Boyhood Homesite
http://www.cr.nps.gov/nr/travel/civilrights/ma2.htm

Index

About the Contributors

NAHFIZA AHMED is a doctoral student at Southampton University in England.

BRIAN C. BLACK is a specialist in landscape and environmental history. He is especially interested in the intersection between ethnicity and ideas of place. He is the author of *Petrolia: The Landscape of America's First Oil Book* (2000). Currently, he is writing about American whaling in the nineteenth century.

AMY BOWLES is an Independent Scholar living in Chevy Chase, Maryland.

MARK S. BRALEY is assistant professor of English at the United States Air Force Academy. His interests include literature and the environment, and he has published on Wallace Stegner.

NIKKI BROWN is a doctoral candidate in history at Yale University.

TIM CEBULA is a journalist in the Great Barrington area.

ROGER CHAPMAN is a doctoral candidate in the American Culture Studies Program at Bowling Green State University (Ohio). His writings have appeared in *Studies in the Social Sciences, Northwest Ohio Quarterly, Encyclopedia of Prisoners of War*, and *St. James Encyclopedia of Popular Culture*.

JAMES L. CONYERS, JR., is an associate professor and chair of Black Studies at the University of Nebraska at Omaha.

PAUL JEROME CROCE is an associate professor and chair of American Studies at Stetson University (Florida), where he also serves on the Africana Studies committee. He is the author of *Science and Religion in the Era of William James: Eclipse of Certainty, 1820–1880* (1995).

LAURA DE LUCA is a Ph.D. candidate in Cultural Anthropology at the University of Colorado, Boulder. She is currently working on an ethnographic study of capitalism in East Africa.

SHAWN R. DONALDSON is associate professor of sociology at Richard Stockton College (New Jersey). Her research interests include race, class, and gender.

DAVID DU BOIS is the son of Shirley Graham Du Bois and the adopted son of W.E.B. Du Bois.

ROBERT FIKES, JR., is a librarian at San Diego State University. He has published four reference books, several monographs, and numerous journal, magazine, and newspaper articles, reviews, and bibliographies largely on African American history and culture.

V. P. FRANKLIN is professor of history at Drexel University. He is the author of *Living Our Stories, Telling Our Truths: Autobiographies and the Making of the African-American Intellectual Tradition* (1995).

LINDA K. FULLER is a professor in the Communications Department of Worcester State College. She is the author of twenty books and was awarded a Fulbright in 1996 to teach in Singapore.

TODD GIBSON is an independent scholar.

RICHARD C. GOODE is an assistant professor at Libscomb University in the Department of History, Politics, and Philosophy. His research emphases center on religion and American culture.

CHRISTINE GRAY is assistant professor of English at Catonsville Community College (Maryland).

EBONY GREEN is a graduate student at Bowling Green State University (Ohio).

SCOT GUENTER is an associate professor of American Studies at San Jose State University (California).

STEPHEN G. HALL is an assistant professor of history at Central State University (Ohio). His areas of interest include African American, American, and African intellectual history.

ANGE-MARIE HANCOCK is a doctoral candidate in political science at the University of North Carolina at Chapel Hill.

JAMIE HART received a Ph.D. in U.S. history from the University of Michigan at Ann Arbor. The author of numerous articles, she is now working on a master's degree in public health.

PETER C. HOLLORAN is the author of *Boston's Wayward Children: Social Services for Homeless Children, 1830–1930* (1989). He teaches American history at Worcester State College and is secretary of the New England Historical Association.

GERALD HORNE is at the University of North Carolina at Chapel Hill.

MALAIKA HORNE is assistant professor of communications at Webster University (Missouri). Her research interests include African Americans and the media.

ALPHINE JEFFERSON is chair of history at the College of Wooster (Ohio).

WILLIAM POWELL JONES is a graduate student in history at the University of North Carolina at Chapel Hill.

MUATA KAMDIBE is a doctoral candidate in Africana Studies at Howard University, Washington, D.C.

AKIL K. KHALFANI is a graduate student at the University of Pennsylvania. His research interests include affirmative action in South Africa and the United States.

WILLIAM M. KING is professor and coordinator of Afroamerican Studies in the Department of Ethnic Studies at the University of Colorado at Boulder. He is the author of two books and numerous articles, essays, and reviews and is the editor of the e-journal *Des: A Scholarly Journal of Ethnic Studies*.

AMANDA LAUGESEN is currently completing a Ph.D. dissertation in the History Program, Research School of Social Sciences, Australian National University.

CATHERINE M. LEWIS is an independent scholar.

KENNETH MOSTERN is assistant professor of English at the University of Tennessee at Knoxville. He is the author of *Autobiography and Black Identity Politics: Racialization in Twentieth Century America* (1999).

BILL MULLEN is an associate professor of English at Youngstown State University (Ohio).

ALLE PARKER is a graduate student at Kunztown State University (Pennsylvania).

BRENDA GAYLE PLUMMER is a professor of history at the University of Wisconsin at Madison. Her latest book is *Rising Wind: Black Americans and U.S. Foreign Affairs, 1935–1968* (1996).

KATHRYN RHOADS is a graduate student of Ohio State University.

CHRISTY RISHOI is associate professor of language and literature at Jackson Community College (Michigan).

JUNIUS RODRIGUEZ is associate professor of history at Eureka College (Illinois) and is the editor of *The Historical Encyclopedia of World Slavery* (1997).

LADONNA RUSH is an assistant professor of psychology at the College of Wooster (Ohio). Her research interests include racism, stereotyping, and social stigma.

PAUL RYAN SCHNEIDER is an independent scholar.

JONATHAN SILVERMAN completed his doctorate at the University of Texas at Austin.

MALIK SIMBA is a professor of history at California State University at Fresno. His teaching and research interests include American constitutional history and African American history.

FAYE P. SNORTON is an independent scholar living in New Jersey.

STEPHEN SOITOS is the author of *The Blues Detective: A Study of African American Detective Fiction* (1996).

JACK STUART is professor of history at California State University at Long Beach.

DREW VANDECREEK is the editor of the electronic version of *Essays in History* published by the University of Virginia.

TRENT WATTS is an independent scholar.

YVONNE WILLIAMS is professor of political science and Black Studies and director of the Black Studies Program at the College of Wooster (Ohio).

MARY ELLEN WILSON is professor of history at Middle Georgia College. Her research interests include southern forest history and environmental history.

COURTNEY YOUNG is assistant instruction librarian and reference librarian at Michigan State University. Her research interests include popular culture and issues of gender.

MARY YOUNG is director of Black Studies at Berea College (Kentucky).